The Theology of Paul Tillich

THE THEOLOGY OF

PAUL TILLICH

Contexts and Key Issues

Christian Danz

MERCER UNIVERSITY PRESS
MACON, GEORGIA

MUP/ P703

28 27 26 25 24   5 4 3 2 1

Books published by Mercer University Press are printed on acid-free paper
that meets the requirements of the American National Standard for
Information Sciences—Permanence of Paper for Printed Library Materials.

Printed and bound in the United States.

This book is set in Adobe Caslon and Georgia

Cover/jacket design by Burt&Burt.

Library of Congress Cataloging-in-Publication Data

Names: Danz, Christian, author.
Title: The theology of Paul Tillich : contexts and key issues / Christian
    Danz.
Description: 1st. | Macon, Georgia : Mercer University Press, [2024] |
    Series: The Mercer Paul Tillich series | Includes bibliographical
    references and index. |
Identifiers: LCCN 2024030336 (print) | LCCN 2024030337 (ebook) | ISBN
    9780881469523 (paperback) | ISBN 9780881469530 (ebook)
Subjects: LCSH: Tillich, Paul, 1886-1965.
Classification: LCC BX4827.T53 D37 2024 (print) | LCC BX4827.T53 (e-
book)
    | DDC 230/.044092--dc23/eng/20240731
LC record available at https://lccn.loc.gov/2024030336
LC ebook record available at https://lccn.loc.gov/2024030337

Contents

List of Abbreviations

AT   *Paul Tillich Ausgewählte Texte.* Edited by Christian
        Danz, Werner Schüßler and Erdmann Sturm.
        Berlin; New York: de Gruyter, 2008.

EW   *Paul Tillich Ergänzungs- und Nachlaßbände zu den
        gesammelten Werken von Paul Tillich.* Edited by
        Ingeborg Henel et. al. Twentyone Volumes to date.
        Stuttgart; Berlin: de Gruyter, 1971ff.

GA   *Karl Barth Gesamtausgabe.* Edited by Hans-Anton
        Drewes, Hinrich Stoevesandt et. al. Fiftysix
        Volumes to date. Zürich: TVZ, 1971ff.

GW   *Paul Tillich Gesammelte Werke.* Edited by Renate
        Albrecht. Fourteen Volumes. Stuttgart:
        Evangelisches Verlagswerk, 1959–1975.

KGA   *Ernst Troeltsch Kritische Gesamtausgabe.* Edited by
        Friedrich W. Graf and Gangolf Hübinger. Twenty-
        four Volumes to date. Berlin; Boston: de Gruyter,
        1998ff.

MW   *Paul Tillich Main Works/Hauptwerke.* Edited by
        Carl H. Ratschow. Six Volumes. Berlin; New York:
        de Gruyter, 1989–1992.

ST   Tillich, Paul. *Systematic Theology.* Three Volumes.
        Chicago: The University of Chicago Press, 1951–
        1964.

Preface

The present book grew out of the idea of bringing together my various English-language publications on Paul Tillich's theology from recent years. However, this proved more difficult than first thought. It soon became apparent that it is not possible to simply put together various articles in order to present Tillich's theology in a systematic way.

Thus, while this study is based on some previously published works, they have been completely revised and supplemented with newly written chapters. This has resulted in a study of Tillich's theology, the first part of which reconstructs the work-historical development of Tillich's theology from his beginnings to his *Systematic Theology*. On this basis, the second part of the book then addresses central themes of Tillich's *Systematic Theology* within a systematic perspective. Through its interlocking of work-historical and systematic perspectives, this account of Tillich's theology brings into focus aspects that have received little attention from previous research.

To formulate German systematic theology in English is not easy. Paul Tillich already knew that. Without the help of Fábio Henrique Abreu (Rio de Janeiro), Charles Fox (Williamstown), and J. J. Warren (Vienna), it would not have been possible to put my "German English" into a more understandable form. I thank them for their efforts with the text. Immanuel Carrara, Dr. Thomas Scheiwiller, Paul Schömann, J.J. Warren, and Sabrine Wolsink (all Vienna) gratefully edited the manuscript for printing and prepared the indexes. I thank Marc Jolley of Mercer University Press for the interest he has shown in this research and for its inclusion in the Mercer University Press publishing program.

Christian Danz
Vienna, April 2023

MERCER UNIVERSITY PRESS

Endowed by

TOM WATSON BROWN
and
THE WATSON-BROWN FOUNDATION, INC.

Notes on first publications

Some of the chapters in this book are based on previously published articles, but have been rewritten throughout and expanded to include sub-chapters.

Chapter II:
"Historicism, Neo-Idealism, and Modern Theology. Paul Tillich and German Idealism," in *The Palgrave Handbook of German Idealism and Existentialism*. Ed. by Jon Stewart. Cham: Springer, 2020, 287–303.

Chapter III:
"From the Religious apriori to Intending the Absolute: Reflections on the Methodological Principles in Otto and Tillich against the Backdrop of their Historical Problematic," in *HTS Teologiese Studies / Theological Studies* 69 (2013) No. 1, 1–7.

Chapter IV:
"Symbol, Dämonie, Angst. Paul Tillich und die Kulturwissenschaftliche Bibliothek Warburg," in *Theologie und Religionsphilosophie in der frühen Weimarer Republik*. Ed. by Michael Moxter and Anna Smith. Tübingen: Mohr Siebeck, 2023, 14–163.

Chapter VII:
"The Significance of Paul Tillich's Christology for Contemporary Discussions," in *Why Tillich? Why Now?* Ed. by Thomas G. Bandy. Macon/Georgia: Mercer University Press, 2021, 51–64.

Chapter VIII:
"Spirit and the Ambiguities of Life: Reflections on Paul Tillich's Pneumatology," in *Les ambiguïtés de la vie selon Paul Tillich. Travaux issus du XXIe Colloque internationla de l'Association Paul Tillich d'expression française*. Ed. by Marc Dumas, Jean Richard and Bryan Wagoner. Berlin; Boston: de Gruyter, 2017, 359–366.

Chapter IX:
"Christianity and the encounter of world religions. Considerations to a contemporary theology of religions," in *Correlatio* 15 (2016) Nr. 2, 9–26.

I.

Prologue: Paul Tillich in the History
of Protestant Theology

In both the United States and Germany, Paul Tillich remains an influential theologian. He started his academic career in Germany as a theologian and in the United States he became one of the best-known public intellectuals of the country. Tillich's work stands, as he himself described it, on the boundary between "native and alien land."[1] However, it was only after almost two decades in his "alien" homeland that he was finally able to complete his main lifework, the *Systematic Theology*. It was published in English during the period from 1951 to 1963. But the history of his theological system goes back to the early days of his German period, as Tillich himself mentioned in the *Preface* to the subsequent German edition of his *Systematic Theology*.[2] In fact, he wrote the first draft of a systematic theology in 1913. It was not until 1925, however, that Tillich began to give regular lectures in dogmatics at Marburg, Dresden, and Leipzig. His first lectures on this topic in the United States were given in 1936 at Union Theological Seminary in New York City under the title *Advanced Problems*

---

[1] Cf. Mary A. Stenger, "Tillich's American Theology on the Boundary between Native and Alien Land," in *Paul Tillich im Exil*, ed. Christian Danz and Werner Schüßler (Berlin; Boston: de Gruyter, 2017), 229–249.

[2] Cf. Paul Tillich, *Systematische Theologie*, vol. I (2nd ed. Stuttgart: Evangelisches Verlagswerk, 1956), 7–8. To the history of the edition of Tillich's *Systematic Theology* both in the USA and in Germany, cf. Friedrich Wilhelm Graf, "Zur Publikationsgeschichte von Paul Tillichs 'Systematic Theology'. 2 parts," in *JHMTh* 23 (2016) 192–217; *JHMTh* 24 (2017) 51–121; Christian Danz, "Textgeschichtliche Einleitung zur deutschen Übersetzung der Systematischen Theologie," in Paul Tillich, *Systematische Theologie*, vol. I–II, ed. Christian Danz (9th ed. Berlin; Boston: de Gruyter, 2017), XV–LXV.

in Systematic Theology. So, it is quite clear that the content of what became the *Systematic Theology* was developed over a very long history of the work. It is not possible, therefore, to understand the full complexity of this work without consulting the earlier history of his theological work in Germany. Indeed, many ideas of his magnum opus are already found in his 1913 draft of a *Systematische Theologie*. Tillich definitely changed certain basic principles of his theological system over the course of the years, but the overall argument and intention of his theological program remained relatively consistent. For Tillich, theology has the task of providing a religious interpretation of the world as a whole. This means that his use of philosophy, sociology, psychology, among other disciplines, have a theological function. This is also true for Tillich's ontology and his famous statement that "God is being-itself."[3] The theological function of his ontology is to criticize theological conceptions that restrict the revelation of God to the process of salvation or to the revelation of God in the figure of Jesus as the Christ. We find this intention already manifest in Tillich's theological writings before the First World War, where he argued that God must be known not only by God's revelation in Jesus Christ, but also by God's revelation in nature and culture.

The development of the theology of Paul Tillich is understandable only against the background of the theological debates he encountered during his university years, which began in early 1904 at the University of Berlin. To give an interpretation of his theology means, therefore, at the same time, to give an interpretation of the history of modern Protestant theology.[4] Without this, it is not possible to integrate Tillich's theology

---

[3] Paul Tillich, *Systematic Theology*, vol. I (Chicago: The University of Chicago Press, 1951), 235.

[4] In his lectures on the history of Protestant theology, Tillich himself placed his own conception in the history of the development of modern Protestantism, interpreting it as a precondition of his own theology. Cf. Paul Tillich, *Perspectives on the 19th and 20th Century Protestant Theology*, ed. Carl E. Braaten (New York; Evanston; London: Harper & Row, 1976), 8: "All this shows that the kind of history of Christian thought to which I will introduce you is, so to speak, the historical dimension of systematic theology." Cf. Folkart Wittekind, "Herrmann, Treoltsch und Tillich über die Konstruktion der Theologiegeschichte," in *Paul Tillich in der Diskussion. Werkgeschichte – Kontexte – Anknüpfungspunkte. Festschrift für Erdmann Sturm zum 85. Geburtstag*, ed. Christian Danz and Werner Schüßler (Berlin; Boston: de Gruyter 2022), 133–170.

into the development of the history of modern Protestant theology. This history is a necessary presupposition for an understanding of his theology both in Germany and later in the United States. Only if we understand how modern Protestant theology works, can we understand what Tillich is doing in his own theology, which he developed in the period before and after the First World War.[5] What, then, is important to the history of modern Protestant theology?

First, there was a fundamental change in the methodological basis of Protestant theology around 1800. After the Enlightenment, theology as a *Wissenschaft*—science—within universities was possible only on the basis of the concept of religion. The reason for this is that the understanding of the theology of the so-called "old Protestantism," as Ernst Troeltsch names it, could not simply be continued. For Martin Luther and the theologians of the sixteenth- and seventeenth-century Protestantism, the holy scripture was the sole basis for theology. This status of the holy scripture presupposes that the Bible was a book made in heaven, so to speak. The words of the Bible are authoritative only insofar as all its words are infallibly true. Therefore, the meaning and signs of the text of the Bible must come directly from God. The truth that God presents of God's self is set down in the Bible. This is the only meaning of the notion of revelation in the old Protestantism. However, the function of the Bible as a foundational theological principle was only one aspect of the old Protestant theological perspective. The other aspect was the metaphysical and cosmological framework of old Protestantism's theology. For Luther, soteriology was the focus of all theology, and more specifically, the individual appropriation of salvation through faith. Luther presupposed as a matter of fact that every human being had a knowledge of God and that Jesus as the Christ was an objective factum of history. Therefore, for Luther the decisive theological problem lay in the appropriation of the salvation made available in Christ as an objective historical reality. Hence, faith is regarded on the one hand, as a performative act (*Vollzug*)[6] which no human can

---

[5] Cf. Folkart Wittekind, "Tillichs Dresdener Dogmatik im theologiegeschichtlichen Kontext," in *Paul Tillich in Dresden. Intellektuellen-Diskurse in der Weimarer Republik*, ed. Christian Danz and Werner Schüßler (Berlin; Boston: de Gruyter, 2023), 247–276.

[6] Throughout this book, the German word "*Vollzug*" will be translated as "performative act" or "performance."

produce, but on the other hand it is a performative act that humans must necessarily realize.[7]

Both presuppositions of the old Protestant theology collapsed during the Enlightenment. The emerging historical criticism of the Biblical text dissolved the so-called "scriptural principle," and the newly emerging critique of knowledge destroyed the so-called "natural knowledge" of God. From this it followed that Protestantism had to find a new basis for its theological science. Around 1800, Protestant theologians found such a new foundation for "theology as a *Wissenschaft*" in the concept of religion, and theologians now began to make a sharp distinction between theology and religion. As Johann Salomo Semler argued at this time, theology is a special branch of science, a *Fachwissenschaft*, and not itself religion.[8] If theology speaks about religion, then it must do so against the backdrop of the differentiation between theology and religion. In this way, the object of theology was no longer God, as in the theology of the old Protestantism, but rather its object became religion. The notion of religion, therefore, replaced the notion of God in the horizon of the modern critical analysis of knowledge undertaken by David Hume and Immanuel Kant, who demonstrated that no knowledge, and therefore no science of God, is possible.[9]

But what, then, is religion? In the shadow of Kant's critique of knowledge, "philosophy of religion" was developed as an independent academic discipline in the 1790s.[10] It is very important to note that this philosophy of religion was quite different from the old *theologia naturalis* (natural theology). The object of the philosophy of religion is not God, as in the traditional natural theology, but rather, the object of this new academic

---

[7] Cf. Christian Danz, *Einführung in die Theologie Martin Luthers* (Darmstadt: Wissenschaftliche Buchgesellschaft, 2013).

[8] Cf. Johann S. Semler, *Versuch einer Anleitung zu nützliche Fleisse in der ganzen Gottesgelehrsamkeit für angehende Studiosos Theologiä* (Halle: Gebauer, 1757). Cf. Marianne Schröter, *Aufklärung durch Historisierung. Johann Salomo Semlers Hermeneutik des Christentums* (Berlin; Boston: de Gruyter, 2012).

[9] Cf. Gary J. Dorrien, *In a Post-Hegelian Spirit. Philosophical Theology as Idealistic Discontent* (Waco: Baylor University Press, 2020).

[10] Cf. Walter Jaeschke, "Um 1800' – Religionsphilosophie in der Sattelzeit der Moderne," in *Philosophisch-theologische Streitsachen. Pantheismusstreit – Atheismusstreit – Theismusstreit*, ed. Georg Essen and Christian Danz (Darmstadt: Wissenschaftliche Buchgesellschaft, 2012), 7–92.

discipline is the human consciousness of God. Religion is now understood as a faculty in the structure of human consciousness. At the same time, consciousness is the general foundation for all cultural acts. On this basis, many theologians and philosophers of the early nineteenth century worked out theories about how religion was rooted in the general structure of human consciousness. There are two important consequences that follow from this new foundation of religion: first, religion is seen as universal because it is an element in the very structure or "faculties" of consciousness, along with thinking, acting, and feeling. Therefore—and this is the key consequence—religion is a universal phenomenon of being human. In this sense, every human being is constitutively religious. Secondly, in this new religious-philosophical framework, we find also a new theological understanding of religion. Theology now relates the Christian religion to an underlying general concept of religion. From this follows that the contents of a historical religion do not refer to objects beyond consciousness. Rather, these religious contents refer only to religion as an element in the general structure of human consciousness or the philosophical theory of religion. Religion becomes self-related, that is to say, it refers only to itself as "religion." Only in this way is religion autonomous, an independent form in culture alongside others.

We find this new understanding of religion as the basis for theology not only in Friedrich Schleiermacher's speeches *Über die Religion* or in his dogmatics *Der christliche Glaube*,[11] but also in many other theologians of the nineteenth and early twentieth centuries.[12] For all of them, religion is understood as an element in the structure of human consciousness or, as

---

[11] Cf. Friedrich Schleiermacher, *On Religion. Speeches to its Cultured Despisers*, ed. and trans. Richard Crouter (Cambridge: Cambridge University Press, 1996); *The Christian Faith*, 2 vol. (Louisville: Westminster John Knox Press, 2016).

[12] As Rudolf Otto advances in his famous book *Das Heilige* from 1917, the numinous feeling is the basis and core of all historical religions. Cf. below chapter III. To the debates about theology as science in the nineteenth century, cf. Johannes Zachhuber, *Theology as Science in Nineteenth-Century Germany. From F. C. Baur to Ernst Troeltsch* (Oxford: Oxford Academic, 2013); Georg Pfleiderer and Harald Matern (eds.), *Die Religion der Bürger. Der Religionsbegriff in der protestantischen Theologie vom Vormärz bis zum Ersten Weltkrieg* (Tübingen: Mohr Siebeck, 2021).

formulated at the end of the nineteenth century, based on a so-called "religious a priori."[13] On the one side, religion is an essential human element and is constitutive for human beings. And on the other side, actual religion is seen as the realization of this a priori potential in various historical and symbolic forms. In this way, the various historical religions are understood as actualizations of the one inner religion as a structural element in human consciousness. This is also true for Christianity as a particular historical realization of human beings' inner religion. Naturally, in the nineteenth century most theologians were convinced that in Christianity the notion of religion finds its historical realization. Therefore, Christianity was seen as the "absolute religion" or "perfect religion."[14]

As we have seen, theology as science is, under the conditions of modernity, possible only on the basis of the concept of religion. In these constructions of theology, religion is understood on the one hand as a part of the structure of consciousness, and on the other hand, the contents of the historical religions—like Christianity—either refer to religion, or they are all expressions of the inner human religion. However, around 1900, we find a change in the theological constructions of religion. Especially in theological debates after the First World War, the foundations of theology that start from religion as the basis of theology became subject to criticism. The object of theology, as many younger theologians now declare, is not religion, but God alone and God's revelation. Consequently, they criticize the concept of religion as the foundation for theology as inadequate. Returning to the task of this book, we must ask the question, how can this theological development in German Protestant theology around 1900, in the time of Tillich's theological beginnings, be understood?

The first response to be considered is the state of the social and cultural development at that time. By 1900 the process of modernization had

---

[13] Cf. Peter Harrison, "'Science' and 'Religion': Constructing the Boundaries," in *The Journal of Religion* 86 (2006) 86–106; Michael Bergunder, "'Religion' and 'Science' within the Global History," in *Aris* 16 (2016) 86–141.

[14] To the discussions around 1900, cf. Ernst Troeltsch, *Die Absolutheit des Christentums und die Religionsgeschichte (1902/1912), mit den Thesen von 1901 und den handschriftlichen Zusätzen* (KGA, vol. V), ed. by Trutz Rendtorff (Berlin; New York: de Gruyter, 1998).

led to a functional differentiation of society and culture.[15] It followed from this that the different cultural systems, such as science, politics, economy, art, and religion, now stood side by side, as it were. All these diverse cultural forms now follow their own autonomous logic without a general unity of the society or the culture. But the increasing differentiation of society and culture is only one aspect of the new situation confronting theology. The academic disciplines dealing with religion had also become much more differentiated around 1900.[16] It was no longer theology alone that was engaged in the study of religion, as was the case during the preceding century. With religious studies, psychology of religion, sociology of religion and other related research fields, academic disciplines, independent from theology, emerged during this period. Thus, in order to remain an autonomous academic discipline alongside other academic disciplines, theology was compelled to develop its own approach to religion. Both aspects mentioned led to a new understanding of theology as science, or as an academic discipline. Against the backdrop of the functional differentiation of culture and society, conceptions of religion which located religion in the general structure of human consciousness became implausible. This can be understood as a consequence of the fact that the unity of culture had been lost. What followed, however, was the task of giving a new determination of religion. Alongside the other scientific disciplines, theology had to work out a new understanding of itself as an autonomous scientific discipline. Otherwise, theology could not be a discipline of its own, as distinct from philosophy of religion, religious studies, and so forth. For theology, this meant that it had to work out its own description of religion— and theology did this with concepts and categories derived from its own doctrinal tradition. It replaced the concept of religion in the sense of a faculty of consciousness by the concept of God and God's revelation. The immediate recourse to the concept of God, which was significant for these theologies, thus had a specific function: it served to redescribe religion.

In the literature about the development of Protestant theology after the First World War, it remains controversial as to how to interpret the

---

[15] Cf. Peter Beyer, *Religion in Global Society* (London; New York: Routledge, 2006), 18–61; Christopher A. Bayly, *Birth of the Modern World. Global Connections and Comparisons* (Oxford: Blackwell, 2004).

[16] Cf. Hans G. Kippenberg, *Die Entdeckung der Religionsgeschichte. Religionswissenschaft und Moderne* (München: C. H. Beck, 1997).

changes associated with the advent of the so-called "dialectical theology."[17] For some interpreters, this represents a return of theology to its own proper foundation, namely, God and God's revelation.[18] For others, the shift is a break, namely, the exit of theology from modern consciousness and the return to a pre-modern form of theology.[19] But both interpretations are one-sided and inadequate. We must see the emergence of dialectical theology against the background of the above-described development of modern culture and its consequences for theology as a "scientific discipline." If we proceed in this manner, we will see that the new change of focus from the notion of religion to a focus on the ideas of God and revelation does not constitute a break with the trajectory of modern theology. On the contrary, the replacement of religion with the notion of God is simply a new determination of religion in a more embracing sense. Religion, as we understand from the critique of religion, is not an element in the general structure of the human consciousness. A religion which is understood as a part of the human being, or as an a priori concept in the human consciousness, is nothing more than a presupposition. However, religion is not a substantive thing that exists independently of the actual religious performative act. Rather, religion is precisely the religious performance. And this performative act happens without a presupposition within human consciousness or in culture. Both the notion of God and the revelation of God describe the performance of religion as an event that has no presupposition in the human being. That is what is meant with the transcendence of God, namely, that the religious performative act exists

---

[17] Cf. Wolfhart Pannenberg, *Problemgeschichte der neueren evangelischen Theologie in Deutschland. Von Schleiermacher bis zu Barth und Tillich* (Göttingen: Vandenhoeck & Ruprecht, 1997); Hermann Fischer, *Systematische Theologie. Konzeptionen und Probleme im 20. Jahrhundert* (Stuttgart; Berlin; Köln: Kohlhammer, 1992); Friedrich W. Graf, *Der heilige Zeitgeist. Studien zur Ideengeschichte der protestantischen Theologie in der Weimarer Republik* (Tübingen: Mohr Siebeck, 2011).

[18] So the statement from Rudolf Bultmann. Cf. Rudolf Bultmann, "Die liberale Theologie und die jüngste theologische Bewegung," in *Glaube und Verstehen*, vol. 1 (Tübingen: Mohr Siebeck, 1958), 1–25, here 1.

[19] In the view of Tillich, the dialectical theology is ambiguous. On the one side he could see himself close to these theologians, and on the other side he names this theology "neo-orthodox" (ST I, 7). Cf. below chapter V.

only as an actual performance that has no foundation in human consciousness. But this performative act of religion is a reflexive one in the self-relation of consciousness. To it belongs the knowledge that it exists only as a performance that arises without a religious precondition in the structure of the human being. This is exactly what the concept of revelation denotes. Revelation is a reflexive category and does not describe anything in terms of content.[20]

The development of Protestant theology during the time of Tillich's study, around 1900 and then after the First World War, led to a new determination of the concept of religion. Religion was now no longer a part in the general structure of human consciousness and, in this way, something that exists without its use by human beings. Against such an understanding, religion can now be understood as a performative act. The task of both theology and the philosophy of religion now becomes, as Tillich formulated in 1922, to overcome the concept of religion—that is, the presupposition of a religious disposition in human beings.[21] For this stands the notion of faith, which now replaces religion as an element in human consciousness. So, the critique of religion from the dialectical theologians is not a critique of religion as such, but a critique of a particular understanding of religion. At the same time, however, the new theological departures after the First World War hold fast to a reflexive understanding of religion. The claim to God has a determined function in the self-referential redefinitions of religion as faith. For even in the theological conceptions of the 1920s, religious contents do not refer to objects outside of religious consciousness; they refer to religion, but no longer to a religion that is an element in the general structure of human consciousness. Religious contents, rather, refer to religion as a performative act that arises in human beings without preconditions. Thus, it becomes the task of theology to describe how religion comes into being together with its contents and its knowledge of being religion.

---

[20] Cf. Paul Tillich, "Die Idee der Offenbarung," in GW VIII, 31–39; Rudolf Bultmann, "Der Begriff der Offenbarung im Neuen Testament," in *Glaube und Verstehen*, vol. 3 (Tübingen: Mohr Siebeck, 1960), 1–34; Karl Barth, *Die kirchliche Dogmatik*, vol. I/1 (8th ed. Zürich: TVZ, 1964), 311–367.

[21] Cf. Paul Tillich, "Die Überwindung des Religionsbegriffs in der Religionsphilosophie," in GW I, 367–388.

With that we have outlined the horizon of the theological debates within which Tillich worked out his own theology, at first during and after his university studies, and then in the period after World War I. His theology can only be understood in this context. Tillich takes up the debates of his time and formulates answers to these theological problems in his writings. The outworking of this process is the subject of the chapters of this book. In the first part of the book – *A. Contexts* –, the development of Tillich's theology is discussed against the background of the theological horizon just described, as revealed in the extant writings from his university student days and in his two dissertations. The other chapters of the first part trace the development and shaping of his theology against the background of contemporary theological and philosophical debates in the 1920s and 1930s. In doing so, the presentation is oriented towards Tillich's understanding of religion in terms of a theology of revelation, which forms the basis of his later method of correlation. In the second part of this book – *B. Key Issues* –, Tillich's doctrine of God, Christology, and pneumatology are discussed in a systematic perspective against the background of the history of the work's development outlined in the first part. With this outline, Tillich's Trinitarian concept of revelation is incorporated. This understanding of revelation is also the basis of Tillich's conception of a theology of the history of religions, which will conclude *Part B*, and which, by its turn, focuses us on the *Systematic Theology*. In this way, the two main parts of the study complement each other to form a whole.

In the final chapter of this book, we must return to the outline of the history of Protestant theology given in this *Prologue*. The reason is that we must deal with the significance of the theology of Paul Tillich for contemporary theological debates. This is only possible, however, if we look at the ongoing debate in theology in the twentieth century against the backdrop of the process of modernization of culture and society.

A.

Contexts

Modern-Positive Theology, Neo-Idealism, and the Young Tillich

One of the unquestioned convictions of Tillich research is that of the fundamental importance of Schelling's philosophy for his theology. Tillich himself referred to it in his autobiography *On the Boundary*, with which he prefaced his 1936 collection of essays *The Interpretation of History*, in order to introduce and recommend himself to his readers in the United States. Here it says:

> Partly by chance of a bargain purchase, and partly by inner af-
> finity I came under the influence of Schelling, whose collected
> works I read through several times with enthusiasm, and con-
> cerning whom I wrote my theses both for the degree of Doctor
> of Philosophy and Licentiate of Theology.[1]

In other writings from his American period, Tillich also repeatedly emphasizes the importance of Schelling for the formation of his own philosophy of religion and theological thought and refers to Schelling as his teacher.[2] Now indeed, it cannot by any means be denied that the young Tillich intensively studied Schelling's philosophy. As Tillich himself mentions in *On the Boundary*, Schelling's philosophy was the subject of his two

---

[1] Paul Tillich, "On the Boundary," in *The Interpretation of History* (New York; London: Charles Scribners Son's, 1936), 3–73, here 31.

[2] Cf. Paul Tillich, "Schelling und die Anfänge des existentialistischen Protestes," in MW I, 392: "He [sc. Schelling] was my teacher, although the beginning of my studies and the year of his death are 50 years apart. In developing my own thought I have never forgotten my dependence on Schelling. [...] My work on the problems of systematic theology would be unthinkable without him." Cf. Tillich, *Perspectives on the 19th and 20th Century Protestant Theology*, 142.

dissertations: *Die religionsgeschichtliche Konstruktion in Schellings positiver Philosophie, ihre Voraussetzungen und Prinzipien,* from 1910,[3] and his so-called theological licentiate-dissertation on *Mystik und Schuldbewußtsein in Schellings philosophischer Entwicklung,* submitted two years later.[4] Apart from his two theses, however, the emphatic accent on Schelling's influence is not evident in the published texts of his German period, but only in those after his emigration to the United States. Is it then the case that Tillich's later self-stylization as a Schellingian is nothing more than a myth?

Tillich's late emphasis on the importance of Schelling to his own theology undermines two fundamental facts for the formation of his theology. First, he did not begin his theological career with Schelling's philosophy. Rather, Tillich received his theological education in Tübingen and Halle under the influence of his two academic teachers Adolf Schlatter and Wilhelm Lütgert, both representatives of the so-called modern-positive theology. Although Tillich mentions Lütgert in his autobiography *On the Boundary,* he most expressly named Martin Kähler as the theological teacher who was decisive for him.[5] On the other hand, Tillich had intensively studied the philosophy of Johann Gottlieb Fichte during his formation. Indeed, Tillich's initial studies of Classical German Philosophy—or German Idealism—began with Fichte during his four-semester period of study with the theological faculty at the University of Halle, from 1905 to 1907. It was only after this period, in 1909, that Tillich turned to an

---

[3] Cf. Paul Tillich, "Die religionsgeschichtliche Konstruktion in Schellings positiver Philosophie, ihre Voraussetzungen und Prinzipien," in EW IX, 156–272.

[4] Cf. Paul Tillich, "Mystik und Schuldbewußtsein in Schellings philosophischer Entwicklung," in GW I, 13–108.

[5] Cf. Tillich, "On the Boundary," 32. In his history of theology, Tillich devotes a separate chapter to Martin Kähler, while he merely mentions Adolf Schlatter and Wilhelm Lütgert. Cf. Tillich, *Perspectives on 19th and 20th Century Protestant Theology,* 213–215. Cf. also "Foreword," in Martin Kähler, *The So-Called Historical Jesus and the Historic Biblical Christ,* trans. Carl E. Braaten (Philadelphia: Fortress Press, 1964), IX-X. To my knowledge, the only passage in Tillich's writings from his German period in which he refers to Martin Kähler as his teacher is found in a review that appeared in the *Vossische Zeitung* in 1926. Cf. "Religiöse Gestalten," in *Vossische Zeitung,* Nr. 52 (1926) 1–2, here 1, reprinted in EW XXI, 131–134, here 133.

intensive study of the work of Schelling. During his time in Halle, it was the young *Privatdozent* in philosophy, Fritz Medicus, who introduced Tillich to German Idealism. Medicus was one of the central figures engaged in the debate over a "Neo-Idealism" around 1900, especially a so-called "Neo-Fichteanism."[6] In 1905, the year in which Tillich began his studies at Halle, Medicus published his important book, *J. G. Fichte. Dreizehn Vorlesungen gehalten an der Universität Halle.*[7] This book title refers to lectures that the young philosopher had given the year before Tillich arrived in Halle.

The engagement of Tillich with Fichte's philosophy, as well as the significance of that philosophy for the genesis of Tillich's theological thinking in the context of the modern-positive theology, have hitherto received only limited attention.[8] In regards to the importance of Fichte for the young theologian's intellectual development, this becomes clear when one takes note of Tillich's excerpts from Fichte's *Grundlage der gesamten*

---

[6] Cf. Friedrich W. Graf and Alf Christophersen, "Neukantianismus, Fichte- und Schellingrenaissance. Paul Tillich und sein philosophischer Lehrer Fritz Medicus," in *JHMTh* 11 (2004) 52–78; Fritz Medicus, "Neufichteanismus," in *Die Religion in Geschichte und Gegenwart*, vol. 4 (2nd ed. Tübingen: Mohr Siebeck, 1930), 498–9.

[7] Fritz Medicus, *J. G. Fichte. Dreizehn Vorlesungen gehalten an der Universität Halle* (Berlin: Reuther & Reichard, 1905).

[8] While there is already some literature on Tillich's Fichte studies, his relationship to his theological teachers Schlatter and Lütgert has not been considered by researchers at all. Cf. Samuel A. Shearn, *Pastor Tillich. The Justification of the Doubter* (Oxford: University Press 2022); Georg Neugebauer, "Freiheit als philosophisches Prinzip – Die Fichte-Interpretation des frühen Tillich," in *Wissen, Freiheit, Geschichte. Die Philosophie Fichtes im 19. und 20. Jahrhundert. Beiträge des sechsten internationalen Kongresses der Johann-Gottlieb-Fichte-Gesellschaft in Halle (Saale) vom 3.–7. Oktober 2006*, vol. 2, (Fichte-Studien, vol. 36), ed. Jürgen Stolzenberg and Oliver-Pierre Rudolph (Amsterdam; New York: Rodopi, 2012), 181–198; Christian Danz, "Theologischer Neuidealismus. Zur Rezeption der Geschichtsphilosophie Fichtes bei Friedrich Gogarten, Paul Tillich und Emanuel Hirsch," in *Wissen, Freiheit, Geschichte. Die Philosophie Fichtes im 19. und 20. Jahrhundert. Beiträge des sechsten internationalen Kongresses der Johann-Gottlieb-Fichte-Gesellschaft in Halle (Saale) vom 3.–7. Oktober 2006*, vol. 2 (Fichte-Studien, vol. 36), ed. Jürgen Stolzenberg and Oliver-Pierre Rudolph (Amsterdam; New York: Rodopi, 2012), 199–215; Marc Boss, *Au commencement la liberté. La religion de Kant réinventée par Fichte, Schelling et Tillich* (Genf: Labor et Fides, 2014).

Wissenschaftslehre (1794) and the *Wissenschaftslehre* from 1804, which, along with Tillich's other literary legacies, are preserved in the Harvard Divinity School Library, Harvard University, Cambridge, Massachusetts. This document stems from around the early period of Tillich's university studies, as he later mentioned in his autobiographical reflection, entitled *On the Boundary*.[9] Moreover, texts posthumously published in recent years—especially a seminar paper from 1906 entitled *Fichtes Religionsphilosophie in ihrem Verhältnis zum Johannesevangelium*,[10] and the doctoral lecture from Breslau in 1910, *Die Freiheit als philosophisches Prinzip bei Fichte*[11]—make clear that Tillich's entry into German Idealism was mediated by Fichte's philosophy, especially as interpreted by Medicus. This picture is further confirmed by an examination paper from 1908, entitled *Welche Bedeutung hat der Gegensatz von monistischer und dualistischer Weltanschauung für die christliche Religion?*,[12] as well as Tillich's correspondence with Friedrich Büchsel between 1907 and 1911,[13] and the scarcely known article from 1912, *Wissen und Meinen*, published on the occasion of Fichte's 150th birthday.[14]

With his Fichte studies, the young theologian, like other theologians and philosophers of his time (such as Emmanuel Hirsch, Friedrich Gogarten, Friedrich Brunstäd, and Emil Lask), found a point of departure for his own intellectual work within the renaissance of German Idealism around 1900. Tillich's occupation with Fichte's philosophy during his

---

[9] Cf. Paul Tillich, "Autobiographische Betrachtungen," in GW XII, 58–77, here 65. Tillich, "On the Boundary," 31.

[10] Cf. Paul Tillich, "Fichtes Religionsphilosophie in ihrem Verhältnis zum Johannesevangelium (1906)," in EW IX, 4–19.

[11] Cf. Paul Tillich, "Die Freiheit als philosophisches Prinzip bei Fichte," in EW X, 55–62.

[12] Cf. Paul Tillich, "Welche Bedeutung hat der Gegensatz von monistischer und dualistischer Weltanschauung für die christliche Religion? (1908)," in EW IX, 28–93 (Urfassung); 94–153 (Schönschrift), here 28: "The necessity to go beyond Kant, which is also recognized by most Neo-Kantians, finally shows itself as a necessity to go in the direction of Fichte."

[13] Cf. Correspondence from Paul Tillich and Friedrich Büchsel, in EW VI, 14–27, 62–74.

[14] Paul Tillich, "Wissen und Meinen. Zu Fichtes 150. Geburtstag am 19. Mai 1912," in *Neue Preußische Zeitung*, Nr. 232 (1912) 2, reprinted in EW XXI, 9–14.

studies is in no way to be seen as merely a stopover on his way to Schelling. Rather, his engagement with Fichte established fundamental convictions for the young thinker on the basis of which he subsequently responded to Schelling's philosophy and also began his initial theological constructions.[15]

But we must ask, why did the young Tillich concern himself with German Idealism? This becomes understandable only if one considers the biblically oriented history of salvation theology of his academic teachers. By taking up idealistic philosophy, first Fichte's and later Schelling's, Tillich's concern was to give modern-positive theology a better grounding than Schlatter and Lütgert were able to work out. This new justification of theology, which Tillich had already worked out before the First World War, consists of a new philosophy of history. In this chapter we need first of all to take a look at the perspectives of Tillich's academic teachers in Halle who introduced him to both theology and philosophy. Tillich's idea of a contemporary concept of theology in the spirit of Fichte's Idealism will be the focus of part two. In the third part we shall discuss Tillich's reception of the philosophy of Schelling, and in part four Tillich's new interpretation of the absoluteness of Christianity. In conclusion, Tillich's early theology must be placed in the context of the modern-positive theologies.

1. Modern-Positive Theology and Neo-Idealism around 1900

"In case authorities such as Schlatter and Schmuhl carry weight with you, then I inform you that I have arrived at the philosophical presupposition of both: the later Schelling" (EW VI, 76). This comment is taken from a 1909 letter of Tillich to his student friend and later brother-in-law, Alfred Fritz, in which he writes about his current reading of Schelling's works. It is revealing that the philosophy of the later Schelling is referred to as the philosophical presupposition for the theology of his Tübingen and Halle teachers, Adolf Schlatter and "Schmuhl," that is, Wilhelm Lütgert. Both

---

[15] For example, the form-substance (*Form-Gehalt*) schema that is constitutive for Tillich's early theology of culture stems from the analysis of Fichte as developed by his teacher, Medicus. Cf. Ulrich Barth, "Religion und Sinn," in *Religion – Kultur – Gesellschaft. Der frühe Tillich im Spiegel neuer Texte (1919–1920)*, ed. Christian Danz and Werner Schüßler (Wien: LIT, 2008), 197–213, here 210–1.

theologians, as the quotation from the 1909 letter shows, were very important to the theological development of the young Tillich. Schlatter and Lütgert were so-called modern-positive theologians. This was a conservative school of theologians with broad influence in the theological debates of their time. Around 1900, the theological faculties of Halle, Greifswald, and also Tübingen were the centers of this version of Protestant theology. These theologians began their reflection from the biblical salvation history, not from the Lutheran Creeds connected with a religious experience, as did the Neo-Lutheran theologians of Erlangen and Leipzig, nor from the revelation of God in Jesus Christ, as did Albrecht Ritschl and his school. In their dissertations and in their later work, many young followers of these theologians had also connected the motifs of their modern-positive theology with the thinking of German Idealism: for example, Friedrich Brunstäd,[16] Erich Schaeder,[17] and others like Tillich's close friend Kurt Leese, a pupil from Schaeder.[18] This was also true of Tillich, for whom the modern-positive theology of Schlatter, Lütgert, and also his father Johannes Tillich formed the background of his own engagement with German Idealism.[19] Indeed, Tillich used the philosophy of Fichte and the later Schelling for an interpretation of the theology of his own teachers.

What was it that made the theology of Schlatter and Lütgert so important for the young student Tillich? It is significant for Schlatter that, since his habilitation in 1881, in Bern, he worked out the program of an

---

[16] Cf. Friedrich Brunstäd, *Die Idee der Religion. Prinzipien der Religionsphilosophie* (Halle: Niemeyer, 1922). Cf. Christoph Schwöbel, "Die Idee der Religion und die Wirklichkeit der Religionen," in *Religion und Religionen im Deutschen Idealismus. Schleiermacher – Hegel – Schelling*, ed. Friedrich Hermanni, Burkhard Nonnenmacher and Friederike Schick (Tübingen: Mohr Siebeck, 2015), 449–475; Julius Trugenberger, *Neuhegelianisches Kulturluthertum. Friedrich Brundstäd (1883–1944)* (Berlin; Boston: de Gruyter, 2021).

[17] Cf. Klaus-Dieter Rieger, *Heiliger Geist und Wirklichkeit. Erich Schaeders Pneumatologie und die Kritik Karl Barths* (Berlin; Boston: de Gruyter, 2017).

[18] Cf. Anton Knuth, *Der Protestantismus als moderne Religion. Historisch-systematische Rekonstruktion der religionsphilosophischen Theologie Kurt Leeses (1887–1965)* (Frankfurt a.M.: Peter Lang, 2005).

[19] Cf. Shearn, *Pastor Tillich*, 38–49.

empirical theology, which is concerned with the knowledge of God in nature and history.[20] His theological realism consists in the fact that he bases God as the cause of nature and history. God is thus always already related to the concrete in the world as its ground of unity. The soul, i.e., the consciousness of human beings, is always already in real contact with the world by perceiving it. Perception means here the affect of reality on the soul, which is given in consciousness as memory pictures and is processed by consciousness by means of a double step of analysis and synthesis. In the faith bound to the self-revelation of God, God discloses God's self to human beings as the cause of both the world and history, so that both become media of God. Theology is, here, knowledge of God, and this knowledge is bound to the revelation of God. For dogmatic theology, this means: "The dogmatic question is thus where and how we experience events that become the revelation of God to us, and the dogmatic proof, the proof of God, consists in showing the events through which our consciousness of God arises and gets its content."[21] Schlatter's student, Wilhelm Lütgert took up his program of a realistic theology.[22] Like his teacher, Lütgert also tied all knowledge of God to God's revelation and distinguished between a universal revelation in creation and a special salvation revelation of God,

---

[20] Cf. Adolf Schlatter, "Habilitationsrede zum Zusammenhang von Dogma und Geschichte," in *Das Verhältnis von Theologie und Philosophie II. Die Berner Vorlesung (1883): Wesen und Quellen der Gotteserkenntnis*, ed. Harald Seubert and Werner Neuer (Stuttgart: Calwer, 2019), 249–258; "Wesen und Quellen der Gotteserkenntnis. Berner Vorlesung im Sommersemester 1883," in *Das Verhältnis von Theologie und Philosophie II. Die Berner Vorlesung (1883): Wesen und Quellen der Gotteserkenntnis*, ed. Harald Seubert and Werner Neuer (Stuttgart: Calwer, 2019), 67–247. Schlatter elaborated his early reflections in his main dogmatic work *Das christliche Dogma*, from 1911. Cf. Adolf Schlatter, *Das christliche Dogma* (2nd ed. Stuttgart: Calwer, 1923).

[21] Schlatter, *Das christliche Dogma*, 11.

[22] Cf. Wilhelm Lütgert, *Die Methode des dogmatischen Beweises in ihrer Entwicklung unter dem Einfluß Schleiermachers* (Gütersloh: Bertelsmann, 1892); *Gottes Sohn und Gottes Geist. Vorträge zur Christologie und zur Lehre vom Geist Gottes* (Leipzig: Deichert'sche Verlagsbuchhandlung, 1905); *Schöpfung und Offenbarung. Eine Theologie des ersten Artikels* (Gütersloh: Gütersloher Verlagshaus Mohn, 1934), 25: "Theology, like every science, starts from facts, observations, perceptions, i.e. from revelation, from seeing and hearing. But the special nature of theological thinking is that this empirical basis is understood from God, because in it God is revealed."

whereby the former forms the basis of the latter. The starting point for their theology was not the revelation of God in Jesus Christ, but rather God's revelation in nature and culture. With this conception, they both rejected the theology of Albrecht Ritschl, who restricted the revelation of God to Jesus Christ. For if, as they argued, we find God only through the revelation in Christ, then both nature and culture play no real, definitive role in theology.[23] That is the reason why Schlatter and Lütgert worked out conceptions of theology that started from God's universal revelation, and then they integrated God's revelation in Christ into this framework. It is also noteworthy that both theologians explicitly connected their theology with philosophical motifs derived from German Idealism.[24] The young Tillich embraced this approach to theological construction. Thus, on the premise of a universal concept of revelation, Tillich proceeded to criticize the dominant theology of Albrecht Ritschl. Already in his essay on monism from 1908 (*Monismusschrift*), Tillich had argued against Ritschl's sharp separation of theology from metaphysics.[25] And, in his work after the First World War, Tillich continued this pattern, as we may note in his differentiation of a foundational revelation (*Grundoffenbarung*) from a salvation revelation (*Heilsoffenbarung*) in his 1924 lecture on *Rechtfertigung und Zweifel*.[26] Such a conception of the basis of theological reflection was quite different from that of Martin Kähler, whom Tillich would describe as "his teacher." Undoubtedly, Kähler was also a modern-positive theologian, but as his main work, *Die Wissenschaft der christlichen Lehre*, shows, he began his theology from the concept of justification—

---

[23] Cf. Schlatter, *Das christliche Dogma*, 18: "Whoever turns his observation immediately and solely to Jesus also has a danger to ward off, namely that of seeing the whole world as dark and godless, and of hiding God's Creator Glory."

[24] Cf. Adolf Schlatter, *Die philosophische Arbeit seit Cartesius. Ihr ethischer und religiöser Ertrag* (Gütersloh: Calwer, 1906); Wilhelm Lütgert, *Die Religion des Deutschen Idealismus und ihr Ende*, 3 vol. (Gütersloh: Bertelsmann, 1923–1925).

[25] Cf. Tillich, „"Welche Bedeutung hat der Gegensatz von monistischer und dualistischer Weltanschauung für die christliche Religion? (1908)," 28.

[26] Cf. Paul Tillich, "Rechtfertigung und Zweifel," in GW VIII, 85–100. Cf. below chapter V.

that is, from the salvation in Christ—rather than from a universal revelation.[27]

As already mentioned, Schlatter and Lütgert connected their theologies with aspects derived from German Idealism. Especially in regards to Lütgert, we can see that he makes use of the interpretation of Fichte from his colleague in Halle, Fritz Medicus. In Lütgert's book *Die Religion des Deutschen Idealismus und ihr Ende*, from 1923—which, as Lütgert wrote in the preface, went back to his lectures in Halle, from 1908—the philosophy of Fichte is understood as the "doctrine of conviction" (*Überzeugungslehre*).[28] This is exactly the interpretation of the idealistic thinker advanced by Fritz Medicus in his book from 1905. This book is also decisive for Tillich's understanding of German Idealism, as we can see in his early texts. According to Medicus, the central point of the philosophy of Fichte is the concept of conviction (*Überzeugung*). In the concept of conviction, Medicus sees the importance of Fichte—the "*Wissenschaftslehrer*"—for his own time and especially for the crisis of historicism.[29]

There are three central aspects in Medicus's interpretation of the philosophy of Fichte. First, the understanding of the I as conviction. That means the I is nothing other than a deed-action (*Tathandlung*), which has a reflexive knowledge about itself. Following Fichte's writing *Ueber den Begriff der Wissenschaftslehre*, Medicus made a differentiation between form and substance (*Gehalt*), and understood the I as action and substance. In this action lies the foundation of the certainty of the I.[30] But in consciousness, this certainty is only present as form, that is to say, as a conviction of the certainty as a proposition.[31] Against the background of this structure, Medicus interpreted the I as conviction as the self-disclosedness of the I. The realization of the I must take up the Not-I in the I. In his book about

---

[27] Cf. Martin Kähler, *Die Wissenschaft der christlichen Lehre von dem evangelischen Grundartikel aus im Abrisse dargestellt* (Leipzig: Deichert'sche Verlagsbuchhandlung, 1905), 5: "Christianity is the first recognizable object of theology; it demands a special science, because its understanding is conditioned by its possession. But that in Christianity, which cannot be grasped without personal Christianity and which constitutes the actual [!] object of theology, is the religious knowledge of God revealed in Christ [!] from his deeds and effects."

[28] Lütgert, *Die Religion des Deutschen Idealismus und ihr Ende*, vol. 1, 37.

[29] Cf. Medicus, *J. G. Fichte*, 14.

[30] Cf. Medicus, *J. G. Fichte*, 70.

[31] Cf. Medicus, *J. G. Fichte*, 71.

Fichte from 1905, Medicus dealt not only with the early *Wissenschaftslehre* from 1794, but he also interpreted the late *Wissenschaftslehre* as a further development of the early conception. This is the second important point. The later philosophy of Fichte, especially the so-called *Wissenschaftslehre* from 1801/02 and 1804, established a differentiation between the absolute and the absolute knowledge (*absolutes Wissen*). It is significant for the later Fichte that the self-disclosedness of the I is now understood as substance, and the knowledge as form. The I is the image (*Bild*) of the absolute. Medicus calls the late philosophy of Fichte with respect to the Gospel of John the "Johannine period" of Fichte. It is interesting to note that Medicus, through a quotation of Wilhelm Lütgert's book *Die johanneische Christologie*,[32] pointed out that Fichte's interpretation of the Gospel of John is wrong.[33] In the first place, Fichte's understanding of sin as a lack of autonomy is different from that of the Gospel of John. For Fichte, sin meant that the I does not grasp itself as I, that is, that it falls behind itself as autonomy in the act of its self-positing.[34] Rather, against such a negative understanding, sin is, according to the Gospel of John, an act and, thus, something positive. The third central aspect is Fichte's conception of history. Medicus interprets Fichte's philosophy of history as a construction of the consciousness of history. There is no connection between empirical history and the philosophy of history.[35] Rather, the philosophy of history constructs a history of self-consciousness (*Geschichte des Selbstbewusstseins*). That is to say, the philosophy of history reconstructs the path of self-consciousness on its way to its own self-understanding. The young Paul Tillich took up this understanding of history from his teacher, Medicus. And, as with Medicus, so also with Tillich, Fichte's conception of history as a history of self-consciousness functions as the basis of a philosophy of history that has the goal of overcoming the crisis of historicism, as Ernst Troeltsch calls it.

---

[32] Cf. Wilhelm Lütgert, *Die johanneische Christologie* (Gütersloh: Bertelsmann, 1899).

[33] Cf. Medicus, *J. G. Fichte*, 225.

[34] Cf. Medicus, *J. G. Fichte*, 226.

[35] Cf. Medicus, *J. G. Fichte*, 220.

2. Sin and Freedom; or, Tillich's
Interpretation of Fichte

During his first semester in Halle in 1905/1906, the young theologian Tillich participated in a seminar offered by Fritz Medicus on the theme of
"Philosophical Exercises (Fichte)."[36] It was for this seminar that Tillich
wrote the paper *Fichtes Religionsphilosophie in ihrem Verhältnis zum Johannesevangelium*. This paper set itself the task of "working out the main
ideas" of Fichte's philosophy of religion, "and comparing them with those
of the Gospel of John" (EW IX, 9). For this purpose, Tillich assumed a
concept of religion according to which the religious consciousness is the
"most central, all determining expression of the spirit" (EW IX, 4). The
functions of thought and will are constitutive for the life of the spirit.[37] For
the theology student, these pre-conditions result in two fundamental types
of religion or notions of God: a voluntaristic type and an intellectualist
type. While Judaism produced a voluntaristic notion of God, an intellectualist formulation was more significant for the ancient Greeks. Tillich
ultimately understands Christianity as a synthesis of voluntarism and intellectualism: "God reveals himself in Christ as a God of grace and truth"
(EW IX, 5).

Against the background of this constellation, Tillich compares
Fichte's philosophy of religion with the Gospel of John on the basis of
three aspects: first the metaphysical basis (i.e., the notion of God and
God's relation to the world), second the "historical significance of Christ
and Christendom," and third its "moral-religious consequences" (EW IX,
9). At this point, a detailed engagement with Tillich's deliberations must
be left aside. Although we must limit ourselves to a systematic aspect of
his interpretation of Fichte, it should nevertheless be pointed out that the
twenty-year-old theologian mainly refers to what he, following Medicus,
calls the third phase of the development of the history of Fichte's philosophy. By this is meant Fichte's *Anweisung zum seligen Leben*, from 1806.
Furthermore, the citations which the theologian assembled from the
works of the philosopher do not appear to go back to his own extensive

---

[36] Cf. Tillich, "Fichtes Religionsphilosophie in ihrem Verhältnis zum Johannesevangelium (1906)," 1.

[37] Cf. Tillich, "Fichtes Religionsphilosophie in ihrem Verhältnis zum Johannesevangelium (1906)," 4.

reading of Fichte, but rather to Medicus's book from 1905, *J. G. Fichte.* However, we must turn now to Tillich's early image of Fichte.

According to the young theologian, Fichte's philosophy of religion had indeed overcome Kant's "subjectivism and skepticism" (EW IX, 7), and had, in the last phase of his works, i.e., the "Johannine phase," advanced a concept that accounted equally for the subjective and objective sides of religion. However, Fichte's interpretation of Johannine Christianity excluded all voluntaristic moments. Thus, his philosophy of religion was intellectualist and did not do justice either to the synthesis arrived at in Christianity, or (as Tillich showed by going through the three above-named aspects) to the Gospel of John. The young theologian's image of Fichte, as expressed in the seminar paper from 1906, was thus quite critical and thereby similar to Medicus's (and also Lütgert's) interpretation. In the comparison of the philosopher with the fourth evangelist, he thoroughly determined Fichte's philosophy as an intellectualist one. This intellectualist trait was reflected, above all, in Fichte's concept of sin. Against Fichte's view, Tillich argued that sin is actually "something totally other than the negative." It is "indeed the powerful positive [*Position*] that rules the world" (EW IX, 13) and, therefore, not a mere "Not-I."

The seminar paper from 1906 represents an intermission. This is most clearly visible if we compare the paper from 1906 with Tillich's examination paper about monism, from 1908. The latter is concerned with a rehabilitation of Idealism for theology, and again it carries distinct traces of Medicus's interpretation of Fichte.[38] The young theologian is now concerned with a monism of the spirit which takes dualism up into itself as a necessary moment of passage. "This is the idealistic interpretation of reality. It moves through a dualism and ends in the monism of the spirit" (EW IX, 54). In this program, certain motifs emerge that will occupy Tillich in all his further works.[39] However, here they are still accomplished thoroughly on the basis of Fichte's philosophy.[40] Yet, we must also leave a detailed reconstruction of the *Monismusschrift* aside, and limit ourselves to

---

[38] Cf. Georg Neugebauer, *Tillichs frühe Christologie. Eine Untersuchung zu Offenbarung und Geschichte bei Paul Tillich vor dem Hintergrund seiner Schellingrezeption* (Berlin; New York: de Gruyter, 2007), 146–155.

[39] Cf. below chapter III.

[40] Cf. Tillich, "Welche Bedeutung hat der Gegensatz von monistischer und dualistischer Weltanschauung für die christliche Religion? (1908)," 61.

considering how Tillich carried forward both of the above-mentioned critiques of Fichte: on the one hand, his intellectualism, and on the other hand, the notion of sin.

While the theology student in his 1906 seminar paper interpreted Fichte's philosophy as intellectualism, his examination paper completely revoked this image. Fichte's philosophy now appears as a synthesis of intellectualism and voluntarism on the basis of practical reason, the freedom of self-determination. The accusation of intellectualism is now turned upon Hegel. "In Fichte and Schelling, Idealism still has both moments [sc. the intellectual and the voluntaristic side of the life of the spirit] in itself, while Hegel already falls back into intellectualism" (EW IX, 72). As a result, the concept of sin appears in a new light. "Sin is the limitation of the spirit that must be overcome, or more precisely: the lack of overcoming the Not-I, the lingering of the spiritual personality [*Persönlichkeit*] behind its *telos*" (EW IX, 68). Though in his seminar paper of 1906 Tillich criticized Fichte's understanding of sin as negation, he now takes it up. Sin is an act of self-determination of the I in which the I does not succeed in taking up the Not-I into its self-understanding. Thus neither self-recognition, nor a representation of God in the overcoming of the Not-I are achieved.[41] In other words, in sin the human being misses autonomy.

Tillich's image of Fichte had changed during the short time between the seminar paper from Halle and the examination paper from Berlin. First, Fichte's interpretation of sin is criticized and rejected. Later, however, it is taken up as the basis of a theological system. This shows both that Tillich resorted to German Idealism in order to solve theological problems, but also that he was not yet able to solve these problems in an adequate way, for he did not yet have the conceptual means to undertake such a task.

3. Formal and Material Freedom; or, Tillich's Interpretation of Schelling

As in the case of Tillich's reception of the philosophy of Fichte, so also his reception of Schelling stands in the horizon of the Halle debates about a modern-positive theology. Tillich had engaged with the thought of the

---

[41] Cf. Tillich, "Welche Bedeutung hat der Gegensatz von monistischer und dualistischer Weltanschauung für die christliche Religion? (1908)," 61.

philosopher from Leonberg within the framework of his dissertation project since 1909.[42] As is well known, he submitted his dissertation to the faculty at the University of Breslau as a philosophical dissertation. Although it was originally planned for the attainment of a theological licentiate degree, Tillich submitted his dissertation to the department of philosophy in order to obtain a secular stipend offered by the city of Berlin. It is no longer possible to determine from the extant sources and documents who proposed the theme of Tillich's dissertation. Against the background of the course of his studies and his early Fichte reception, an engagement with Schelling does not immediately suggest itself, even if it is undoubtedly within the sphere of the contemporary *Idealismusrenaissance*. But it is worth noting that Fritz Medicus wrote a review of the works of Schelling in 1908.[43] Although the examination paper from 1908 documents a strong affinity with German Idealism, Schelling in particular does not play a fundamental role in it. That changed around 1909, however, as attested by the previously quoted statement from the letter to Alfred Fritz. "On every page" of Schelling, writes Tillich in the letter, "I discover a new cornerstone of Schmuhl's thought, up to the very last psychologumena: I am utterly surprised, that we should rediscover one another here" (EW VI, 76). The engagement with Schelling led to a new placement of Fichte. This new placement of Fichte's philosophy had to do with a question which that already surfaced in the seminar paper from 1906, and which did not find a fitting solution in the *Monismusschrift* two years later. I refer to the concept of freedom and the correlative understanding of sin as negation. Tillich's reading of Schelling led to a deepening of his concept of freedom, which became at the same time the basis for a new philosophy of history and religion. The foundation of both history and religion is the absolute. The philosophical dissertation he submitted to Breslau in 1910, under the title *Die religionsgeschichtliche Konstruktion in Schellings positive Philosophie*, and the series of theses from 1911 on *Die christliche Gewißheit und der historische Jesus*, indicate Tillich's new understanding of the concept of freedom in connection with the absolute and history. We must now discuss this new understanding by referring to the philosophical dissertation on

---

[42] Cf. the letter to Alfred Fritz from 1909, in EW VI, 76–7; cf. Neugebauer, *Tillichs frühe Christologie*, 155–158; Shearn, *Pastor Tillich*, 75–103.

[43] Cf. Fritz Medicus, "Review of F. W. J. Schelling, Werke, Auswahl in drei Bänden [...], ed. Otto Weiss," in *Kant-Studien* 13 (1908) 317–328.

Schelling from 1910 and the Breslau post-doctoral lecture, *Die Freiheit als philosophisches Prinzip bei Fichte*, from 22 August 1910.

Tillich construed Schelling's philosophical development as a whole as the result of the critical questions raised by Immanuel Kant.[44] Thus, the two basic phases that Tillich distinguished in Schelling's development were both understood as having arisen from within the horizon of the questions posed by Kant. The difference Tillich saw between these two phases was a matter of the changed way in which the philosophy of history was understood. Concerning Schelling's late philosophy, Tillich says: "The knowledge of God is also the knowledge of history and not, as in the earlier Schelling, the knowledge of nature" (EW X, 20). Tillich believed that Schelling's new assessment of history—an assessment that Schelling arrived at in his work of 1809, *Philosophische Untersuchungen über das Wesen der menschlichen Freiheit*—was the consequence of Schelling's new idea of God. What was new in this concept of God was that Schelling no longer conceived of the absolute as an immediate identity, as in his early so-called philosophy of identity. Rather, Schelling took up contradiction and difference into the concept of the absolute.

> When we describe the absolute not as thesis, but as synthesis, we thereby take up contradiction into the absolute. In so doing we also take up the irrational into the absolute. Just why it is the case that the absolute should posit itself as determined both by unity and by contradiction is something that is absolutely underivable. (GW I, 78)

Schelling's new conception of the absolute is connected with a new understanding of freedom. His concept of the potencies leads to an interpretation of the absolute spirit as freedom that can contradict itself. Freedom is not only autonomy, like in the theories of Kant and Fichte, but is rather the possibility of self-contradiction. "Without self-contradiction [*Selbstentgegensetzung*] there is no living self-positing [*Selbstsetzung*], and without living self-positing there is no perfect freedom, and without perfect freedom there is no spiritual personality of God" (EW IX, 175). If freedom is the possibility of the self-contradiction of freedom, then sin is

---

[44] Cf. Paul Tillich, "Gott und das Absolute bei Schelling," in EW X, 9–54, here 12.

a positive act and not merely negative. Therefore, for the concept of freedom, it is necessary to complete the material concept of freedom through a formal understanding of freedom. Sin is, as Tillich wrote in his draft *Gott und das Absolute bei Schelling* from 1910, "freedom and not absence, disharmony, not absence of harmony, separateness that wants to be unity, not unconnectedness [*Unverbundenheit*]" (EW X, 32).

In the dissertation lecture from August 1910, Tillich pronounced his new understanding of freedom, which led him to an interpretation of Fichte's philosophy as the completion of Kantian critical philosophy. The theologian, still following Fritz Medicus, perceives the pre-condition for this claim in the notion of autonomy, which makes up the foundation of the system. "An observation of the principle of the Fichtean philosophy, the concept of freedom in Fichte, teaches us that this process does indeed have an inner congruity. In it, the motifs of critical philosophy take full effect" (EW X, 55).[45] And yet, the completion of critical philosophy means simultaneously "a narrowing of scope" (ibd.). The lecture works out this thesis in two lines of argument: first, with reference to Fichte's "consistent execution of Kantian anti-empiricism," and second, with reference to "Kantian anti-dogmatism" (EW X, 56). In both sequences of thought, which cannot be considered here, it is the notion of autonomy that bears the whole weight of explanation. The I is not an object, but a deed-action (*Tathandlung*), inasmuch as it grasps itself in its unconditional validity through its self-positing. But of importance for our line of inquiry is a distinction that Tillich introduces in this context as an aside.[46]

> In the *Kritik der praktischen Vernunft*, the postulate of freedom is posited as the faculty of the free [*willkürlichen*] incorporations of maxims. This concept of freedom—in contrast to the principle of rational autonomy, as something to be formally characterized—disappears in Fichte. It has no place in the implemented system of reason. (EW X, 58).

The basis of the completed system of reason is a material concept of freedom, namely, freedom in the sense of moral autonomy. Against the background of this concept of freedom, sin can only be conceived of as

---

[45] Cf. Medicus, *J. G. Fichte*, 57.
[46] Cf. Danz, *Theologischer Neuidealismus*, 200–204.

negation. Herein lies now—in 1910—the reductionism of Fichte's conception. In order to understand sin as a positive act, the material concept of freedom (autonomy) must be supplemented by a formal concept of freedom.[47] Freedom is only fittingly conceived of when it is understood as the power of self-contradiction (formal freedom), and not merely as the submission of the will to the moral law. To have introduced this concept of freedom in continuity with the Kantian critical philosophy is the accomplishment of the "second Schelling." Insofar as this is the result of the development of the German Idealism, Tillich concludes:

> As if in an ellipse, idealistic philosophy can be grouped around the two focal points of the double concept of freedom. In one focal point stands Fichte and the principle of his system, freedom as the self-positing of reason. On the other [side], Schelling and the principle of his philosophy of religion, freedom as the power to contradict itself. (EW X, 62)

4. Tillich's Interpretation of the Absoluteness of Christianity

Tillich's new understanding of freedom as the possibility of self-contradiction solves the problems of his interpretation of sin in his seminar paper and also in his examination paper about monism. Sin is not only a lack of autonomy, but it is now (as already in the seminar paper on Fichte and the Gospel of John from 1906) a positive act, namely the act of contradiction. At the same time, this new concept of freedom gives Tillich the possibility for a construction of history and religion in a universal dimension. But this universal history is similar to Medicus's previously-mentioned understanding of history as a structural description of religious consciousness and not an empirical history. Tillich discovered such a concept of the history of religion in the philosophy of Schelling.

According to Tillich, Schelling's understanding of the absolute as a synthesis is documented from the publication of his *Philosophische Untersuchungen über das Wesen der menschlichen Freiheit*, from 1809. Therefore, God is an identity into which the irrational contradiction is taken up. The concrete and individual, whose character as "posited" cannot be derived

---

[47] Cf. Tillich, "Die religionsgeschichtliche Konstruktion in Schellings positiver Philosophie," 174–176.

from God, is at once both the necessary and the contradictory representation of the self-relatedness of God (EW IX, 175). Taken up in this manner into the identity of its own self-relatedness, the concrete and individual is in unity with God. According to Tillich, Schelling's concept of history results from the irrational contradiction of the individual against essential being, and the reaction of essential being against the contradiction of the individual.[48] History thus understood is a history of self-consciousness in which consciousness understands itself in the reflexivity and historicity that is internal to itself. The inner structuring of this history of self-consciousness, as it takes place both in mythology and in revelation, is something that Schelling interprets as a gradual increase of reflexivity in consciousness. While mythological consciousness does not become transparent to itself in its own historicity, things are different with regard to revelation. In God's revelation in Christ, self-consciousness understands itself in the inner reflexivity of its self-relatedness. As Tillich expresses this:

> In Christianity God becomes personal, spiritual, historical to consciousness; he can only be intuited here in a historical personality. But being historical means sacrificing oneself in one's natural status [*Natürlichkeit*] in order to rediscover oneself in one's spiritual status [*Geistigkeit*]. This intuition was given in Christ, and therefore God became personal to human beings in him. (EW IX, 271)

The quote speaks of the revelation of God in Jesus Christ. This revelation introduces a personal and historical view of reality into history. And this personal and historical view of reality takes place exactly by the fact that Jesus Christ as a special person negates and cancels his particularity. Only in this way is Christ, as an individual spirit, a representation of the absolute spirit. By negating itself and becoming the medium of the absolute spirit, the world returns to God. Christ, then, is the image of the self-representation of the history of the absolute spirit. Tillich takes up this

---

[48] Cf. Tillich, "Die religionsgeschichtliche Konstruktion in Schellings positiver Philosophie," 174: "But that is the irrational will, the principle of subjectivity, whose contradiction to the principle of objectivity, the will of love, is the condition of particularity [*Einzelheit*], selfhood [*Selbstheit*] and creaturehood [*Kreatur*]. For through the contradiction the world process begins to flow, the task of which is to reconcile that which contradicts [*des Widersprechenden*]."

construction of Schelling's history, but he contradicts it at one point. Tillich makes the criticism that it is not necessary for God to become empir-
ically incarnate.[49] The content of the history of religion is solely the process
in which the absolute spirit grasps itself in its relation to itself. This is the
case in the revelation of God in Jesus Christ. But it is the individual spirit,
the human consciousness, which becomes aware of itself as a moment in
the history of the absolute spirit. Religion consists in this self-perception
of the individual spirit. Tillich identifies this process, which he calls with
Hegel the returning of the finite to the infinite, with the Holy Spirit.
Therefore, history "in its innermost character is the history of religion"
(GW I, 100). History for Tillich is not an outwardly unfolding process.
Rather, history is the history of self-consciousness in which self-conscious-
ness understands itself in its inner historicity.

Tillich reads the later philosophy of Schelling against Ernst Troeltsch
as a new foundation of the absoluteness of Christianity.[50] But the absoluteness of Christianity does not consist in a content of the Christian religion, but in the consciousness of history. This historical consciousness entered history with Jesus Christ. Therefore, as Tillich writes, the philosophy
of history "was the first and from the beginning of time the most important
form in which Christianity became conscious of its own claim to absoluteness. The verdict (*Urteil*): Jesus as the Christ contains the seeds of all
Christian philosophy of history" (EW X, 53).

5. Tillich's Modern-Positive Theology

Tillich had already worked out an independent theology before the First
World War. Against the background of historicism and in debate with it,
this theology aims at a new foundation for modern-positive theology. Besides the two dissertations on Schelling, Tillich elaborated his theology in

---

[49] Cf. Tillich, "Die religionsgeschichtliche Konstruktion in Schellings positiver Philosophie," 272.

[50] This becomes clear in the manuscript of the 1910 dissertation, which is
entitled *Die Absolutheit des Christentums und die Religionsgeschichte in Schelling's positiver Philosophie*. The unpublished manuscript is in Paul Tillich's estate at the
Harvard Divinity School Library, Harvard University, Cambridge, Massachusetts
(bMS 649/101[2]).

his 1911 theses, *Die christliche Gewißheit und der historische Jesus*,[51] and in his 1913 draft, *Systematische Theologie*.[52] What is significant for this theological conception is that it starts from the speculative principle of absolute truth as the basis of the system.[53] Thus, Tillich transfers Schelling's speculative philosophy of religion to the modern-positive theology of his teachers Adolf Schlatter and Wilhelm Lütgert in order to give their theology a better justification from his point of view. For this purpose, he takes up the speculative concept of truth, i.e., the relation between absolute and individual spirit. This concept of truth is supposed to be the basis for Christian certainty and to make possible a new justification of the absoluteness of Christianity based on it. According to this understanding of truth, all self-positing acts of human consciousness *are* truth. These acts are the carrying out of the "synthesizing of the manifold in the unity of consciousness" (EW VI, 41). On this assumption, the certainty of consciousness must be found in the relation of consciousness to itself: Certainty exists in the relationship of consciousness to itself when the spirit says "yes" to itself, namely to the idea of truth.[54] Consciousness posits the determinate qualities that characterize individual and concrete beings. Tillich understands the individuality and concreteness that are posited in this way to be simultaneously necessary and contradictory, and he believes that this necessity and this contradictoriness make up the very nature of historical truth. There can be certainty with respect to the individual only to the extent that the individual is "taken up into the synthesis of consciousness,"

---

[51] Paul Tillich, "Die christliche Gewißheit und der historische Jesus," in EW VI, 31–50 and 50–61.

[52] Paul Tillich, "Systematische Theologie von 1913," in EW IX, 278–434.

[53] Cf. Tillich, "Die christliche Gewißheit und der historische Jesus," 41; cf. Folkart Wittekind, "'Sinndeutung der Geschichte'. Zur Entwicklung und Bedeutung von Tillichs Geschichtsphilosophie," in *Theologie als Religionsphilosophie. Studien zu den problemgeschichtlichen und systematischen Voraussetzungen der Theologie Paul Tillichs*, ed. Christian Danz (Wien: LIT, 2004), 135–172.

[54] Cf. Tillich, "Systematische Theologie von 1913," 278; cf. Christian Danz, "Theologie als normative Religionsphilosophie. Voraussetzungen und Implikationen des Theologiebegriffs Paul Tillichs," in *Theologie als Religionsphilosophie. Studien zu den problemgeschichtlichen und systematischen Voraussetzungen der Theologie Paul Tillichs*, ed. Christian Danz (Wien: LIT, 2004), 73–106, here 74–80.

as Tillich puts it (EW VI, 41). In this manner, the individual spirit becomes a representation or a medium of the self-relatedness of the absolute spirit.

Starting from this basis of theoretical principles, Tillich conceives a philosophy of history that is not only designed to overcome the criticism that historicism brings to bear against historical elements of religious faith. This philosophy of history is also intended to interpret religion as the knowledge of the necessarily concrete character of historical truth, and to describe religion as the place where history is constituted as history.[55] As Tillich works this all out, religion is understood as a particular kind of consciousness. Religion is the consciousness for which the inner reflexivity of its own self-relatedness has become transparent. Therefore, faith is a consciousness of history which has become reflexive. Tillich has a special name for the contingent self-understanding of consciousness in its historicity: he calls it "paradox," and he connects paradox in this sense with religion and the theological standpoint. "The sphere of paradox is religion; because religion is the return of freedom to truth, the relative to the absolute without sublation [*Aufhebung*] of the freedom and the relative" (EW IX, 315). This means that religious certainty has the character of a paradox. The paradox resides in the absolute spirit: even though the spirit *is* absolute truth on the grounds of its being self-related, the spirit can only understand absolute truth as a concrete truth that is the content of its own awareness.[56] Concreteness and historicity are, as such, moments of the absolute certainty. But the necessarily concrete character of truth that Tillich insists upon stands in tension with his definition of the spirit as "a gradually increasing reaction of essential being against contradiction, against that which contradicts it" (EW VI, 41).[57] Thus, the concreteness of history here seems to become only a moment of passage of the absolute spirit on the way to its self-realization. But, with it, the concreteness of history is dissolved and annulled.

The basic structure of Paul Tillich's theology before the First World War, as it is present in his two dissertations, the 128 theses of 1911, as well as the draft of a *Systematische Theologie* of 1913, is clearly indebted to

---

[55] Cf. Tillich, "Die christliche Gewißheit und der historische Jesus," 42.

[56] Cf. Tillich, "Systematische Theologie von 1913," 281.

[57] Cf. Tillich, "Mystik und Schuldbewußtsein in Schellings philosophischer Entwicklung," 100.

the modern-positive theology of his teachers Schlatter and Lütgert. For both, too, God already underlies the process of nature and history, so that faith bound to God's revelation consists in God's being revealed as the ground and unity of this process. The task of theology is to describe this process of knowing God. Tillich takes up and continues this program of a modern-positive theology. With the philosophies of Fichte and Schelling, on which Tillich falls back, he tries to give this theological program a new and better foundation. In doing so, however, Tillich, with Schelling, transforms Schlatter's empiricist justification of theology into a speculative theology that understands the world process as God's self-revelation.

III.

Religious A Priori; or, Directedness Towards the Unconditioned:

Tillich's Understanding of Religion and the Religious-Philosophical Debate of his Time

> Through H[eidegger] and O[xner] (I no longer recall who takes precedence here) I became aware of your book about the Holy last summer and it had a strong impact on me like hardly any other book in years. Allow me to put my impression like this: It is a first beginning for a phenomenology of the religious, at least after everything that does not go beyond a pure description and analysis of the phenomena themselves.[1]

With these words from March 5, 1919, Edmund Husserl described to his former Göttingen colleague, Rudolf Otto, the impression that his reading of the latter's work, *Das Heilige*, had made upon him. Despite the critique that Husserl directed at Otto's book, he acknowledged that it would nevertheless "retain a permanent place in the history of genuine philosophy of religion or of phenomenology of religion. It is a beginning and goes back, that is its meaning, to the 'beginnings,' 'origins,' that is, it is 'original' in the most beautiful sense of the word."[2]

Whoever it was that brought Otto's book to Husserl's attention, we know—from volume 60 of the collected works of Martin Heidegger, published in 1995 and entitled *Phänomenologie des religiösen Lebens*—that

---

[1] Edmund Husserl to Rudolf Otto, March 5, 1919, in Hans Walter Schütte, *Religion und Christentum in der Theologie Rudolf Ottos* (Berlin: de Gruyter, 1969), 141.

[2] Husserl to Otto, March 5, 1919, in Schütte, *Religion und Christentum in der Theologie Rudolf Ottos*, 142.

Heidegger not only worked on a discussion of *Das Heilige*, but also undertook a phenomenology of the religious.[3] Furthermore, among the drafts and outlines of a lecture on *Die philosophischen Grundlagen der mittelalterlichen Mystik*, planned for the winter semester of 1918/19, one finds the groundwork of a review of Otto's book.[4] Heidegger's notes on Otto, his outlines for the planned lecture, and above all his own lecture from the winter semester of 1920/21, entitled *Einleitung in die Phänomenologie der Religion*, indicate the horizon of the problems which also characterize Paul Tillich's work at this time.[5] Regarding the concept of religion, the general horizon of the problems may be seen as standing between neo-Kantianism and phenomenology against the backdrop of the debates concerning the absoluteness of Christianity.[6] The establishing of the validity of religion in a religious a priori was increasingly perceived as being problematic. Such a conception not only raises the question as to how religion must be classified within the structure of consciousness—with its necessarily realized a priori functions—but also that of its relation to the other functions of consciousness. Furthermore, the a priori functions of consciousness are necessarily realized. Yet, if this is the case, how must the underivability and contingency that are constitutive for religion be understood? As we can see, with the understanding of religion as an element in the inner structure of the faculties of human consciousness, the problem of a religion that is given before the use of religion by human beings becomes inevitable. But

---

[3] Cf. Martin Heidegger, *Phänomenologie des religiösen Lebens* (Gesamtausgabe. II. Abteilung: Vorlesungen, vol. 60), (Frankfurt a.M.: Klostermann, 1995).

[4] Cf. Martin Heidegger, "'Das Heilige' (Vorarbeiten zur Rezension von Rudolf Otto, Das Heilige, 1917)," in *Phänomenologie des religiösen Lebens* (Frankfurt a.M.: Klostermann, 1995), 332–334.

[5] Concerning Heidegger's early philosophy of religion, cf. Christian Danz, "Religion der konkreten Existenz. Heideggers Religionsphilosophie im Kontext von Ernst Troeltsch und Paul Tillich," in *Kerygma und Dogma* 55 (2009) 325–341; Matthias Jung, *Das Denken des Seins und der Glaube an Gott. Zum Verhältnis von Philosophie und Theologie bei Martin Heidegger* (Würzburg: Königshausen & Neumann, 1990).

[6] Cf. Karl Heim, "Ottos Kategorie des Heiligen und der Absolutheitsanspruch des Christentums," in *Zeitschrift für Theologie und Kirche* 28 (1920) 14–41. On the debates concerning philosophy of religion around 1900, cf. Georg Pfleiderer, *Theologie als Wirklichkeitswissenschaft. Studien zum Religionsbegriff bei Georg Wobbermin, Rudolf Otto und Max Scheler* (Tübingen: Mohr Siebeck, 1992).

this is a construction that loses its plausibility under the conditions of the modern culture around 1900. Against the background of the problems indicated here, it is no wonder that in the contemporary controversies, the attempt was made to carry *cum grano salis* neo-Kantian conceptions forward—by incorporating phenomenological motifs—toward a performance-bound (*vollzugsgebundene*) theory of religion. Into this horizon, Heidegger's early phenomenology of religion seamlessly assimilates itself.[7] Heidegger did away with establishing the validity of religion in a religious a priori and replaced it with a determination of religion as the reflexive transparency and expression of actual life.[8] However, religion here acquires a new description, that is, it becomes determined as an underivable performance that only exists as such.

Because this chapter aims to deal with the methodological foundations of Rudolf Otto's and Paul Tillich's theories of religion, the history of the problems described above must also be addressed. Therefore, we must begin with a short glance at the theories of religion and methodological groundworks of Wilhelm Windelband and Ernst Troeltsch because the transcendental explanations of religion in the structure of human consciousness, which they both propounded, constitute the context of Otto's and Tillich's theories of religion. In the second section of this chapter, Otto's theory of religion is sketched in the perspective of the history of the work (*werkgeschichtlichen*) against the background of the horizon of the history of the problems (*problemgeschichtlichen*) introduced above. In his post-World War I writings, the young Tillich endeavored to develop, like Otto, a theory of religion in which transcendental and phenomenological motifs were intertwined. In doing so, Tillich also referred to Otto's book *Das Heilige*. Tillich's justification of religion is the subject of the concluding third section of this chapter. The focus here is on understanding the way in which Tillich's pre-war theology, discussed in the second chapter, was further developed by him after the war vis-à-vis contemporary debates in the philosophy of religion.

---

[7] Cf. Heidegger, "Das Heilige," 334: "Windelband ('The Holy') shows the insight into almost the same abundance of religious phenomena, albeit in a strongly rational formulation, but above all it shows that the decisive factor is this principle of problem formulation as such and that the structure of the problem groups and the *methodical* approaches depend on it."

[8] Cf. Heidegger, *Phänomenologie des religiösen Lebens*, 105.

1. From the Holy to the Religious A Priori;
or, The Place of Religion Within the
Structure of Human Consciousness

In 1902, Wilhelm Windelband, the well-known neo-Kantian from Heidelberg, put forward the sketch of a philosophy of religion that was concerned with a transcendental foundation for religion within the structure of human consciousness. It is according to this way of construing the problem that Windelband describes the task of the philosophy of religion. This task consists in showing "the place which religion occupies in the purposeful interconnectedness of the functions of the reasonable consciousness, and from this to understand and evaluate all its particular manifestations of life."[9] A philosophy of religion committed to the methodological insights of critical Idealism has the task of determining the place and function of religion within the structure of consciousness. In terms of a theory of validity, religion is founded when a function to which religion can be assigned becomes nameable within the internal structure of consciousness. In the first part of his essay, Windelband undertook just such a transcendental foundation, while dedicating the second part to a formal theory of the categories of religious consciousness. In the following, we must limit ourselves to Windelband's transcendental foundation of religion.

The point of departure of Windelband's transcendental theory of religion is constituted by the necessary a priori functions of consciousness: thought, action, and feeling, which correspond to the three sciences, viz., logic, ethics, and aesthetics. It is by means of these necessary a priori functions of consciousness that culture is constituted.[10] The question thereby

---

[9] Wilhelm Windelband, "Das Heilige. Skizze zur Religionsphilosophie," in *Präludien. Aufsätze und Reden zur Philosophie und ihrer Geschichte*, vol. 2 (7th ed. Tübingen: Mohr Siebeck, 1921), 295–332, here 295.

[10] Cf. Wilhelm Windelband, "Kulturphilosophie und transzendentaler Idealismus," in *Logos* 1 (1910/11) 186–196, here 191: "For by culture, after all, we understand nothing other than the totality of that which human consciousness, by virtue of its rational determination, works out of the given: and the point of departure of transcendental philosophy is Kant's insight that already in that which we are accustomed to accept as given, as soon as it presents itself as universally valid experience, there is a synthesis according to the laws of 'consciousness in general', according to comprehensive, objectively valid forms of reason."

RELIGIOUS A PRIORI; OR, DIRECTEDNESS
TOWARDS THE UNCONDITIONED

arises as to which of these three functions religion must be assigned. Windelband's answer, which is significant for the debate on the philosophy of religion around 1900, is that religion indeed constitutes a separate cultural force, but is distinct from the three functions of consciousness.[11] Thus, Windelband classifies religion within the transcendental structure of consciousness in such a way that it is neither linked to one of the three cultural functions, nor does it constitute, in and of itself, a separate function of consciousness. Nevertheless, religion must have a "rational cause"[12] and must correlate with the cultural functions. Otherwise, not only would the unity of consciousness be abolished, but the contribution that religion makes to modern culture would also no longer be evident. Windelband accomplishes this task by referring religion to a problem that arises in each of the three cultural functions, but which cannot be dealt with in any of them. "This," says Windelband, "could be nothing other than the antinomy of consciousness, which becomes manifest in the relation between should [*Sollen*] and must [*Müssen*], between norms and the laws of nature."[13] For Windelband, the reference point of religion is an antinomy of consciousness, namely, the tension between ideal validity and empirical facticity. And such an antinomy appears in all three functions of consciousness.

However, the question as to where and how Windelband sees the essence of religion is not thereby answered. "*Religion*," according to Windelband's basic determination, "*is transcendent life*; it is essential for it to transcend the experience, the consciousness of belonging to a world of spiritual values, not being satisfied with the empirical reality."[14] Windel-

---

[11]Cf. Windelband, "Das Heilige," 297: "From this it follows that philosophy of religion cannot be accommodated in any of the three basic philosophical disciplines alone, that it cannot be treated as part or appendage of logic or ethics or aesthetics." Cf. also "Kulturphilosophie und transzendentaler Idealismus," 192–3. Cf. also Hermann Cohen, *Der Begriff der Religion im System der Philosophie*, ed. Andrea Poma (Hildesheim; Zürich; New York: Olms, 1996). Cf. Frederick C. Beiser, *The Genesis of Neo-Kantianism, 1796–1880* (Oxford: Oxford University Press, 2014), 492–530.

[12] Windelband, "Kulturphilosophie und transzendentaler Idealismus," 193; cf. "Das Heilige," 299.

[13] Windelband, "Das Heilige," 300.

[14] Windelband, "Das Heilige," 305.

band understands religion as the contingent becoming aware of the transcendental sphere of validity in terms of its dimension of unity and totality, or as he himself says, as the "normal consciousness" (*Normalbewusstsein*), which is already engaged in the three necessary, a priori cultural functions of consciousness.[15] Obviously, this cannot take place except in the cultural functions of consciousness, where it nevertheless must not be thought to seamlessly collapse into them. For Windelband, religion represents the unity of culture, or respectively, the unity of the three cultural functions of thought, action, and feeling, a unity that cannot be grasped in and through any of those functions alone.[16] In his value-theoretical philosophy of religion, Windelband removed religion from any connection with a particular function of consciousness, referring religion to consciousness as such.

It was also around 1900 that Ernst Troeltsch, under the influence of southwestern German neo-Kantianism, especially of Heinrich Rickert, began to develop his philosophy of religion, and above all his philosophy of history. However, Troeltsch did not follow Windelband's philosophy of religion. To be sure, like his colleague in Heidelberg, Troeltsch also wishes to demonstrate that religion is based on a transcendental function of consciousness. Yet, beginning in 1904, he gives this function the title of a "religious a priori."[17] With this formulation of the problem, one sees

---

[15] Windelband, "Das Heilige," 305: "Thus the content of the holy cannot be determined otherwise than through the quintessence of the norms that govern logical, ethical and aesthetic life. [...] But they are holy to us because they are not products of the individual life of the soul, nor products of empirical social consciousness, but values of a higher rational reality in which we are allowed to participate, which we are allowed to experience [*erleben*] in ourselves."

[16] Cf. Windelband, "Kulturphilosophie und transzendentaler Idealismus," 193: "Their special functions, insofar as they draw their reason grounds from the logical, ethical or aesthetic contents, participate in their transcendental essence, and the only reason inherent in religion consists in the postulate of experiencing the totality of all reason values in an absolute unity that cannot be grasped by any of the forms of our consciousness."

[17] Cf. Ernst Troeltsch, *Psychologie und Erkenntnistheorie in der Religionswissenschaft. Eine Untersuchung über die Bedeutung der Kantischen Religionslehre für die heutige Religionswissenschaft* (2nd ed. Tübingen: Mohr Siebeck, 1922), 24. Cf. also "Zur Frage des religiösen Apriori. Eine Erwiderung auf die Bemerkungen von Paul Spieß," in *Zur religiösen Lage, Religionsphilosophie und Ethik* (Gesammelte

Troeltsch's concern with the task to connect and at the same time to distinguish in the structure of the religious consciousness a "historic-psychological-causal" element and a creative, productive element, which creates, from inner necessity, the effective truth of religion.[18]

As developed in the 1895/96 essay *Die Selbständigkeit des Religion*,[19] published in the *Zeitschrift für Theologie und Kirche*, Troeltsch's philosophy of religion orients itself first around an empirical analysis of religion. This analysis is represented in a historiography of religions that proceeds by means of the psychology of religion. An empirical description and assessment of the religious life, however, does not yet imply anything concerning "the substance of truth and reality" of religious phenomena.[20] The interest in an explanation of religion, which is not and cannot be accomplished by means of empirical description, leads Troeltsch to supplement the psychology of religion with an epistemology—of Kantian provenance—of the theory of validity.[21] Thus, Troeltsch set out to combine the empirical study

---

Schriften, vol. 2) (2nd ed. Tübingen: Mohr Siebeck, 1922), 754–768. For Troeltsch's philosophy of religion, cf. Frank W. Veauthier, "Das religiöse Apriori: Zur Ambivalenz von E. Troeltschs Analyse des Vernunftelements in der Religion," in *Kant-Studien* 78 (1987) 42–63; Ulrich Barth, "Religionsphilosophisches und geschichtsmethodologisches Apriori. Ernst Troeltschs Auseinandersetzung mit Kant," in *Gott als Projekt der Vernunft* (Tübingen: Mohr Siebeck, 2005), 359–394; Christian Danz, "Die geschichtsphilosophische Grundlegung der Theologie bei Ernst Troeltsch," in *Gott und die menschliche Freiheit. Studien zum Gottesbegriff in der Neuzeit* (Neukirchen-Vluyn: Neukirchener, 2005), 69–87.

[18] Troeltsch, "Zur Frage des religiösen Apriori," 755. Cf. also "Ethik und Geschichtsphilosophie," in *Fünf Vorträge zu Religion und Geschichtsphilosophie für England und Schottland* (KGA, vol. 17) (Berlin; Boston: de Gruyter, 2006), 68–104, here 68.

[19] Ernst Troeltsch, "Die Selbständigkeit der Religion," in *Schriften zur Theologie und Religionsphilosophie (1888–1902)* (KGA, vol. 1) (Berlin; New York: de Gruyter, 2009), 364–534.

[20] Troeltsch, *Psychologie und Erkenntnistheorie in der Religionswissenschaft*, 17.

[21] Cf. Ernst Troeltsch, "Das Historische in Kants Religionsphilosophie. Zugleich ein Beitrag zu den Untersuchungen über Kants Philosophie der Geschichte," in *Kant-Studien* 9 (1904) 21–154; "Zur Frage des religiösen Apriori," 756. Cf. additionally Barth, "Religionsphilosophisches und geschichtsmethodologisches Apriori," 371–382; Mark D. Chapman, *Ernst Troeltsch and Liberal Theology. Religion and Cultural Synthesis in Wilhelmine Germany* (Oxford: Oxford University Press, 2001), 111–137.

of religion with rational epistemology. While the task of the psychology of religion is to study "the religious experience without prejudice for or against" in order "to grasp it in its characteristic peculiarity,"[22] it behooves epistemology to establish the validity and truth of religion by reducing them to a law of reason in order to defend its reality against the psychological appearance.[23]

Thus, by means of a modified appropriation of Kant, Troeltsch names this law of reason *religious a priori*.

> It lies in the absolute relationship of substance, which must be realized from the essence of reason, by virtue of which all that is real and, in particular, all values are related to an absolute substance as starting point and yardstick [*Maßtab*]. With that is already said that this religious a priori is dependent on the connection with the other a priori and that it gives their inner unity the solid substance basis in the first place.[24]

Of course, the religious a priori that is supposed to carry the burden of the theoretical validity of the reasoning in Troeltsch's theory of religion is anything but clear. Two things are obvious:[25] first, by referring religion to a religious a priori, Troeltsch wants to understand religion, as it were, as a phenomenon of the a priori functions of consciousness. Accordingly, religion is a necessary phenomenon of reason, and consequently, not a false consciousness as the critique of religion wrongly suggests. Thus, religious consciousness must be understood as a valid consciousness. As a specific consciousness of truth, it originates in the essence of reason. However, the way in which this religious a priori must be classified within the structure

---

[22] Troeltsch, *Psychologie und Erkenntnistheorie in der Religionswissenschaft*, 10. Cf. also "Empirismus und Platonismus in der Religionsphilosophie. Zur Erinnerung an William James," in *Zur religiösen Lage, Religionsphilosophie und Ethik* (Gesammelte Schriften, vol. 2) (2nd ed. Tübingen: Mohr Siebeck, 1922), 364–385; "Wesen der Religion und der Religionswissenschaft," in *Zur religiösen Lage, Religionsphilosophie und Ethik* (Gesammelte Schriften, vol. 2) (2nd ed. Tübingen: Mohr Siebeck, 1922), 452–499, here 492–494.

[23] Cf. Troeltsch, *Psychologie und Erkenntnistheorie in der Religionswissenschaft*, 22; "Wesen der Religion und der Religionswissenschaft," 494–5.

[24] Troeltsch, "Wesen der Religion und der Religionswissenschaft," 494–5.

[25] Cf. Troeltsch, "Zur Frage des religiösen Apriori," 757. Cf. Barth, "Religionsphilosophisches und geschichtsmethodologisches Apriori," 369.

of reason—whether it is on the same level with, or whether it underlies the reason-functions of thought, action and feeling—was left open by Troeltsch. Second, and still more serious: a balancing out of the tension between the transcendental concept of religion as a necessary and legitimate phenomenon of reason, and the idea of God, which, since his early works, Troeltsch understands as a consciousness-transcending reality,[26] becomes inconceivable.[27]

How then do the religious theories of Otto and Tillich come to stand in the outlined horizon of the history of the problems between "normal consciousness" and a religious a priori?

2. Between Validity and History: The Holy as an Interpretive Category of the Spirit

In his discussion of Rudolf Otto's book, *Das Heilige*, published in the *Kant-Studien* of 1918 under the title *Zur Religionsphilosophie*, Ernst Troeltsch favorably aligns himself with Otto's overall approach, while harshly criticizing the manner in which it is carried out in the particulars, a criticism that was followed in the ulterior philosophical discussion. "If Otto believes," thus Troeltsch summarizes the classification of the work from 1917,

> that he has described the rational elements in the first book [sc. *Kantisch-Fries'sche Religionsphilosophie*] and now [sc. *Das Heilige*] only "supplements" this presentation with the irrational ones, then in my opinion he is hiding a total change of front, and that is precisely why the main task of the book, that is, the task of determining the relationship between the rational and the irrational, has been so unsuccessful.[28]

---

[26] Cf. Troeltsch, "Die Selbständigkeit der Religion," 399; "Die christliche Weltanschauung und ihre Gegenströmungen," in *Zur religiösen Lage, Religionsphilosophie und Ethik* (Gesammelte Schriften, vol. 2) (2nd ed. Tübingen: Mohr Siebeck, 1922), 227–327, here 301.

[27] Cf. Barth, "Religionsphilosophisches und geschichtsmethodologisches Apriori," 370–1.

[28] Ernst Troeltsch, "Zur Religionsphilosophie. Rudolf Otto: Das Heilige," in *Rezensionen und Kritiken (1915–1923)* (KGA, vol. 13) (Berlin; New York: de

THE THEOLOGY OF PAUL TILLICH

However one may judge Troeltsch's discussion, it certainly did not escape his notice that Otto's methodological groundwork of religion in a validity-theoretical a priori departs considerably from his own considerations concerning a transcendental explanation of religion. On the whole, it is quite possible to read Otto's philosophy of religion as an analysis of and counter project to Troeltsch's own, against the backdrop of a shared set of problems. As with Troeltsch, so with Otto the issue is not only to establish the independence of religion between the poles of naturalism and historicism,[29] but also at issue is the intertwining of an explanation of the theoretical validity of religion with a psychology of religion. Additionally, an explanation of the validity of Christianity in the history of religions is needed. In this respect, Otto's and Troeltsch's conceptions belong to the context of the debates concerning self-understanding within the Ritschl-school during the first decades of the twentieth century. Similar to Troeltsch, Otto differentiates the task of a philosophy of religion that, in the form of a psychology of religion, is in accord with the basic principles of modernity, and a theoretical philosophy of the validity of religion in the strict sense. As he explains in his book *Kantisch-Fries'sche Religionsphilosophie*, the latter has the double task of investigating "how religion and religious convictions and religious experience [*Erleben*] arise in the rational spirit itself, from what faculties and dispositions [*Anlagen*] of this spirit religion arises and what claim to validity it has as a result[30] On the basis of the transcendental explanation of religion, the philosophy of religion must undertake a "metaphysics of religion" (as Otto, following Kant, calls it) as

Gruyter, 2010), 412–425, here 425. On the debate between Troeltsch and Otto, cf. Chapman, *Ernst Troeltsch and Liberal Theology*, 120–122.

[29] Cf. Rudolf Otto, "Darwinismus von heute und Theologie," in *Theologische Rundschau* 5 (1902) 483–496; "Die mechanische Lebenstheorie und die Theologie," in *Zeitschrift für Theologie und Kirche* 13 (1903) 179–213; "Die Überwindung der mechanistischen Lehre vom Leben in der heutigen Naturwissenschaft," in *Zeitschrift für Theologie und Kirche* 14 (1904) 234–272. On the philosophy of religion from Otto, cf. Peter Schüz, *Mysterium tremendum. Zum Verhältnis von Angst und Religion nach Rudolf Otto* (Tübingen: Mohr Siebeck, 2016); Jörg Lauster, Peter Schüz, Roderich Barth and Christian Danz (eds.), *Rudolf Otto. Theologie – Religionsphilosophie – Religionsgeschichte* (Berlin; Boston: de Gruyter, 2014).

[30] Rudolf Otto, *Kantisch-Fries'sche Religionsphilosophie und ihre Anwendung auf die Theologie. Zur Einleitung in die Glaubenslehre für Studenten der Theologie* (Tübingen: Mohr Siebeck, 1909), VI.

well as the metaphysical first principles of the theory of religion.[31] How, then, does Otto classify religion within the framework of the human spirit? In what does its specific character consist and in what relation does it stand to the cultural functions of the spirit?

> Religion is itself the experience of the mystery as such [*Erleben des Geheimnisses schlechthin*]; not a mystery that would only be one for the uninitiated, but would be resolved for higher degrees, but the tangible mystery of all temporal existence in general and the shining through of eternal reality through the veil of temporality for the open minded [*das aufgeschlossene Gemüth*].[32]

As Otto advances in his *Kantisch-Fries'sche Religionsphilosophie*, the specific character of religion results neither from theoretical nor from practical reason—no matter how inevitable and necessary both faculties are for the realization of religion—but rather from a separate province of the *Gemüt*, from feeling. The concept of feeling (*Gefühl*) already functions here as a "pre-conceptual evidential experience,"[33] which represents the dimension of the unity of the spirit in a way that is conceptually inexpressible.[34]

---

[31] Otto, *Kantisch-Fries'sche Religionsphilosophie*, VII.

[32] Otto, *Kantisch-Fries'sche Religionsphilosophie*, 75. Cf. also "Mythus und Religion in Wundts Völkerpsychologie," in *Theologische Rundschau* 13 (1910) 251–275 and 293–305, here 298: "It is a disposition. And with that we also have the real psychological and sufficient explanation for the fact that we mentioned above and to which we must, in the history of religions work, pay even more attention than before, namely, that in becoming religious we are dealing with a drive, and indeed with one of a power like few others." Cf. also "Mythus und Religion in Wundts Völkerpsychologie," 305.

[33] Ulrich Barth, "Theoriedimensionen des Religionsbegriffs. Die Binnenrelevanz der sogenannten Außenperspektive," in *Religion in der Moderne* (Tübingen: Mohr Siebeck, 2003), 29–87, here 43. Cf. also Otto, "Mythus und Religion in Wundts Völkerpsychologie," 302: "But by 'feeling' we understand here, as well as our language itself, an undeveloped, confused and dark imaginative content with a corresponding peculiarly determined state of mind. The latter is never able to dissolve into clear concepts. It attaches itself to images and ideas that must somehow be analogous to it, without it being possible to specify what the analogy actually consists of and how far it extends."

[34] Cf. Otto, *Kantisch-Fries'sche Religionsphilosophie*, 75: "This subordination does not occur by means of a clear middle term, but purely in feeling, in a feeling

THE THEOLOGY OF PAUL TILLICH

For this reason, the "understanding of religion and pre-religion [...] must be primarily an analysis of feeling."[35] Unlike Schleiermacher (but together with Jakob Friedrich Fries and Kant's *Kritik der Urteilskraft*), Otto docs not grasp feeling as a pre-reflexive, self-referential state of consciousness.[36] Rather, feeling appertains primarily to a specific way of qualifying the consciousness of objects.

> Here it is not conclusions and conceptual reflections, but the immediate judgement of feeling that subsumes a process under the "idea." And hence the immediate violence with which the religious shiver seizes the experiencer [*Erlebenden*] when experiencing [*Erleben*] the "inexplicable."[37]

Thus, one can summarize Otto's considerations in the *Kantisch-Fries'sche Religionsphilosophie* as follows: religion arises from its own source of reason; that is to say, in religion, the concrete, determined consciousness represents the dimension of the unity of consciousness in a pre-conceptual manner, which simultaneously arises as a specific determination of feeling.

In *Das Heilige*, Otto adheres to the methodological basis of the philosophy of religion that he developed both in the *Kantisch-Fries'sche Religionsphilosophie* and in his review of Wilhelm Wundt's *Völkerpsychologie*,

---

that cannot be dissolved conceptually ('unfinished terms' according to Kant). Such an understanding, which cannot be expressed conceptually and which only takes place in feeling, is called 'forbode' [*Ahnen*] in our language. But that this foreboding of the idea can make this powerful impression on us, extending through all degrees of experience, is precisely because the 'idea' has always been 'schematized' in the dark interior of our mind, has enlivened itself with the great 'practical' contents of which we have spoken."

[35] Otto, "Mythus und Religion in Wundts Völkerpsychologie," 264.

[36] Cf. Otto, *Kantisch-Fries'sche Religionsphilosophie*, 117; *Das Heilige. Über das Irrationale in der Idee des Göttlichen und sein Verhältnis zum Rationalen* (7th ed. Breslau: Trewendt & Granier, 1922), 9–12. Cf. Barth, "Theoriedimensionen des Religionsbegriffs," 44; Chapman, *Ernst Troeltsch and Liberal Theology*, 122–128.

[37] Otto, *Kantisch-Fries'sche Religionsphilosophie*, 115.

which appeared a year later in 1910.[38] *Das Heilige* also offers a transcendental explanation of religion which relies on Kantian and Friesian critical Idealism. Of course, as it is evident in the first few methodological chapters of his classic, Otto more sharply emphasized the embeddedness of religion in the performative act, which is already inherent in the concept of experience (*Erlebnis*) that is fundamental to his entire theory of religion.[39] Here one sees Otto's concern in avoiding the problem of the necessary realization of the functions of consciousness, inherent in the concept of a religious a priori, that is, the exclusion of the contingency which is constitutive for the emergence of religion.[40] The holy, according to Otto's well-known determination, is a "category of interpretation and evaluation that occurs only in religious areas."[41] The a priori category of the holy, located in the self-relation of human consciousness, constitutes the religious sphere. As Otto makes clear in response to and over against Wilhelm Wundt, religion is not an epiphenomenon that is derivable from other sources, such as animism. As Otto states in his famous sentence: "*Religion begins with itself,* and is itself already active in its 'preliminary stages' of the mythical and demonic."[42] Indeed, the holy is a complex category. It represents a unity-in-tension of irrational and rational moments. Unlike Troeltsch, the irrational moment does not rest in the "irrational actuality" of religion.[43] Instead, it belongs, together with the rational elements, to the categorial principles of religion in the self-understanding of the spirit. Hence, Otto assumes the underivable experientiality of religion in its a priori spirit-philosophical groundwork. Religion originates in an underivable way within concrete, determined consciousness of the world, in that "I attach to the object a predicate, namely a predicate of meaning

---

[38] Concerning the question of continuity in the history of the development of Otto's philosophy of religion, cf. Schütte, *Religion und Christentum in der Theologie Rudolf Ottos*, 10; Pfleiderer, *Theologie als Wirklichkeitswissenschaft*, 108–114; Schüz, *Mysterium tremendum.*

[39] Cf. Otto, *Das Heilige*, 8.

[40] Otto is already aware of this problem in his study of the *Kantisch-Fries'sche Religionsphilosophie.* Cf. Otto, *Kantisch-Fries'sche Religionsphilosophie*, 3–4; "Mythus und Religion in Wundts Völkerpsychologie," 305.

[41] Otto, *Das Heilige*, 5.

[42] Otto, *Das Heilige*, 163.

[43] Troeltsch, *Psychologie und Erkenntnistheorie in der Religionswissenschaft*, 22.

[*Bedeutungs-prädikat*], which does not or cannot give me the sensory experience, but which I spontaneously attribute to it of my own accord."[44] Religious consciousness articulates itself as a breakthrough of reflexivity in and upon concrete, determined consciousness, so that the contentual determinations function, by means of the transparency of the spirit with reference to its depth-structure, as representations—or, as Otto calls them, ideograms and schematizations.

In *Das Heilige*, Otto combines his determination of the specific character of religion, which is based on a philosophy of spirit, with an interpretation of the history of religion, which reaches its summit in Christianity. The point of departure is constituted by the transcendental structure of the spirit.

> The *disposition* [*Anlage*] that human reason brought with it at the entry of the genus man into history, once, partly through stimuli from outside, partly through its own pressure from within, also became a *driving force* for it, namely, a religious one that, in a groping movement, in a searching formation of ideas, in an ever advancing generation of ideas, wants to become clear about itself and becomes clear a priori through the development of the dark basis of ideas, from which it itself also originated.[45]

On the methodological basis of his philosophy of spirit, Otto interprets the history of religion as the spirit's path to self-awareness.[46] The aim of the processes of the history of religion constitutes the self-transparency of the spirit in its depth-structure. To be sure, the numinous, represented in feeling, is to a certain extent the depth-dimension of religion. Yet, in its historical development, religion is only able to become a religion of culture and humanity if the two moments of the irrational and rational "stands in healthy and fine harmony."[47] This is the case with the founding figure of Christianity. For Otto, the historical image of Jesus Christ, which for him is taken up from the "accidentally fluctuations of exegetical results and the

---

[44] Otto, *Das Heilige*, 165–6.

[45] Otto, *Das Heilige*, 144–45.

[46] Cf. Otto, *Das Heilige*, 214: "Who wants history of spirit, must want qualified spirit; who means history of religion, means history of a spirit qualified for religion."

[47] Otto, *Das Heilige*, 173.

agony of historical legitimation,"[48] is the expression of the true religion in history.

Thus far we have seen how Otto combines transcendental philosophy, the concept of experience (*Erlebnis*), and the history of religion into a tension-laden unity. Therefore, true religion is feeling, which is a part of human consciousness, but this feeling, the numinous, is, as the core of all religion, not accessible. Like in Troeltsch's philosophy of religion and history, only the symbolic expressions of the inward feeling are accessible.

3. From the Religious A Priori to the Intention of the Absolute; or, Religion in Paul Tillich

When *Das Heilige* was published in 1917, the young Tillich was fascinated. On May 9, 1918, Tillich enthusiastically wrote to his friend Emmanuel Hirsch about the impression that Otto's work made on him.[49] According to his correspondence, Tillich saw in the book the spirit of the late Schelling, and he identified in Otto a congenial theological conception to his own theology. Not surprisingly, we find the notion of the holy in Tillich's writings all the time after the First World War and indeed right up through the late *Systematic Theology*. In 1923, Tillich wrote a review of Otto's book in the journal *Theologische Blätter*[50] and, two years later, an article about Rudolf Otto in the newspaper *Vossische Zeitung*.[51] But this is only one side in the relation between Tillich and Otto. At the same time, Tillich completely rejected Otto's justification of a religious feeling as an element in the structure of the consciousness. For Tillich, the basis of religion cannot be conceived as a religious a priori in the structure of the faculties of the human spirit. Rather, religion has a different basis. This is already evident in Tillich's 1910 philosophical dissertation on Schelling's philosophy of religion, whose systematic foundations were discussed in the

---

[48] Otto, *Das Heilige*, 211.

[49] Cf. the letter from Paul Tillich to Emmanuel Hirsch, May 9, 1918, in EW VI, 123–127, here 123–4.

[50] Cf. Paul Tillich, "Die Kategorie des 'Heiligen' bei Rudolf Otto," in GW XII, 184–186.

[51] Cf. Paul Tillich, "Der Religionsphilosoph Rudolf Otto," in GW XII, 179–183.

second chapter.[52] The notion of religion outlined here by Tillich refers not only to the contemporary debates on the philosophy of religion, but also claims to overcome the difficulties bound up with current "concepts of idealistic-history-of-religions" (EW IX, 158-7), namely those of Ernst Troeltsch and also of Otto.

In the third part of the philosophical dissertation from 1910, Tillich turns his attention to Schelling's concept of religion. In Tillich's judgment, the basic methodological insight of Schelling's later philosophy is that the latter did not postulate an "independent a priori of the religious appearances" (EW IX, 232). "The essence of religion must not be sought in any form of spiritual activity, but in the spirituality [*Geistigkeit*] of man as such." (EW IX, 233) The young Tillich sees Schelling's contribution to the contemporary debates on the philosophy of religion in that the latter constructs the concept of religion on the basis of the concept of God.[53] Just as in modern-positive theology, God is the foundation of religion, not religious consciousness.[54] Those explanations of religion, which reduce religion to a religious a priori, i.e., to a specific function of consciousness, are thus eliminated as inadequate.

Tillich understands Schelling's speculative philosophy of religion as follows: Schelling interlocks the concept of God and the theory of consciousness in a concept of religion, and construes religion as the self-relation of God. "The pure substance of human consciousness is what posits

---

[52] Tillich, "Die religionsgeschichtliche Konstruktion in Schellings positiver Philosophie," 154–272. Concerning the background of Tillich's philosophy dissertation, cf. Neugebauer, *Tillichs frühe Christologie*, 155–158 and 392–399.

[53] Cf. Tillich, "Die religionsgeschichtliche Konstruktion in Schellings positiver Philosophie," 235.

[54] Cf. also Tillich's doctoral thesis from 1912: "The concept of religion must be derived from the concept of God, not vice versa." (MW I, 25) Cf. Hermann Brandt, "Konstanz und Wandel in der Theologie Paul Tillichs im Lichte der wiedergefundenen Thesen zu seiner Lizentiaten-Dissertation," in *Zeitschrift für Theologie und Kirche* 75 (1978) 361–374.

God *natura sua*: human consciousness stands in a real, substantial relationship to God, and this relationship is religious." (EW IX, 235)[55] The concept of a pure substance of consciousness stands for the synthetic and unifying function in the self-relation of consciousness that already underlies all actions.

The basis of this determination of the general concept of religion is a speculative philosophy of spirit, which connects the absolute with the individual spirit. The absolute spirit posits the particular or individual spirit as distinct from itself and recognizes itself in the particular spirit. The particular spirit is therefore nothing for itself, but a representation or medium of the absolute spirit.[56] Religion, in this self-referential version of the concept of religion, is understood as the identity of the individual with the absolute spirit, which functions as the basis of the latter. Tillich connects this concept of the essence of religion with history. The latter arises from the contradiction of the subject against the absolute spirit. Thereby the subject is something for itself and no longer medium of the self-representation of the absolute. As absolute and individual spirit diverge through the contradiction of the subject, the substantial religious relation of consciousness is not abolished, but is realized in history in the three functions

---

[55] Cf. Georg Neugebauer, "Die religionsphilosophischen Grundlagen der Kulturtheologie Tillichs vor dem Hintergrund seiner Schelling- und Husserlrezeption," in *Paul Tillichs Theologie der Kultur. Aspekte – Probleme – Perspektiven*, ed. Christian Danz and Werner Schüßler (Berlin; Boston: de Gruyter, 2011), 38–63, here 41–47; *Tillichs frühe Christologie*, 169–175. For Schelling's construction of myth, cf. Christian Danz, "Das Werden Gottes im Bewusstsein der Menschheit. Der Begriff des Mythos bei Schelling," in *Gott und die menschliche Freiheit. Studien zum Gottesbegriff in der Neuzeit* (Neukirchen-Vluyn: Neukirchener 2005), 28–44.

[56] Cf. Tillich, "Die religionsgeschichtliche Konstruktion in Schellings positiver Philosophie," 234: "The method becomes speculative. It begins with the apprehension of the principles in the self-apprehension of the spiritual personality. It shows that in this self-apprehension there is an immediate going beyond the individual subjectivity, insofar as this is based on a reversal of the principles, the untruth of which comes to consciousness at the same time as the truth of the supra-individual spiritual. In this way it ascends to the idea of God, in order to descend from there again to the philosophy of nature and at the end of the same to reach its goal in anthropology and at the same time to speculatively justify its starting point."

of consciousness: thinking, acting, and feeling. Thus, Tillich transfers Schelling's doctrine of potency to the neo-Kantian faculty-theory (*Vermögenstheorie*) of consciousness in order to describe the realization of religion in history. Even through this integration, however, religion is not attributed to a function of consciousness. Rather, the principle of religion is realized historically in the functions of consciousness. In contrast to the pre-Christian religions, in the revelation of God the absolute spirit grasps itself in the individual, so that its selfhood is negated and it becomes again the medium of the absolute. Religion is consequently the return of the particular to the absolute and to truth.[57]

This speculative concept of religion, which Tillich, following Schelling, had developed since 1910, forms the basis of the theses of 1911, the theological dissertation from 1912, as well as the *Systematische Theologie* of 1913. What is of importance for the early understanding of religion is, on the one hand, the rejection of a religious a priori and, on the other hand, the interlocking of philosophy of religion and philosophy of history. God is the basis of religion and history, which is understood as a process of self-knowledge of the absolute in the individual spirit. Thus, the particular and concrete is included as a necessary moment in the speculative construction of history. But the concreteness of history is only a moment of passage on the way of the absolute spirit towards its self-knowledge. For religion is, as it is said in *Systematische Theologie* of 1913, the "return of freedom to truth, of the relative to the absolute" (EW IX, 315). As a result, Tillich's early speculative construction of history leads to its devaluation of history since it cannot assign any intrinsic meaning to the concreteness of history. The further development of Tillich's theology and philosophy of religion results from the treatment of this problem of his early conception in the context of modern-positive theology. It leads to a complete reconstruction of the earlier principled-theoretical foundation in the post-World War I period.

During the First World War, Tillich reshaped his early speculative justification of religion in the idea of God while also holding on to earlier concepts and motives, continuing them in his new conception and making

---

[57] Cf. Tillich, "Die religionsgeschichtliche Konstruktion in Schellings positiver Philosophie," 228: "*For this is the content of all history, because it is the essence of the spirit: to sacrifice itself in its naturalness in order to find itself again in spirit and truth.*"

their change difficult to reconstruct. In a lecture that Tillich gave in Halle around 1912/13 on the subject of the *Hauptprobleme der Geschichtsphiloso-phie*,[58] he still follows the speculative conception just described.[59] The Halle habilitation thesis is also still completely in line with it. New tones sound in untitled sketches from the years 1915/16, edited from the estate, from the context of the Halle habilitation proceedings.[60] In these sketches, which were published under the title *Theodicee*, Tillich initially also ties in with older thoughts that go back to the 1908 *Monismusschrift*. The lecture juxtaposes two series in which the problem of God and theodicy are dealt with: a dualistic as well as a monistic one. Tillich finally transforms both series into a monism that is realized dualistically. When compared to the previous version, there are two new aspects, however. On the one hand, the older model of history as self-knowledge of the absolute spirit in the individual is clearly criticized as insufficient,[61] and on the other hand, the construction amounts to the concrete in the present, which is included in the thought of God.[62] The only little developed train of thought of these

---

[58] Cf. Paul Tillich, "Das Problem der Geschichte," in EW X, 85–100. Erdmann Sturm, who edited the text, assigns it to Tillich's apologetic lectures. However, the previously lost handwritten manuscript of Tillich's lecture is in the estate of Wilhelm and Marion Pauck. The title page indicates that it is a lecture that Tillich gave under the title *Hauptprobleme der Geschichtsphilosophie* in the philosophical society in Halle. Cf. Paul Tillich, "Hauptprobleme der Geschichtsphilosophie," in The Wilhelm and Marion H. Pauck Manuscript Collection, Wright Library, Princeton Theological Seminary, Box 42.

[59] Cf. Tillich, "Das Problem der Geschichte," 91: "What is effective in the ultimate ground of the history is, after all, nothing other than the idea in which the contradiction is eternally suspended."

[60] Cf. Paul Tillich, "Theodicee," in EW X, 101–106 (1st draft), 107–113 (2nd draft). Cf. Folkart Wittekind, "'Allein durch den Glauben'. Tillich's sinn-theoretische Umformulierung des Rechtfertigungsverständnisses 1919," in *Religion – Kultur – Gesellschaft. Der frühe Tillich im Spiegel neuer Texte (1919–1920)*, ed. Christian Danz and Werner Schüßler (Wien: LIT, 2008), 39–65, esp. 46–52.

[61] Cf. Tillich, "Theodicee," 105: "all negative is developmental; all suffering and dying is passage of the Absolute to itself."

[62] Cf. Tillich, "Theodicee," 106: "The entrance of God into the relative is Christology, is doctrine of the cross; [...] Theodicee becomes Christology. God suffers with us. Every [!] grave cross is a symbol of God's victorious struggle with actuality."

sketches seems to transfer the former speculative construction of the relation of absolute and individual spirit to the self-relation of consciousness and to use it for the structuring of the self-relation of consciousness.[63] The considerations from the habilitation lecture *Der Begriff des christlichen Volkes* of 1915 also point in this direction.[64] A first complete and comprehensive elaboration of the new conception is found in the draft *Rechtfertigung und Zweifel* of 1919.[65] However, what does this mean for Tillich's understanding of religion in the context of the debates on the philosophy of religion around 1900?

The draft *Rechtfertigung und Zweifel* also falls back on older motifs, such as the idea that the principle, that is, the idea of the absolute, is realized dualistically.[66] But unlike the *Systematische Theologie* of 1913, the draft begins with the theological standpoint and no longer leads to such a theological standpoint through a speculative grounding. Thus, also the paradox, which is a key concept in Tillich's works since 1910 as well as in the 1919 draft, receives a new determination. It is now connected with faith and no longer functions as a return of the finite to the absolute.[67] Likewise, God is retained as the starting point of the system, and with it the rejection of a religious a priori as the basis of religion, as in the conceptions of Ernst Troeltsch and Rudolf Otto. But God is now tied to the present events of faith, so that the idea of God no longer forms the speculative basis of the system as in the early work. The draft of 1919 dismantles the speculative system foundation in the absolute spirit, which recognizes itself in the individual, and replaces this with a consciousness-theoretical version. It is solely from this consciousness-theoretical foundation that not only the new basic concepts of the unconditioned (*Unbedingte*) and meaning (*Sinn*)

---

[63] This is the interpretation of Wittekind, "Allein durch den Glauben," 51–2.

[64] Paul Tillich, "Der Begriff des christlichen Volkes. Habilitationsvortrag," in EW X, 114–116 (1st version), 117–126 (2nd version).

[65] Paul Tillich, "Rechtfertigung und Zweifel," in EW X, 128–185 (1st version), 185–249 (2nd version).

[66] Cf. Tillich, "Rechtfertigung und Zweifel," 189–90.

[67] Cf. Tillich, "Rechtfertigung und Zweifel," 218: "Faith in the unconditionality of the absolute paradox is precisely the meaning of faith also in the field of cognition."

result—concepts that Tillich employs in the reformulation of his system[68]—but also the new determination of religion as affirmation of the absolute paradox.[69]

Tillich bases his new definition of religion on the structure of consciousness. In its reflexive self-referentiality, consciousness itself is the basis and precondition for all positing of reality in consciousness. This means that in every concrete theoretical or practical act of consciousness, the latter is already claimed as something that has been reflexively disclosed (*erschlossenes*) to itself. Tillich designates this general basic structure of consciousness with the concept of the unconditioned. As such, the unconditioned underlies all acts of consciousness. Religion, now determined as faith, is the disclosedness (*Erschlossensein*) of this general basic structure in the individual consciousness. Faith is therefore a performative act that cannot be derived from consciousness and that, therefore, cannot be produced by it. Thus, solely in the act of faith is its disclosedness given in consciousness, which forms the basis of all its acts. Tillich understands faith, therefore, as an act of reflexivity in consciousness. He thus binds all knowledge of God to a revelation of God. For the act of faith arises in an underivable way in consciousness. Faith as religion is consequently not a form of consciousness either, for all forms of consciousness are posited by consciousness itself. Therefore, faith as religion is rather the becoming-reflexive of forms.

The reflexive disclosedness claimed by consciousness in each of its acts, determined by Tillich as the unconditioned, is itself indeterminate and in principle indeterminable, since it is the basis of all determinations in consciousness. In the performative act of faith, the unconditioned is disclosed to consciousness. The unconditioned is neither an object nor the I.[70] The unconditioned is the reflexive disclosedness of consciousness, "the meaning that paradoxically reveals itself to the experiencing [*erlebenden*] I, the meaning that signifies an unconditioned yes and an unconditioned no simultaneously about the doubter" (EW X, 219). The certainty of faith

---

[68] Cf. Wittekind, "Allein durch den Glauben," 59–61.

[69] Cf. Tillich, "Rechtfertigung und Zweifel," 218–221 (*E. Faith as the Affirmation of the Absolute Paradox*).

[70] Cf. Tillich, "Rechtfertigung und Zweifel," 219.

consists in its performative act.[71] The concept of meaning, which Tillich has used since 1918 to explain the unconditioned,[72] thus refers, like the unconditioned, to a new determination of consciousness and describes the performative dimension of faith, i.e., the reflexive disclosedness of consciousness in its performative act. The individual experience (*Erleben*) of the meaning in which the unconditioned is grasped consists in grasping the indeterminateness (*Bestimmungslosigkeit*) of the reflexivity of consciousness. Any content in which the disclosedness of consciousness is grasped in consciousness misses this reflexivity because it is posited by consciousness itself. Tillich's justification-theological description of the religious performative act applies to its reflexive structure.[73] For the contents of religious consciousness, this means that they constitute the reflexive structure of the religious performance. In Tillich's self-referential understanding of religion, religious consciousness refers to itself with its contents and represents itself in them. The "God above God" (EW X, 219), already here the aim of the reflections on the certainty of faith, does not refer to an actual or true God behind the images produced by consciousness. Rather, the God above God represents the reflexive structure of the religious performance *for* and *in* the religious consciousness.[74] It is here, as

---

[71] Cf. the doctrine of certainty newly taken up in "Rechtfertigung und Zweifel" (EW X, 204–218). In this new conception, Tillich incorporates his old reflections on conviction (*Überzeugung*) following Fichte, Fritz Medicus, and Wilhelm Lütgert (cf. EW X, 210–1). Cf. above chapter II.1.

[72] On the neo-Kantian and phenomenological backgrounds of Tillich's concept of meaning, cf. Ulrich Barth, "Die sinntheoretischen Grundlagen des Religionsbegriffs. Problemgeschichtliche Hintergründe zum frühen Tillich," in *Religion in der Moderne* (Tübingen: Mohr Siedbeck, 2003), 89–123. On the difficulty to translate Tillich's understanding of the German word "*Sinn*" into English, cf. Steven Cassedy, "What is the Meaning of *Meaning* in Paul Tillich's Theology?" in *HTR* 111:3 (2018) 307–332; *What Do We Mean When We Talk about Meaning?* (New York: Oxford University Press, 2022). Here and henceforth the English word "meaning" is employed for the German word "*Sinn.*"

[73] Cf. Christian Danz, "Critique and Formation. Paul Tillich's Interpretation of Protestantism," in *The Courage to Be. International Yearbook for Tillich Research*, vol. 13, ed. Christian Danz, Marc Dumas, Werner Schüßler, Mary A. Stenger and Erdmann Sturm (Berlin; Boston: de Gruyter, 2018), 237–244.

[74] Cf. chapter VI below.

early as 1919, that Tillich lays the foundation for the later theory of sym-bols.[75] It is not the referential structure that is constitutive for Tillich's un-derstanding of symbol. Rather, with the concept of symbol, Tillich desig-nates the reflexive position of the fundamentally symbol-productive consciousness to its contents.

Tillich's new conception of religion, as he systematically elaborated it in his draft *Rechtfertigung und Zweifel* after the First World War, com-pletely transforms the older, speculative version of religion into a reflexive description of the structure of the religious performance in consciousness. With the new justification-theological version of religion, he structures its performance, which exists and has its validity in itself. For every justifica-tion of religion, including Tillich's former speculative one in the absolute spirit, can only be a produced one, which is subject to doubt. The new version of religion refers to the present, to modernity as an age of reflexive autonomy. This is what doubt stands for, which is incorporated into the theological system. Faith, understood as a performative act of reflection in consciousness, is no longer the overcoming of doubt,[76] but the recognition that doubt is the realization of the unconditioned in history.[77] Conse-quently, history also acquires now a new version. It is no longer a mere moment of passage of the absolute spirit on the way to its self-knowledge, but the concrete and individual is, at the same time, the necessary and failed form in which God reveals God's self in history. Only then does history acquire, as it is said in the writings of the 1920s, "unconditional meaning" (GW VI, 79).

In his writings after the First World War, especially the lecture *Die Überwindung des Religionsbegriffs in der Religionsphilosophie*, published in 1922, and the *Religionsphilosophie*, written a year later and not published

---

[75] Tillich uses the concept of symbol in the first version of "Rechtfertigung und Zweifel" (EW X, 172), but this does not yet function as a leading concept. In the second version, Tillich also no longer used the concept of symbol. On Tillich's concept of symbol, cf. Lars Heinemann, *Sinn – Geist – Symbol. Eine systematisch-genetische Rekonstruktion der frühen Symboltheorie Tillichs* (Berlin; Boston: de Gru-yter, 2017). Cf. below chapter IV.3.

[76] Like in the *Systematische Theologie* of 1913. Cf. Tillich, "Systematische Theologie von 1913," 314–317.

[77] Cf. Tillich, "Rechtfertigung und Zweifel," 218: "that in this state of doubt [sc. of reflexive disclosedness of consciousness] he [sc. modern human being] oc-cupies the only possible position vis-à-vis the unconditioned."

until 1925, Tillich further elaborated his new understanding of religion. Its basic structures will be discussed in the following chapters. Before that, Tillich's understanding of religion must still be related to the debates on the concept of religion discussed in this chapter. Even in the new version of the concept of religion elaborated during and after the war, the rejection of a religious a priori remains. Similar to Windelband, Tillich detaches religion from the cultural functions of consciousness and at the same time relates religion to these functions. This is the difference between Tillich's understanding of religion and that of Troeltsch and Otto. Despite Tillich's appreciative references to Otto's understanding of religion in *Das Heilige*, Tillich dissolves Otto's foundation of religion in a religious disposition already given to human being. Religion is not based on an a priori given in the general structure of the foundation of consciousness, but solely in the performance of religion to which it is bound. Tillich's new, performance-bound (*vollzugsgebundene*) philosophy of religion stands in the context of the new theologies as they were conceived after the First World War. He himself drew attention to this parallel.[78] At the same time, Tillich's new understanding of religion, which starts from the unconditioned, can also be understood as an epistemic-critical further development of modern-positive theology,[79] which has parallels in contemporary conceptions of its

---

[78] Cf. Tillich, "Die Überwindung des Religionsbegriffs in der Religionsphilosophie," 367: "It is therefore factually justified if I refer to the spiritual community in which I find myself in the following thoughts with men of the religious word, such as Barth and Gogarten."

[79] It is in this sense that Tillich's engagement with Karl Heim's apologetic theology, which occupies a large space in the draft "Rechtfertigung und Zweifel," must be understood. Tillich had already dealt with Heim's book *Das Gewißheits-problem in der systematischen Theologie bis zu Schleiermacher* – on a different systematic basis – in *Systematische Theologie* of 1913. Cf. Tillich, "Systematische Theologie von 1913," 321. Cf. Karl Heim, *Das Gewißheitsproblem in der systematischen Theologie bis zu Schleiermacher* (Leipzig: J. C. Hinrichs, 1911); *Glaubensgewißheit. Eine Untersuchung über die Lebensfrage der Religion* (Leipzig: J. C. Hinrichs, 1916). Cf. Folkart Wittekind, "Von der Bewußtseinsphilosophie zur Christologie. Theologie und Moderne bei Karl Heim, Paul Tillich und Hans Joachim Iwand," in *Der "frühe Iwand" (1923–1933)*, ed. Gerard den Hertog and Eberhard Lempp (Waltrop: Spenner, 2008), 59–114.

younger representatives, such as Paul Althaus's theology of faith[80] or Rudolf Hermann's philosophy of religion.[81]

---

[80] Cf. Paul Althaus, "Theologie des Glaubens [1924/25]," in *Theologische Aufsätze* (Gütersloh: Bertelsmann, 1929), 74–118.

[81] Cf. Rudolf Hermann, "Zur Grundlegung der Religionsphilosophie," in *Zeitschrift für Systematische Theologie* 1 (1923) 92–106. Cf. Folkart Wittekind, "Das Erleben der Wirklichkeit Gottes. Die Entstehung der Theologie Hans Joachim Iwand aus der Religionsphilosophie Carl Stanges und Rudolf Hermanns," in *Neue Zeitschrift für Systematische Theologie und Religionsphilosophie* 44 (2002) 20–42; Heinrich Assel, *Der andere Aufbruch. Die Lutherrenaissance – Ursprünge, Aporien, Wege: Karl Holl, Emanuel Hirsch, Rudolf Hermann (1910–1935)* (Göttingen: Vandenhoeck & Ruprecht, 1994).

IV.

The Religious Symbol, the Demonic, and Anxiety: Paul Tillich and the *Kulturwissenschaftliche Bibliothek Warburg* in Hamburg

> The anxiety of fate returned with the invasion of the late antiquity. 'Fortuna' became a preferred symbol in the art of the Renaissance, and even the Reformers were not free from astrological beliefs and fears. And the anxiety of fate was intensified by fear of demonic powers acting directly or through other human beings to cause illness, death, and all kinds of destruction.[1]

The passage is taken from Paul Tillich's 1952 publication *The Courage to Be*, one of the most successful texts of the Protestant theologian who emigrated to the United States in 1933. The astrological superstition of the Reformers mentioned by the theologian alludes to Aby Warburg's study *Heidnisch-antike Weissagung in Wort und Bild zu Luthers Zeiten*, which discusses the afterlife of the ancient stellar faith in the age of the Reformation.[2] Tillich's reference is a trace or engram in his work, which echoes his little-known contacts with the *Kulturwissenschaftliche Bibliothek Warburg* in Hamburg, dating back to the 1920s.

---

[1] Paul Tillich, *The Courage to Be* (3rd ed. New Haven; London: Yale University Press, 2014), 55.

[2] Cf. Aby Warburg, *Heidnisch-antike Weissagung in Wort und Bild zu Luthers Zeiten* (Heidelberg: Carl Winters Universitätsbuchhandlung, 1920).

What connects the religious socialist theologian Tillich with the art historian Aby Warburg and his library, which he characterized as a "collection of documents on the psychology of human expression"?[3] The methodological innovation of Warburg and his collaborators consists in a cultural-theoretical extension of art history,[4] which focuses on the function of symbols for a theory of social memory.[5] I will show in this chapter that this also applies to Paul Tillich's understanding of the Christian religion in the horizon of culture whose fundamentals were discussed in the third chapter. However, it is not only the concept of symbols which is the focus of the works of Warburg and Tillich, but also other concepts such as the demonic and the phenomenon of anxiety, which are intrinsically related to symbol theory. In the work of the theologian, these terms, initially that of the symbol, find their way into the early 1920s, i.e., at the time when Tillich established his contacts with the *Kulturwissenschaftliche Bibliothek Warburg*. While it cannot be proven that the theologian adopted Warburg's concept of symbolism, it is a fact that Tillich worked out his understanding of the symbol in the 1920s when he was in touch with the scholars of the *Kulturwissenschaftliche Bibliothek Warburg*, above all Ernst Cassirer. As the passage from *The Courage to Be* quoted at the beginning shows, this contact left traces even in his late work.

This is the subject of the following reflections on Paul Tillich and the *Kulturwissenschaftliche Bibliothek Warburg*. The traces of Warburg's "*Problem-Bibliothek*" in the work of the theologian must be followed. In particular, I will trace the concepts of symbol, the demonic, and anxiety. This will be done in three sections, starting with Tillich's encounter with the *Kulturwissenschaftliche Bibliothek Warburg*, followed by the discussion of

---

[3] Aby Warburg, "Reise-Erinnerungen aus dem Gebiet der Pueblo Indianer in Nordamerika," in *Werke in einem Band. Auf der Grundlage der Manuskripte und Handexemplare*, ed. Martin Treml, Sigrid Weigel and Perdita Ladwig (Berlin: Suhrkamp, 2018), 566–600, here 582.

[4] Cf. Fritz Saxl, "Die Kulturwissenschaftliche Bibliothek Warburg in Hamburg [1930]," in Dorthea McEwan, *Fritz Saxl – Eine Biographie. Aby Warburgs Bibliothekar und erster Direktor des Londoner Warburg Instituts* (Wien; Köln; Weimar: Böhlau, 2012), 265–270, here 267: "This expands the concept of image history [*Bildgeschichte*] by making it a source for the history of religion and science beyond its artistic substance [*künstlerischen Gehalt*]."

[5] Cf. Bernd Villhauer, *Aby Warburgs Theorie der Kultur. Detail und Sinnhorizont* (Berlin: Akademie Verlag, 2002), 66.

Aby Warburg's theory of social memory, and concluding with Tillich's work on these themes in his own writings.

1. "The unifying bond of all these works is the idea of the Warburg Library"; or, Paul Tillich and the *Kulturwissenschaftliche Bibliothek*

In May 1921, the publishing house B. G. Teubner in Leipzig published Aby Warburg's study *Heidnisch-antike Weissagung in Wort und Bild zu Luthers Zeit.*[6] Its subject matter is the belief in stars in Luther's and Melanchthon's Wittenberg, i.e., the afterlife and overlapping of pagan-ancient magic and mathematics in the battle for the sovereignty of astral images in the Reformation. The Viennese art historian Fritz Saxl, who, due to Warburg's severe mental illness, had been acting deputy director of the *Kulturwissenschaftliche Bibliothek Warburg* since April 15, 1920, and who promoted its transformation into a research institute, was instrumental in publishing Warburg's research. Saxl was also the *spiritus rector* behind the organization of the library as an academic institution, intensifying the library's network with numerous scholars at home and abroad.[7] It was due to his initiative that regular lectures were held from October 1921 onwards and the two series of research publications of the *Kulturwissenschaftliche Bibliothek Warburg*, the *Studien der Bibliothek Warburg* and *Vorträge der Bibliothek Warburg*, were published by Teubner publishers. They institutionalized the library's research.

Saxl took great personal interest in the reception of Warburg's Luther study by writing to scholars from a wide variety of research fields and asking them to review the book.[8] He sent the book to art historians, who had been in touch with Warburg, to historians of religion, to Reformation scholars, as well as theologians such as Otto Eißfeld, Hugo Gressmann,

---

[6] The article first appeared in the proceedings of the Heidelberg Academy of Sciences. Philosophical-historical class 1920, 26th paper, received October 25, 1919, submitted by Franz Boll.

[7] Cf. McEwan, *Fritz Saxl*, 52–64.

[8] Cf. McEwan, *Fritz Saxl*, 65–71; "Making a Reception for Warburg: Fritz Saxl and Warburg's Book Heidnisch-antike Weissagung in Wort und Bild zu Luthers Zeiten," in *Art History as Cultural History. Warburg's Projects*, ed. Richard Woodfield (Abingdon: Routledge, 2001), 93–120.

Hermann Gunkel, Karl Ludwig Schmidt, Walther Köhler, Otto Scheel, and Karl Holl. Among the scholars was the Berlin *Privatdozent*, Paul Tillich. On October 12, Saxl wrote to him: "Am I very immodest if I ask you whether you could show Professor Warburg's booklet somewhere?"[9] However, Saxl's efforts to have the *Privatdozent* discuss the book on Luther remained unsuccessful, since no such review by Tillich has come to light.[10] But how did Saxl even get the idea of asking Tillich, still relatively unknown at the beginning of the 1920s, to review Warburg's book?

The name Tillich is mentioned alongside Karl Ludwig Schmidt's in a letter to Lydia Stöcker, a church historian, dated June 6, 1921, in which Saxl reported on his efforts to find reviewers for the book on Luther.[11] He expressed his hope, as the letter went on to say, that both Tillich and Schmidt would come to Hamburg for lectures. Eighteen days later, on June 24, Saxl finally informed Warburg in Kreuzlingen, that Paul Tillich would visit the library and write a report about it in academic theological journals.[12] Who exactly introduced the young theologian to the *Kulturwissenschaftliche Bibliothek Warburg* is not yet known. Presumably it was the New Testament scholar Karl Ludwig Schmidt, a student of Hugo Gressmann, who, like Tillich, was a *Privatdozent* in the Faculty of Theology at University of Berlin,[13] and whom Warburg had consulted in the course of

---

[9] Fritz Saxl to Paul Tillich, October 12, 1921 (Warburg Institute Archive London [WIA], NL-Signatur GC/13206). Already on August 9, 1921, Saxl wrote to Wilhelm Waetzholdt that Tillich would write a review of the book on Luther for the *Internationalen Monatshefte*. Cf. Fritz Saxl to Wilhelm Waetzholdt, August 9, 1921 (WIA GC/13123). Cf. McEwan, "Making a Reception for Warburg," 119, note 141. However, it is possible that the article about the library was confused with the review.

[10] Half a year later, on January 6, 1922, Warburg—who was impatiently waiting for resonance for his study in Kreuzlingen—asked Saxl again why Tillich had not written a review of the book on Luther. Cf. Aby Warburg to Fritz Saxl, January 6, 1922 (WIA, GC/13865). Cf. McEwan, "Making a Reception for Warburg," 109.

[11] Cf. Fritz Saxl to Lydia Stöcker, June 6, 1921 (WIA GC/13185).

[12] Cf. Fritz Saxl to Aby Warburg, June 24, 1921 (WIA GC/13326).

[13] For Schmidt cf. Andreas Mühling, *Karl Ludwig Schmidt. "Und Wissenschaft ist Leben"* (Berlin; New York: de Gruyter, 1997). But Mühling's study on Schmidt does not address his relationship to the Warburg Library.

his research on Luther.[14] Shortly afterwards, Saxl wrote to Tillich that he was looking forward to showing him the library in the following week and assured him that he would cover Tillich's travel costs, board, and lodgings.[15]

From July 3 to 5, 1921, Tillich visited the *Kulturwissenschaftliche Bibliothek Warburg* in Hamburg. As Saxl told Warburg ten days later, Tillich was enthusiastic and—like Ernst Cassirer—would like to be sentenced to a lengthy "prison term" there in order to work in the library.[16] Mary Warburg also wrote how much Tillich had enjoyed his stay in Hamburg. She had met him, with the Saxls and the Cassirers for dinner on Sunday evening, July 3.[17] In the correspondence between Saxl and Tillich, as well as between Saxl and Warburg, there was talk again and again about Tillich's promised report about the *Kulturwissenschaftliche Bibliothek Warburg*. It was not yet decided in which journal the report would be published, but Saxl promised to find the most appropriate one. The letter to Warburg mentioned the journal *Logos*,[18] then the *Internationale Monatsschrift*.[19] Tillich's article *Renaissance und Reformation. Zur Einführung in die Bibliothek*

---

[14] This is pointed out by McEwan, "Making a Reception for Warburg," 107. Cf. also 118, note 131.

[15] Cf. Fritz Saxl to Paul Tillich, June, 22, 1921 (WIA GC/13201).

[16] Fritz Saxl to Aby Warburg, July 13, 1921. Tillich's visit to the library was also mentioned by Saxl in his annual report for 1921: "Dr. Tillich, lecturer in the history of religion in Berlin, came here for several days and was so strongly influenced by the idea of the library that he wrote an essay about it which will appear in a scientific journal in 1922." [Fritz Saxl,] Bericht über die Bibliothek Warburg für das Jahr 1921, in Tilmann von Stockhausen, *Die Kulturwissenschaftliche Bibliothek Warburg. Architektur, Einrichtung und Organisation* (Hamburg: Dölling & Galitz, 1992), 124–132, here 129.

[17] Cf. Mary Warburg to Aby Warburg, July 4, 1921 (WIA GC/35635). Thomas Meyer probably referred to Tillich's visit to the library and the evening spent together with Mary Warburg. A teaching activity of Tillich in Hamburg, as Meyer claimed, did not emerge from the correspondence and has not yet been proven. Cf. Thomas Meyer, *Ernst Cassirer* (Hamburg: Ellert & Richter, 2006), 103.

[18] Cf. Fritz Saxl to Aby Warburg, July 13, 1921 (WIA GC/13331).

[19] Cf. Fritz Saxl to Wilhelm Printz, July 14, 1921 (WIA CG/13080). On August 16 Saxl wrote to Tillich that he had just received a message from Wilhelm Waetzoldt, "that he is willing to approach Professor Cornicelius for an article on

Warburg finally appeared one year later in the December issue of the journal *Theologische Blätter*, edited by his friend Karl Ludwig Schmidt.[20]

In his *Einführung in die Bibliothek Warburg*, Tillich not only mentioned his own visit to Hamburg in July 1921, but he emphasized above all its significance for theological and religious-historical work, anchored in the "energy with which everything is related to the basic problem, whereby every user of the library is irresistibly caught up by the problem of the Renaissance" (GW XIII, 267). He went on to assess this impact and found it in the historical-philosophical interpretation of one's own present and its formation, which were put into a new direction by the studies of Warburg and his library. Over against simplistic contrasts of cultural Renaissance and religious Reformation as well as theories of "closed cultural circles as expression and creation of particular cultural souls [*Kulturseelen*]" (GW XIII, 265), the library made their complex interaction clear. The Renaissance could not simply be understood as the first stage of an autonomous liberation from the heteronomous Middle Ages, but rather a "shaking of the religious consciousness of the European peoples," i.e., itself a shape (*Gestalt*) of religious consciousness whose forms of expression owe

the Warburg Library through the mediation of the *Ministerialrat* Richter, the advisor in the Ministry for the *Internationalen Monatshefte*." As soon as Tillich finishes his article, Saxl continues, he should send it to him. "I will then pass it on to the *Monatshefte*." Fritz Saxl to Paul Tillich, August 16, 1921 (WIA GC/13204).

[20] Cf. Paul Tillich, "Renaissance und Reformation. Zur Einführung in die Bibliothek Warburg," in *Theologische Blätter* 32 (1922) 265–267, reprinted in GW XIII, 137–140. As can be seen from a letter to Hannah Gottschow, his future wife, from September 1921, Tillich had worked on the article during this time and probably sent it to Saxl at the beginning of October, who received it on October 12, and informed Tillich that, as announced in his letter of August 16, he would forward the contribution via Waetzholdt and Richter to Max Cornicelius, the editor of the *Internationale Monatshefte*, and also to Warburg. Cf. Paul Tillich to Hannah Gottschow, n. d. (Harvard Divinity School Library, Harvard University, Cambridge, Mass., Hannah Tillich Papers, 1896–1976, bMS 721/2[17]); Fritz Saxl to Paul Tillich, October 12, 1921 (WIA GC/13206). On February 11, 1922, Karl Ludwig Schmidt asked Saxl where Tillich's contribution appeared (WIA GC/13711). Saxl replied, on February 18, that he did not know it, but informed him that the article would not be published in the *Internationale Monatsschrift* and asked Schmidt whether he knew a publisher for Tillich's article (WIA GC/13712). On May 8, 1922, Saxl wrote to Schmidt that he was expecting Tillich's contribution and would like to see it published (WIA GC/13717).

their existence to the transforming recourse of "mystical-religious" (ibid.) late antiquity. Only when the "astral-mythological and demonological" (ibid.) elements were combined with rational ones, did the Renaissance become understandable. The picture Tillich painted of the *Kulturwissen-schaftliche Bibliothek Warburg* clearly evoked Warburg's article on the after-life of pagan astral beliefs in the Reformation. No wonder that people in Hamburg and Kreuzlingen were enthusiastic about the article of the young theologian.

Tillich's article on the *Kulturwissenschaftliche Bibliothek Warburg* in the *Theologische Blätter* was not the only literary expression of his contacts with the scholars around Aby Warburg. The theologian's literary estate also contains a hitherto unknown review of the two publication series of the *Kulturwissenschaftliche Bibliothek Warburg*. On July 14, 1925, Teubner publishers informed the *Kulturwissenschaftliche Bibliothek Warburg* that Paul Tillich had agreed to review the library's publication series for the *Kairos* yearbook.[21] In its first volume, which appeared in 1926, there is a list of book publications at the end, but it does not mention the scholarly output of the *Kulturwissenschaftliche Bibliothek Warburg*.[22] As can be seen from Tillich's manuscript, which was written around 1928, it was ear-marked to appear in the second *Kairos* volume,[23] but this did not happen.[24]

Tillich's review interpreted the "idea of the Warburg Library" as the "unifying bond of all these writings," namely the problem of the afterlife of antiquity in the European image memory (*Bildgedächtnis*). As in his 1922 article on the *Kulturwissenschaftliche Bibliothek*, he pointed to the ex-pansion of art history through the history of religion, which he saw as part of the methodological innovation of the scholars around Aby Warburg. Precisely in this fact he saw the importance of the *Kulturwissenschaftliche Bibliothek Warburg* for contemporary theology, which was characterized by

---

[21] E. Triepel to Warburg Library, July 14, 1925 (WIA GC/16894).

[22] Christian Herrmann, "Bücherschau," in *Kairos. Zur Geisteslage und Geis-teswerdung*, ed. Paul Tillich (Darmstadt: Reichl, 1926), 467–483.

[23] Cf. Paul Tillich, "Vorträge und Studien der Bibliothek Warburg," in EW XXI, 359–363.

[24] Paul Tillich (ed.), *Protestantismus als Kritik und Gestaltung. Zweites Buch des Kairos-Kreises* (Darmstadt: Reichl, 1929).

a shift away from considerations on the history of religion and a predominance of the principle which was critical of religion.[25] Of course, this shift was in Tillich's mind specifically associated with the so-called dialectical theology of Friedrich Gogarten and Karl Barth, which had gained increasing influence during the early 1920s. However, their theological approach meant that the formative moment (*gestaltende Moment*) receded behind the critical one and brought with it an isolation of theology from the formative cultural reality. "But as soon as the formative moment comes again more clearly into its right, also the view on the history of religion and the immeasurable abundance of forms it contains will become freer."[26]

The history of religion and formation (*Gestaltung*): these are the aspects highlighted by Tillich, with which he summarized the importance of the *Kulturwissenschaftliche Bibliothek Warburg* for contemporary theology. What did it mean in detail?

2. Symbolism as a "Function of Gravity in the Mental Household"; or, Aby Warburg's Theory of Symbol

> Is it possible to understand what we call symbol as a function of social memory, because this is where the inhibiting or driving organ is created, ... between the instinctive-suffering kinesis and the ordering cosmological theory, the consciousness and the will for compensatory sophrosyne [*Besonnenheit*] as the highest cultural power?[27]

With this statement written in a letter to the classical philologist Ulrich von Wilamowitz-Moellendorf, Warburg shows that the symbol has a fundamental function for social memory. Without symbols there is no social memory. But what does Warburg understand by "symbol" and what is the function of a symbol for social memory? In order to answer these questions, it is necessary to follow Warburg's article *Heidnisch-antike Weissa-*

---

[25] Cf. Tillich, "Vorträge und Studien der Bibliothek Warburg," 362.

[26] Cf. Tillich, "Vorträge und Studien der Bibliothek Warburg," 362.

[27] Aby Warburg to Ulrich von Wilamowitz-Moellendorf, 1924. Cit. after Villhauer, *Aby Warburgs Theorie der Kultur*, 67.

gung in Wort und Bild, of 1921, his Kreuzlingen lecture on the *Pueblo Indians*, of April 21, 1923, and his introductory notes to the *Mnemosyne-Atlas*, of 1929.

Warburg's theory of symbols is the result of his lifelong reflections on the structure and function of symbols. His occupation with the study of symbols can be traced back to important impulses he received already as a student.[28] Significant for his concept of symbolism is the intention of working on a scientific foundation of symbolism, which should lead to a methodical re-foundation of art history in the sense of a cultural studies program.[29] It is therefore not surprising that psychological and theoretical programs based on natural sciences acted as a frame of reference, but also as a plausibility enhancer for Warburg's theory of symbols. A psychological theory, which he adopts from the anthropologist and evolutionary theorist Tito Vignoli, is fundamental to answering the cultural-theoretical question about the origin of symbols.[30] Pictorial symbols banished anxiety, kept them at a distance by objectifying them in an image. The symbolic images created by humanity were thus understood as a reaction to a stimulus, as it were, as a "defensive measure" (*Abwehrmassregel*).[31] Culture is thus based on anxiety, which gives it the power to create culture by capturing the phobic stimulus in the image and keeping it at bay. In this sense, symbols are first and foremost images of meaning, which, as stated in the quote above, react to an instinctive, suffering kinesis by setting a cosmological image that creates order and orientation.

Such image-settings (*Bildsetzungen*) that transform the phobic stimulus into an orienting image and thus make reality habitable for humans

---

[28] Cf. Claudia Wedepohl, "Pathos – Polarität – Distanz – Denkraum. Eine archivarische Spurensuche," in *Warburgs Denkraum. Formen, Motive, Materialien*, ed. Martin Treml, Sabine Flach and Pablo Schneider (München: Fink, 2014), 17–49; Villhauer, *Aby Warburgs Theorie der Kultur*, 15–51. Cf. also Ernst H. Gombrich, *Aby Warburg. Eine intellektuelle Biographie* (Hamburg: Philo Fine Arts, 2006), 42–62.

[29] Cf. the contributions in Frank Fahrenbach and Cornelia Zumbusch (eds.), *Aby Warburg und die Natur. Epistemik, Ästhetik, Kulturtheorie* (Berlin; Boston: de Gruyter, 2019).

[30] Cf. Tito Vignoli, *Mythos und Wissenschaft* (Leipzig: Brockhaus, 1880).

[31] Warburg, "Reise-Erinnerungen aus dem Gebiet der Pueblo Indianer," 587. Cf. also 579: "Through the substituting image, the impressive attraction is objectified and created as an object of defense."

by wresting away their horrors and keeping them at a distance, are called by Warburg "circumference determination" (*Umfangsbestimmung*).[32] What is meant by this is that human beings appropriate their environment through an expansion of their self-image.[33] Such images are always abstractions. Through images created by an individual, reality is assimilated. This is initially done by the act of grasping or gripping, i.e., by extending the human touch over media such as tools, jewelry, etc. Humanity, by appropriating its environment, by seizing it, reduces the distance between it and itself. However, this is only one side of the image-setting composition. The consequent second side is one called by Warburg a "symbolic act," which means that, by reducing the distance between humanity and its environment with the help of the image, the distance is restored through a spiritual act in the composition of the image-setting.[34] Both, i.e., removing the distance and its spiritual restoration, belong together in the composition of the image-setting. A symbol is thus not only a meaningful image, but also a symbolic act that restores the difference between the individual and his environment. In a project outline that he drew up in the late 1890s in order to summarize the theoretical foundations of his symbol theory in a condensed form, Warburg called this composition of the image-setting

---

[32] Cf. Warburg, "Reise-Erinnerungen aus dem Gebiet der Pueblo Indianer," 573–4. Cf. Villhauer, *Aby Warburgs Theorie der Kultur*, 68–70.

[33] Cf. Warburg, "Reise-Erinnerungen aus dem Gebiet der Pueblo Indianer," 574–5: "The attempt of a magical influence is thus first of all an attempt to appropriate a natural event in its living, similar circumferential structure: the lightning is lured by mimic appropriation, not destroyed by magnetic, inorganic, device-like attraction into the ground as in modern culture. Such behavior towards the environment differs from our behavior in that the mimic image is intended to force the connection, while we strive for mental and real distance."

[34] Cf. Aby Warburg, "Bilder aus dem Gebiet der Pueblo-Indianer in Nord-Amerika," in *Werke in einem Band. Auf der Grundlage der Manuskripte und Handexemplare*, ed. Martin Treml, Sigrid Weigel and Perdita Ladwig (Berlin: Suhrkamp, 2018), 524–566, here 561: "In the struggle for the spiritual connection between man and his environment, mythical and symbolic thinking create the space as a space of devotion or thinking, which the electrical momentary connection robs of, unless a disciplined humanity stops the inhibition of conscience again."

"symbolism as circumference determination" (*Symbolismus als Umfangsbestimmung*).[35]

In human imagery, reality is not only appropriated and, as it were, incorporated, but also simultaneously kept at a distance. Through symbols, human beings constantly expand their world and keep it at a distance. The symbolic act thus includes reflexivity, an interruption of stimulus and reaction, which enables what Warburg calls "thought space" (*Denkraum*) and "sophrosyne" (*Besonnenheit*). Without the act of distancing, empowered by symbolic images, neither culture nor orientation is possible. As Aby Warburg writes in his notations introducing the *Mnemosyne* project in 1929, "consciously creating distance between oneself and the outside world" is the "basic act of human civilization."[36]

Warburg's theory of social memory is thus based on the previously discussed structure of the symbol as "circumference determination." In the image memory of humankind, the images that banish the horrors of reality are deposited and overlap one another at the same time. Material images are externalized memories: they compose an archive of stimulus reactions that have become images.[37] The cultural memory of images is based on an affective reaction of stimuli, a religious emotion, as it were, in which the decisive forms of expression were shaped and are preserved.[38] The images

---

[35] Aby Warburg, "Symbolismus als Umfangsbestimmung," in *Werke in einem Band. Auf der Grundlage der Manuskripte und Handexemplare*, ed. Martin Treml, Sigrid Weigel and Perdita Ladwig (Berlin: Suhrkamp, 2018), 615–628; cf. Villhauer, *Aby Warburgs Theorie der Kultur*, 127–130.

[36] Aby Warburg, "Mnemosyne Einleitung," in *Werke in einem Band. Auf der Grundlage der Manuskripte und Handexemplare*, ed. Martin Treml, Sigrid Weigel and Perdita Ladwig (Berlin: Suhrkamp, 2018), 629–639, here 629.

[37] Cf. Warburg, "Reise-Erinnerungen aus dem Gebiet der Pueblo Indianer," 582: "Memory is only a selected collection of answered irritation symptoms through vocal expressions."

[38] Cf. Warburg, "Mnemosyne Einleitung," 631: "In the region of orgiastic mass emotion, the embossed work is to be sought, which hammers into memory the expressions of maximum inner emotion, as far as it can be expressed in sign language, with such intensity that these engrams of passionate experience survive as a memory-preserving heritage and exemplarily determine the outline that the artist's hand creates as soon as maximum values of sign language want to emerge in the daylight of the design by the artist's hand."

stored in the archive of social memory are appropriated through empathetic re-experiencing, in that they evoke corresponding feelings in their recipients, which enable them to understand the represented expression. In doing so, Warburg combines his theory of social memory and an evolutionary interpretation of cultural development, which was formulated in terms of symbol theory following Theodor Vischer.[39] In early texts such as *Symbolismus als Umfangsbestimmung*, Warburg still assumed a cultural-historical development from religion to science. He structured this development with Vischer's differentiation of the concept of symbol, which resulted from different assignments of image and meaning. At the beginning of the cultural development, humanity was imbued with religious-mythical consciousness, to which a "darkly confusing" meaning-image (*Sinn-Bild*) corresponded. At the end of this process there was scientific culture, in which signs and what was designated were differentiated. Between these two cornerstones of cultural development stood a quasi-scanning as well as removing relationship between image and meaning, namely art.[40] Warburg transformed this developmental scheme from myth to science or from image to sign in his late work into a circular model. Steps in this direction are visible in the later entries on the draft for *Symbolismus als Umfangsbestimmung*.[41]

What does that mean for Warburg's understanding of culture? It means that the development of culture follows a tragic trajectory, which consists in the fact that the distance that made culture possible in the first place is reduced by culture itself. Warburg then understands the re-experiential appropriation of the forms of expression stored in the image

---

[39] Friedrich Theodor Vischer, "Das Symbol," in *Philosophische Aufsätze. Eduard Zeller zu seinem fünfzigjährigen Doctor-Jubiläum gewidmet* (Leipzig: Fues's Verlag, 1887), 151–193.

[40] Cf. Warburg, "Symbolismus als Umfangsbestimmung," 626.

[41] Cf. Warburg, "Symbolismus als Umfangsbestimmung," 622. The entry is from December 8, 1899. Cf. Hans C. Hönes, "Spielraum der Rationität. Warburg und die Wahrscheinlichkeitsrechnung," in *Aby Warburg und die Natur. Epistemik, Ästhetik, Kulturtheorie*, ed. Frank Fehrenbach and Cornelia Zumbusch (Berlin; Boston: de Gruyter, 2019), 33–48.

memory as a polarity or as a pendulum movement between magical religion and science.[42] In his study on astrological politics in the Reformation Age of 1921, which is also an analysis of the image propaganda during the First World War, he succinctly works out the coexistence of logic and magic, of trope and metaphor, by means of the afterlife of the ancient astral faith.[43] While the constellations enable people to orient themselves by opening up a space of thought as images created by them, they destroy this space when, in the appropriation of these images, their affective, sensorial dimension (*affektive sinnliche Dimension*) predominates and the symbolic act, which restores the distance between the sign and the signified in the spirit, is absent. The image that provides orientation then gains a demonic power over humanity, to which humanity is not only subjected, but which also destroys culture itself, because the thought space that makes this possible in the first place is dissolved. The constellations become demonic powers that "experience a renewal of blood from the battle-ravaged social and political present time, which makes them, to a certain extent, momentary political gods."[44]

---

[42] Cf. Warburg, "Mnemosyne Einleitung," 629: "The memory of the collective personality as well as of the individual comes to the aid of man, who thus vacillates between religious and mathematical worldview, in a very peculiar way: not without creating further space for thought, but strengthening the tendency to calm observation or orgiastic devotion at the border poles of psychic behavior." Cf. also "Bilder aus dem Gebiet der Pueblo-Indianer," 559: "The replacement of the mythological cause by the technological one thus takes away the horror that primitive man feels. Whether this liberation from the mythological view really helps him to answer the riddles of existence sufficiently, we do not want to claim without further ado."

[43] Cf. Warburg, *Heidnisch-antike Weissagungen in Wort und Bild*, 427: "*Logic*, which *creates* the *space of thought*—between man and object—by means of conceptually special *designation,* and *magic*, which *destroys* this very *space of thought* again by superstitiously *contracting*—idealistic or practical connection of man and object, we still observe in the prophetic thinking of astrology as a uniformly primitive device with which the astrologer can measure and at the same time conjure."

[44] Warburg, *Heidnisch-antike Weissagen in Wort und Bild*, 428. Cf. Roland Kany, *Die religionsgeschichtliche Forschung an der Kulturwissenschaftlichen Bibliothek Warburg* (Bamberg: Wendel, 1989), 14: "Human beings then succumbed to the power of images instead of using them in service. Ancient art, which had grown out of the various ancient religions, could have a healing as well as a pernicious influence on the people of Europe."

The image memory is ambivalent. On the one hand, it enables culture to be shaped, and on the other hand it prevents it by exercising an almost demonic power over humanity. The way out of this tragedy of culture is nothing else but a new conquest of the "thought space," that is, the distance between image and reality. "Athens," said Warburg, "wants to be reconquered again and again by Alexandria."[45]

3. Criticism and Formation (*Gestaltung*); or, Paul Tillich's Theology of Culture

In his *Einführung in die Bibliothek Warburg* as well as in his review of the publication series of the *Kulturwissenschaftliche Bibliothek Warburg*, the young Paul Tillich acknowledged their significance for theology in that they not only offered a more complex image of the historical emergence of modernity than monolinear constructions of development, but also brought the problem of the growth of culture into focus. Both aspects are also the focus of his own work on a theology of culture, which he elaborated after the First World War. Tillich also used the concept of "symbol" for this.[46] The concept of symbol is employed in his writings for the first time in a review of two art-historical studies entitled *Religiöser Stil und religiöser Stoff in der bildenden Kunst*,[47] which appeared in 1921, the same year that he visited the Warburg Library. The discussion continues with considerations from the 1919 lecture *Über die Idee einer Theologie der Kultur*,[48] as well as from the sketch *Rechtfertigung und Zweifel*, written in the same year, in which he did not yet use the term "symbol" in a technical sense. Tillich progressively expanded his theory of symbols in the 1920s,

---

[45] Warburg, *Heidnisch-antike Weissagen in Wort und Bild*, 485.

[46] For the symbolic concept of Tillich cf. Heinemann, *Sinn – Geist – Symbol*, 410–549; Christian Danz, "Symbolische Form und die Erfassung des Geistes im Gottesverhältnis. Anmerkungen zur Genese des Symbolbegriffs von Paul Tillich," in *Das Symbol als Sprache der Religion. Internationales Jahrbuch für die Tillich-Forschung*, vol. 2, ed. Christian Danz, Werner Schüßler and Erdmann Sturm (Wien: LIT, 2007), 59–75. Cf. also below chapter VI.

[47] Paul Tillich, "Religiöser Stil und religiöser Stoff in der bildenden Kunst," in MW II, 88–99.

[48] Paul Tillich, "Über die Idee einer Theologie der Kultur," in *Ausgewählte Texte*, ed. Christian Danz, Werner Schüßler and Erdmann Sturm (Berlin; New York: de Gruyter, 2008), 26–41.

incorporating the elements of the demonic and anxiety already encountered in Warburg's writing. In the essay *Das religiöse Symbol,* published in 1928, his understanding of symbol found its final expression. This was due to the impact of discussions with scholars of the Warburg circle, especially with Ernst Cassirer's *Philosophie der symbolischen Formen.*[49] At this point, we must ask the question, what does Tillich mean by symbols and how does his understanding differ from Warburg's?

Tillich elaborated his understanding of the symbol within the framework of a theology intended to enable a religious interpretation of reality.[50] As a result, his theoretical considerations of symbols primarily serve to describe the specific nature of religion as opposed to cultural forms. Against the background of Neo-Kantianism, phenomenology, and German Idealism, Tillich gave his theory of symbols a more reflexive version than Warburg from the outset. Warburg's psychological foundation of his symbol theory was replaced by a structural theory of consciousness. Tillich, the theologian, also determines religion differently from Warburg, the theorist of social memory. As we saw in chapter three, religion for Tillich is no longer a cultural form alongside other cultural forms, but a kind of reflexive awareness of the cultural process.[51] Religion is thus dissolved as a special cultural form, but only in order to assert its generality. Although not a faculty of human consciousness, religion is the foundation of culture as a whole. It stands for that awareness of consciousness, which is the precondition of all cultural creation processes. Tillich himself describes religion as directedness towards the unconditioned, which in turn is explained as

---

[49] Ernst Cassirer, *Philosophie der symbolischen Formen,* 3 vol. (9th. ed. Darmstadt: Wissenschaftliche Buchgesellschaft, 1994). Cf. Christian Danz, "Die politische Macht des mythischen Denkens. Paul Tillich und Ernst Cassirer über die Ambivalenz des Mythos," in *Die Macht des Mythos. Das Mythosverständis Paul Tillichs im Kontext,* ed. Christian Danz and Werner Schüßler (Berlin; Boston: de Gruyter, 2015), 119–141.

[50] Cf. above chapter II. and III.

[51] Cf. the determination of religion as directedness towards the unconditioned, as Tillich has successively elaborated it since the lecture about theology of culture of 1919 in the 1920s: Tillich, "Über die Idee einer Theologie der Kultur," 30; "Das System der Wissenschaften nach Gegenständen und Methoden," in GW I, 111–293, here 228: "The precondition of this view is the recognition that *religion* is not a sphere of meaning alongside others, but an attitude in all spheres: The immediate directedness towards the unconditioned."

meaning (*Sinn*). It corresponds to what Warburg called a "thought space" (*Denkraum*), now transferred to religion in order to describe its peculiarity in contrast to cultural action.

Tillich first used the concept of symbol to describe the contents of religion. These contents, i.e., the religious images of God, do not refer to objects of a heavenly or historical nature. Rather, religion describes, with its contents, the disclosedness of the unconditionality of consciousness, which is the prerequisite and basis of all cultural action. To put it in religious language: God is as much before the knowledge of God as meaning is before the interpretation of meaning.[52] But humanity cannot produce the event of the disclosedness of consciousness with regard to its structured precondition, that is, the origin of religion in the individual human being. Religion, as knowledge of God, arises in human beings bound to the revelation of God. In it, however, the awareness of the unconditionality of consciousness remains transcendent and therefore cannot be represented in principle. However, the unconditionality of consciousness must be represented, otherwise no religion would be able to develop in human beings and become recognizable in culture. Religion as the disclosedness of consciousness with regard to its presuppositional structure must be represented in images, but at the same time these images always miss religion. God comes into the world only in an image of God's self, which, at the same time, is always a false image. Tillich calls this opposing structure a religious symbol, that is, an image that must be posited and then negated again, since something that is, in principle, unrepresentable becomes represented in and with it.[53] Because of the paradoxical intuitiveness (*Anschaulichkeit*) intrinsic to the religious symbol, every religious symbol is inauthentic, as the 1928 essay on symbols states, in contrast to Cassirer's

---

[52] Cf. Tillich, "Rechtfertigung und Zweifel," GW VIII, 91–2: "The breakthrough of this divine foundational revelation, which stands above all doubt and searching, brings the liberation in that it puts every action of knowledge in second place and reveals the presence of God before the knowledge of God and the meaning before the knowledge of meaning."

[53] Cf. Paul Tillich, "Das religiöse Symbol," in GW V, 196–212, here 198: Religious symbols "have no other right than that of representing the unintuitable-transcendent (*Unanschaubar-Transzendenten*), which does not need them to come into existence." The religious symbol differs from cultural symbols solely by the reflexive position of the religious consciousness to its contents.

understanding of the symbol.[54] Symbols do not constitute any objectivity (*Gegenständlichkeit*), but rather religion is articulated in the symbol. A difference belongs to the religious symbol, namely, that of the image content and the intended religion. The expressive character of religious symbols, similar to Warburg, is thus constitutive. Symbols are "the expression of the religious; they are its creatures and its bearers" (MW II, 96).[55]

Tillich uses the concept of symbol to describe the substance of religious consciousness. However, this substance is always embedded in a concrete history—a social memory—in which certain symbolic forms were shaped and are passed on as an expression of religion. Therefore, in addition to inauthenticity (*Uneigentlichkeit*) and intuitiveness (*Anschaulichkeit*), self-depthness (*Selbstmächtigkeit*) and sociality (*Sozialität*) are constitutive for the religious symbol.[56] Similar to Warburg, this is also about embossed forms that are stored and passed on in a religious community as carriers of the expression of religion in various media such as in the Bible and in images. They are characterized by the fact that there is "no particular meaning to be overcome" in them (MW II, 96), since they are given in social memory as carriers of religious expressions, so to speak.[57] This constitutes, however, only one side of the discussion of religious symbols. In addition, there is another side, through which they only come into being together with religion as an expression of it. Without an individual appropriation of the prefigured forms of expression, there is neither religion nor religious symbols. Tillich connects the appropriation of the traditional symbol worlds with the revelation of God, i.e., the emergence of religion in humanity. It takes the place of Warburg's empathetic experience of the forms of expression preserved in the image memory. Therefore, the symbolic act, that posits the difference between image and reality, is no longer understood by Tillich as just an invariant anthropological feeling to which a certain expression corresponds, but as an act of reflexivity in the structure of consciousness. To this, however, a general validity is also attributed, even if it arises in the individual only in a underivable way.

---

[54] Cf. Tillich, "Das religiöse Symbol," 183.

[55] Tillich, "Religiöser Stil und religiöser Stoff in der bildenden Kunst," 96.

[56] Cf. Tillich, "Das religiöse Symbol," 196–198.

[57] Tillich, "Religiöser Stil und religiöser Stoff in der bildenden Kunst," 96.

Religious symbols, the two sides of which have been briefly discussed above, are representations of the unrepresentable. For them, a specific difference is constitutive, for with the religious image it is the disclosedness of consciousness—that which is meant—and not the content of the cultural image itself. For this disclosedness of consciousness, however, an image must be posited and then negated again. The religious consciousness, however, can hold fast to the posited image and, as it were, withdraw it from negation, in order to preserve it as a concise expression of itself and its self-disclosedness. Tillich describes such a religious image-positing as demonic.[58] Like the revelation of God, it too is based on a disclosedness of consciousness and presents this disclosedness in an image. But this disclosedness is fixed as an image of God. The symbolic act that establishes the difference between the image and the intended religion, through which the intuitive substance (*der anschauliche Gehalt*) becomes a symbol in the first place, is suppressed here. Although humanity is no longer subject to the superiority of a sensory stimulus reaction, as with Warburg, Tillich nonetheless argues with him that human beings are subject to the demonic power of images, which lead to the destruction of the subject and culture.

As explained above, for Warburg culture is based on anxiety, which is captured in the image and kept at a distance. Tillich also included this aspect in his symbol-theoretical concept of religion in the mid-1920s. In the background, of course, lies not so much Warburg's anthropological theory of culture, but rather an existential-anthropological reformulation of the foundations of Tillich's theology following the emerging philosophical anthropology and existentialism.[59] Unlike Warburg, the theologian uses the concept of anxiety as a structural description of human existence and only secondarily as a subjective affect. According to Tillich, anxiety is

---

[58] Cf. Paul Tillich, "Das Dämonische. Ein Beitrag zur Sinndeutung der Geschichte," in GW VI, 42–71. Cf. Christian Danz, "Das Dämonische. Zu einer Deutungsfigur der modernen Kultur bei Georg Simmel, Georg Lukács, Leo Löwenthal und Paul Tillich," in *Das Dämonische. Kontextuelle Studien zu einer Schlüsselkategorie Paul Tillichs*, ed. Christian Danz and Werner Schüßler (Berlin; Boston: de Gruyter, 2018), 147–184.

[59] Cf. Martin Fritz, *Menschsein als Frage. Paul Tillichs Weg zur anthropologischen Fundierung der Theologie* (Berlin; Boston: de Gruyter, 2024) (pending publication).

human beings becoming aware of their own freedom and finitude.[60] This is exactly what drives people to make anxiety disappear in a self-image and worldview that, thereby, become demonic.

What, then, is the way out of the demonic power of images? Nothing less than the establishment of a renewed distance from these images. Unlike Warburg, however, Tillich combines the recovery of thought space with religion because it denotes a reflexive consciousness, an image praxis that is aware of the difference between image and meaning. It realizes itself in history as the critique and formation (*Gestaltung*) of cultural forms, as knowledge of the necessity of concrete forms of cultural representation and their simultaneous inadequacy. Tillich takes up Warburg's psychological-anthropological foundation of cultural theory in the interruption of the phobic stimulus reaction in the changed framework of his cultural theology, which he had worked out in the 1920s in discussion with the *Kulturwissenschaftliche Bibliothek Warburg*. Even in his late writing *The Courage to Be*, with its implicit reference to Warburg's study on Luther, Tillich claims that an absolute faith, which consists in the knowledge of the difference between image and meaning, is a way out of the tragedy of modern culture. This faith, now called the courage to be, *"is rooted in the God who appears when God has disappeared in the anxiety of doubt."*[61]

---

[60] Cf. Christian Danz, "Anxiety is finitude, experienced as one's own finitude.' Werkgeschichtliche Anmerkungen zu Paul Tillichs Ontologie der Angst in *Der Mut zum Sein*," in *International Yearbook for Tillich Research*, vol. 13, ed. Christian Danz, Marc Dumas, Werner Schüßler, Mary A. Stenger and Erdmann Sturm (Berlin; Boston: de Gruyter, 2018), 25–46.

[61] Tillich, *The Courage to Be*, 175. Cf. below chapter VI.3.

V.

General and Special Revelation of God. Paul Tillich's Discussion with Karl Barth and the Formation of the Method of Correlation

In 1935, the *Journal of Religion* published a contribution from Paul Tillich entitled *What is wrong with the "Dialectic" Theology?*, in which he shows very significantly his interpretation of the theological development in Germany after the First World War and, at the same time, his own position in relation to Karl Barth's theology. "When Barth's commentary on Romans was published, a wide circle of theologians of the same age attached themselves to the school for which Barth had prepared the way. Some did so publicly, and some—like the author of this article—in a 'subterranean' group of fellow-laborers."[1] The catchword "'subterranean' group of fellow-laborers" describes this relation and contains agreement as well as criticism of Barth's theology, which Barth elaborated since the First World War. Tillich appreciates Barth and his colleagues as "the most important tendency in the present German Protestant theology" (GW XII, 187).[2] However, from the beginning, Tillich's agreement with Barth is also connected

---

[1] Paul Tillich, "What is wrong with the 'Dialectic' Theology?" in *The Journal of Religion* 15 (1935) 127–145, here 136.

[2] Cf. also Paul Tillich, "Barths 'Römerbrief,'" in *Vossische Zeitung*, no. 513 (1922) 1; "Dialektische Theologie," in *Religion und Politik. Internationales Jahrbuch für die Tillich-Forschung*, vol. 4, ed. Christian Danz, Werner Schüßler and Erdmann Sturm (Wien: LIT, 2009), 149–174; "Karl Barth," in GW XII, 187–193.

with a criticism of his theology that aimed first at his construction of the concept of God[3] and then at his alleged supranaturalism.[4]

In this same direction, Tillich had already described his position on dialectical theology twelve years earlier in his controversy with Karl Barth and Friedrich Gogarten, which appeared under the title *Kritisches und positives Paradox* in the journal *Theologische Blätter*.[5] Already here Tillich criticizes the dialectical theologians' understanding of revelation as tending toward supranaturalism.[6] Barth and Gogarten responded to Tillich's criticism,[7] and both criticized Tillich's proposal of a theology of positive paradox and vehemently rejected it as a philosophy of culture.[8]

What was at stake in this dispute between Tillich, Barth, and Gogarten in 1923? Did an open cultural-theological position and a narrow doctrinaire monism of revelation clash in the controversy, as the texts

---

[3] So in the lecture *Die prinzipiellen Grundlagen und die nächsten Aufgaben unserer Bewegung* from 1919, which Tillich hold in direct answer to the Tambacher meeting from September 1919. Already here he criticizes Barth's concept of God as advanced in his 1919 lecture *Der Christ in der Gesellschaft*. According to Tillich, Barth's concept of God is merely constructed as critical negativity. Cf. Paul Tillich, "Die prinzipiellen Grundlagen und die nächsten Aufgaben unserer Bewegung," in EW X, 237–249, here 239: "The idea of God on which the Swiss is based: God as absolute, world-destroying being of will [*Willenswesen*]."

[4] Tillich, *Systematic Theology*, vol. I, 4.

[5] Paul Tillich, "Kritisches und positives Paradox. Eine Auseinandersetzung mit Karl Barth und Friedrich Gogarten," in GW VII, 216–225.

[6] Cf. Tillich, "Kritisches und positives Paradox," 217: "There is thus a positive, a serious, which makes criticism and humor possible in the first place. But everything depends on the determination of this point; here it is decided whether the theology of the crisis still knows an absoluteness forbidden by it, or whether it is willing to recognize the positive version of the paradox presupposed in the critical one." Cf. also "Antwort," in GW VII, 240–243, here 243.

[7] Karl Barth, "Von der Paradoxie des 'positiven Paradoxes'. Antworten und Fragen an Paul Tillich," in GW VII, 226–239; Friedrich Gogarten, "Zur Geisteslage des Theologen," in GW VII, 244–246.

[8] Cf. Barth, "Von der Paradoxie des 'positiven Paradoxes'," 232: "Where remains the *paradox* of the 'positive paradox', if it is possible to insert this quantity into any calculation at the decisive point as given and on the basis thus laid – now by no means dialectically broken, but most unbroken, to storm straightforwardly and surely the edifice of true gnosis toward the clouds?" Cf. also Gogarten, "Zur Geisteslage des Theologen," 246.

themselves seem to suggest and as it has often been seen in the history of the impact of the controversy?[9] Such a reading of the controversy over the positive paradox, however, tends to marginalize the systematic problems that were disputed as well as their significance for the further development of Paul Tillich's theology, in particular in the 1920s.[10] For, in the controversy, theoretical problems of Tillich's foundation of theology from the beginning of the 1920s became visible, to which he reacted in the years after 1923 with a differentiation of the concept of revelation. For this reason alone, his controversy with Barth and Gogarten is of not inconsiderable importance for understanding the development of Tillich's theology in the 1920s.

The focus of the controversy between Tillich and the dialectical theologians lies on their new understanding of theology, which they worked out in the years after the First World War. Tillich's reshaping of his pre-war theology during and after the World War was discussed in the third chapter.[11] In this chapter, the further development of this new grounding of theology in Tillich's writings up to 1923 will be presented first. I will then discuss how Tillich transfers this understanding of theology to the new theologies conceived by Karl Barth and Friedrich Gogarten after the war, which proceed from the concept of God's self-revelation in Jesus Christ. After that, Barth's critique of Tillich's theology of positive paradox must be presented. For this purpose, the history of the work development

---

[9] On Tillich's controversy with Barth and Gogarten, cf. Hermann Fischer, "Theologie des positiven und kritischen Paradoxes. Paul Tillich und Karl Barth im Streit um die Wirklichkeit," in *Neue Zeitschrift für Systematische Theologie* 31 (1989) 195–212; Joachim Track, "Paul Tillich und die Dialektische Theologie," in *Paul Tillich. Studien zu einer Theologie der Moderne*, ed. Hermann Fischer (Frankfurt a.M.: Athenäum, 1989), 138–166; Werner Schüßler, "Paul Tillich und Karl Barth. Ihre erste Begegnung in den zwanziger Jahren," in *"Was uns unbedingt angeht." Studien zur Theologie und Philosophie Paul Tillichs* (2nd ed. Münster: LIT, 2004), 119–130.

[10] In an argumentation-analytical perspective, the controversy has so far only been examined by Folkart Wittekind, "Grund- und Heilsoffenbarung. Zur Ausformung der Christologie Tillichs in der Auseinandersetzung mit Karl Barth," in *Jesus of Nazareth and the New Being. International Yearbook for Tillich Research*, vol. 6, ed. Christian Danz, Marc Dumas, Werner Schüßler, Mary A. Stenger and Erdmann Sturm (Berlin; New York: de Gruyter 2011), 89–119.

[11] Cf. above Chapter III.3.

of Barth's theology must be included. Against this background of the re-constructed controversy between Tillich and Barth, the further develop-ment of Tillich's theology in the 1920s and early 1930s must be presented with regard to Barth's objections, which finally leads to the development of the method of correlation.

1. Revelation of God as Critique of Religion in Paul Tillich

In the years that followed the war, Paul Tillich continued to develop the foundations of a theology of faith, which was worked out in the 1919 draft *Rechtfertigung und Zweifel*. The starting point of this theological concep-tion is faith understood as the revelation of God, which in turn is under-stood as the affirmation of the absolute paradox. In this, as in his writings before the First World War, Tillich starts from an understanding of reve-lation that is not limited to the revelation of God in Jesus Christ, but rather one that denotes the disclosedness of consciousness. The unconditioned, as the presupposition and foundation of consciousness, can only be grasped in the non-producible performance of faith as an affirmation of the abso-lute paradox. This foundation of theology can still be read as a further epistemological-critical development of the modern-positive theology of his teachers Adolf Schlatter and Wilhelm Lütgert. With his teachers, Til-lich adheres to a universal understanding of revelation as the basis of the-ology, as his writings from the early 1920s and his engagement with dia-lectical theology underline. The epistemological-critical moment in Tillich's theology, which connects him with the theological comrades of his generation, namely, Barth and Gogarten, consists in the strict tran-scendence of God, that is, the opposition of God and world, as well as the binding of the knowledge of God to divine revelation. The linking of God's knowledge to divine revelation also forms the starting point for Til-lich's post-war theology. This becomes clear in his lecture *Die Überwin-dung des Religionsbegriffs in der Religionsphilosophie* from 1922, which pre-sents, as it were, a sketch of the *Religionsphilosophie* written one year later.[12]

---

[12] In order to understand the development of Tillich's theology in the history of his work, it is important to note that the *Religionsphilosophie* dates from 1923 but was not published until 1925. Otherwise, it is not possible to understand why the distinction between foundational revelation (*Grundoffenbarung*) and salvation

In his lecture *Die Überwindung des Religionsbegriffs in der Religion-sphilosophie*, Tillich offers, in continuation of *Rechtfertigung und Zweifel* and of the considerations on the philosophy of history from his 1922 *Kairos* essay,[13] a classification of his own, new determination of religion in the debates of the philosophy of religion of the time. For this task, he makes use of the drafts of Max Scheler and Heinrich Scholz's work, from which Tillich distinguishes his own conception. Tillich's conception has to do with a philosophy of religion that starts from the unconditioned and, in this way, is supposed to overcome the opposition between culture and religion. From this arises the question of the lecture: "It is to be proved that the concept of religion contains in itself a paradox. 'Religion' is the concept of a thing [*Sache*] which is destroyed precisely by this concept." (GW I, 368) How does Tillich determine religion or the certainty of faith in *Die Überwindung des Religionsbegriffs in der Religionsphilosophie*?

Also in the essay of 1922, Tillich's approach remains with a revela-tion-theological determination of religion, which is set apart from a con-cept of religion, i.e., a faculty-theoretical (*vermögenstheoretischen*) founda-tion of religion. As in the writings before the First World War, religion is not part of the general faculty-structure of consciousness, but a performa-tive act in consciousness. What is new vis-à-vis the draft *Rechtfertigung und Zweifel*, from 1919, is the description of the general grounding struc-ture of consciousness as a substantially religious consciousness, which is distinguished from an intentionally religious consciousness:

> There is no such thing as a consciousness that is unreligious in substance, but there is in intention. In every apprehension of the I [*Ich-Erfassung*], the relation to the unconditioned is contained as the ground of reality; but it is not intended [*gemeint*] in every one; according to this, the two positions of consciousness differ. (GW I, 378)[14]

---

revelation (*Heilsoffenbarung*), introduced by Tillich in 1924 as a reaction to Barth's criticism, does not play a role in the *Religionsphilosophie*.

[13] Paul Tillich, "Kairos," in *Ausgewählte Texte*, ed. Christian Danz, Werner Schüßler and Erdmann Sturm (Berlin; New York: de Gruyter, 2008), 43–62.

[14] Tillich's 1923 *Religionsphilosophie* also determines the general essence of religion in this same direction. Cf. Paul Tillich, "Religionsphilosophie," in GW I, 319–321.

Tillich continues his reflections on the foundation of religion in such a way that he understands the unconditioned as a constitutive part of the general foundational structure of consciousness, which is already given in every consciousness. He calls this general foundational structure the religious substance of consciousness. This is a substance in and for consciousness, namely, the reflexive disclosedness of consciousness as the basis and presupposition of all concrete acts of consciousness. From this new consciousness-theoretical construction, Tillich distinguishes the religious substance of consciousness in the 1922 lecture from the substantially God-positing (*Gott-setzenden*) consciousness of the two Schelling dissertations from 1910 and 1912.[15] For, with this earlier determination, Tillich described the speculative relationship between absolute and individual spirit.

From the substance of consciousness, which is laid out as a general foundation structure in every consciousness, Tillich distinguishes an intentionally religious consciousness. With this, the determination of religion as intention (*Meinen*) of the unconditioned is taken up out of *Rechtfertigung und Zweifel*. Religious and cultural consciousness differ by the intention. Religious consciousness is intentionally directed towards the unconditioned and thus it is, by its nature, directedness towards the unconditioned. The cultural consciousness is different; it is also based on the religious substance, but it is not directed towards the unconditioned, but rather towards the forms produced by consciousness and their unity.[16] With religion as directedness towards the unconditioned, Tillich thus designates the event of disclosedness (*Erschlossensein*) of the general substance-basis of consciousness in the individual consciousness. Religion consequently arises in consciousness through a transition from culturally determined consciousness to the intention of the unconditioned, or from implicitly to explicitly religious consciousness.[17] In the 1922 lecture, too, the transition to the explicit religious intention, that is, to the directedness towards the unconditioned, is bound to a performative act in consciousness

---

[15] Cf. chapters II and III above.

[16] Cf. Tillich, "Die Überwindung des Religionsbegriffs in der Religionsphilosophie," 377–8; "Religionsphilosophie," 319–20.

[17] Cf. Tillich, "Die Überwindung des Religionsbegriffs in der Religionsphilosophie," 378: "There is therefore no certainty at all in which the certainty of God is not implicitly contained; but whether it is also explicitly contained, that makes the decisive religious difference."

in and through which consciousness becomes aware of its foundational structure, which Tillich calls religious substance. How must this transition, in which religion first arises in human beings, be understood more precisely?[18]

Religion as directedness towards the unconditioned, i.e., as the disclosedness of the substance-basis of consciousness in consciousness, cannot be produced by human beings. The emergence of religion owes itself to the revelation of God, a breakthrough of the unconditioned through the conditioned, as Tillich's formula reads. Since all contents of consciousness are contents produced by it, the substance of consciousness or the unconditioned cannot be a content of consciousness. No path leads from human beings to God. God is strictly transcendent and distinct from the world. Therefore, the basic structure of consciousness can only be disclosed to human beings in consciousness. With this construction, Tillich incorporates the critique of religion into his justification of religion. All contentual determinations of consciousness are, since they are produced by it, conditioned and cannot grasp the substance-basis laid out in consciousness. This is by definition indeterminate, so that each of its determinations misses the substance. The fact that God is disclosed in consciousness is thus bound to a performance of consciousness that consciousness itself cannot produce. How must one understand this performative act of consciousness?

The disclosedness of the foundational dimension of consciousness in consciousness, that is, the emergence of religion as directedness towards the unconditioned, is not a special performative act in consciousness. Tillich explicitly excludes the notion of religion as a special form. If it were, then it would be a form of consciousness among others. The lecture *Die Überwindung des Religionsbegriffs in der Religionsphilosophie* aims to overcome such a definition of religion.[19] Religion is not based on a special performance of consciousness. This means that the religious performative act

---

[18] Cf. also Wittekind, "Grund- und Heilungsoffenbarung," 95–98.

[19] Cf. Tillich, "Die Überwindung des Religionsbegriffs in der Religionsphilosophie," 380: "Now there is a function of the spirit that neither stands beside the others nor is their unity, but is expressed in and through them: the function of unconditionality; it is the root function, the one in which the spirit breaks through all its forms down to its ground." Cf. also "Das System der Wissenschaften nach Gegenständen und Methoden," 228; "Religionsphilosophie," 329.

of reflection can only present itself and appear *in* and *on* the functions of consciousness, namely, as a simultaneity of use and negation of the forms produced by consciousness.[20] From this follows the determination of the paradox that is constitutive for religion. Religion as the disclosedness of consciousness in consciousness, so Tillich's considerations can be summarized, arises as the negation of the determinacy of consciousness. But what is this disclosedness of the basic structure of consciousness in consciousness itself, which is not supposed to be a particular performative act, like? Does it not already presuppose a knowledge of the indeterminable substance in consciousness, which precisely as a knowledge, is supposed to be excluded? Otherwise, consciousness could not even know that the substance of consciousness cannot be grasped in any determination of consciousness. Tillich does not discuss this question but answers it by referring to the substance-basis already given in consciousness.[21]

Religion as directedness towards the unconditioned arises in consciousness as a negation of the determined consciousness. With this construction of religion, Tillich wants to hold on to its generality. Religion can be universal only if it itself is not something determinate, i.e., no particular performance. In other words, religion can be universal only if it is indeterminate and realizes itself as negation or critique of every determinacy of consciousness. What is disclosed in the religious performative act is the general foundational structure of consciousness, which already underlies all acts of consciousness. This general foundational structure of consciousness, namely, the relation of the transcendent God and world, is universal and always already implicitly given. Thus, all religions and their contents are illustrations of this general foundational structure or of the

---

[20] Cf. Tillich, "Die Überwindung des Religionsbegriffs in der Religionsphilosophie," 381: "Now here is the place to bring the dialectic of the concept of religion to complete transparency: as soon as consciousness is directed towards the unconditioned, the duality of act and object arises. Now the religious act is not a particular [!]; it is real only in the other acts [sc. of consciousness]. It must therefore give these acts a formation in which the religious quality is visible. This formation is the paradox, i.e., the simultaneous affirmation and negation of the autonomous form. Religious thinking, intuition [*Anschauung*], is therefore a thinking, an intuition, which simultaneously uses and breaks the autonomous forms of thinking and intuition at the same time."

[21] Cf. the lucid reconstruction by Wittekind, "Grund- und Heilsoffenbarung," 96–7.

paradoxical unity of God and human.[22] This is also true for Jesus Christ; he illustrates the general structure of the relationship between the unconditioned and the conditioned, which is already claimed in every consciousness and is grasped in religion—the becoming explicit of the implicit structure—and represented in an image produced by consciousness.[23] In order to hold on to the universal validity of religion and to be able to abolish the opposition between religion and culture, Tillich dissolves religion as a particular form. This in turn has the consequence that religion as a special form in culture can only exist as an indication that a special religious form is not allowed to exist. But precisely this, according to Tillich's reasoning, must be represented once again in culture itself. In this respect, religious forms in which the spirit's directedness towards the unconditioned is represented in consciousness and its determinations are justified when these very forms are themselves once again negated. For religion as directedness towards the unconditioned is itself not a particular form or act of consciousness, but the critique and negation of the particular acts of consciousness.

With this, Tillich's foundation of religion in the revelation of God, as he elaborated it in his writings until 1923, has been discussed to such an extent that we can now consider"] his examination of the positive paradox of Karl Barth's and Friedrich Gogarten's dialectical theology. Before doing so, however, we must briefly sketch the history of the development of Karl Barth's theology up to 1923, since it forms the point of reference for Tillich's criticism along with that of Gogarten.[24]

---

[22] Cf. Tillich, "Die Überwindung des Religionsbegriffs in der Religionsphilosophie," 382: "Every religion is relative as religion, because every religion is objectification of the unconditioned. But every religion can be absolute as revelation: for revelation is the breakthrough of the unconditioned in its unconditionality. Every religion is absolute insofar as it is revelation, i.e., insofar as the unconditioned in it emerges as unconditioned in contrast to all the relative things that come to it as religion."

[23] As a special representation of the general basic construction, the revelation of God in Jesus Christ, like every other religion, has the—as it is called in the *Religionsphilosophie*—"general characteristic of symbolic power" (GW I, 337).

[24] Friedrich Gogarten's new theology, as he conceived it after the First World War, will not be specifically discussed here. Tillich's engagement with Gogarten's,

2. Revelation of God as Critique of
Religion in Karl Barth

Karl Barth's answer to Paul Tillich's criticism in 1923 presupposes the formation of his new dialectical theology during the First World War, which is based on a further development of his early reflections on the foundation of theology from the time before the First World War.[25] Already the young Barth, following his teacher Wilhelm Herrmann and criticizing Ernst Troeltsch, had rejected a justification of religion by means of a religious a priori.[26] Nevertheless, Barth also assumes a consciousness-theoretical basis of religion, which, however, is not conceived in faculty-theoretical (*vermögenstheoretisch*) terms. This becomes clear in a philosophy of religion sketch entitled *Ideen und Einfälle zur Religionsphilosophie*, from

---

however, is still a desideratum of Tillich research. In the 1920s, Tillich consistently referred in his writings to the theology of Gogarten, who was regarded as the representative of a new theology like no other at that time. On Gogarten's theology cf. Christian Danz, "Glaube als Evident-Werden Gottes. Die Überwindung des Historismus bei Friedrich Gogarten," in *Gott und die menschliche Freiheit. Studien zum Gottesbegriff in der Neuzeit* (Neukirchen-Vluyn: Neukirchener, 2005), 88–101; D. Timothy Goering, *Friedrich Gogarten (1887–1967). Religionsrebell im Jahrhundert der Weltkriege* (Berlin; Boston: de Gruyter, 2017).

[25] The development of Barth's theology was placed in the self-understanding debates of the younger Ritschl-school by the more recent Barth research, which is referenced here: cf. Georg Pfleiderer, *Karl Barths praktische Theologie. Zu Genese und Kontext eines paradigmatischen Entwurfs systematischer Theologie im 20. Jahrhundert* (Tübingen: Mohr Siebeck, 2000); Folkart Wittekind, *Geschichtliche Offenbarung und die Wahrheit des Glaubens. Der Zusammenhang von Offenbarungstheologie, Geschichtsphilosophie und Ethik bei Albrecht Ritschl, Julius Kaftan und Karl Barth (1909–1916)* (Tübingen: Mohr Siebeck, 2000); Bruce L. McCormack, *Karl Barth's Critically Realistic Dialectical Theology. Its Genesis and Development, 1909–1936* (Oxford: Oxford University Press, 1995).

[26] Cf. Karl Barth, "Rezension der Zeitschrift für wissenschaftliche Theologie, 51. Jahrgang, 1. und 2. Heft," in *Vorträge und kleinere Arbeiten 1905–1909* (GA III), ed. Hans-Anton Drewes and Hinrich Stoevesandt (Zürich: TVZ, 1992), 367–372, here 368. Cf. Christian Danz, "Ursprungsphilosophie und Theologiebegriff. Heinrich Barth im Kontext der dialektischen Theologie Karl Barths," in *Existenz. Facetten, Genese, Umfeld eines zentralen Begriffs bei Heinrich Barth*, ed. Harald Schwaetzer and Christian Graf (Regensburg: Roderer, 2007), 104–122, here 107–111.

1910.[27] The concern of this sketch is to develop a religious-philosophical foundation of religion that functions as the basis of a modern dogmatics. The central task of this religious-philosophical foundation consists in its assignment to cultural consciousness on the one hand and the resulting determination of the nature of religion on the other.[28] It is important for Barth's considerations to observe that, following Hermann Cohen, he detaches religion from the transcendental-legal structure of consciousness. Thus religion is independent of the three faculties of thinking, acting, and feeling, but at the same time it is said to be related to cultural consciousness. For, as Barth asserts against Herrmann, it is not sufficient "to prove the otherness of religion apart from the other functions of consciousness, rather religion must be placed, if otherwise a unified overall view of consciousness is the task of scientific theology, in an intrinsically *necessary* connection with that."[29] What does Barth understand by religion and how does he assign it to consciousness and its transcendental structure?

Barth assigns religion to the individual realization of cultural consciousness, which is not yet given with the general transcendental structure of consciousness. Thus religion is on the one hand independent of the transcendental functions of consciousness and on the other hand related to them. The necessity of religion for cultural consciousness, which he claims to be the case, results from its binding to truth and reality with regard to its individual realization. It is true that consciousness can only be realized individually, but this realization is oriented toward the (critical) idea of truth. Barth calls this *"reality-relation"* (*Realitätsbeziehung*) and *"truth-substance"* (*Wahrheitsgehalt*) in his sketch on the philosophy of religion.[30] Thus, it follows that religion is the individual self-consciousness of truth and reality of cultural consciousness. In religion, individual self-consciousness grasps itself in its directedness towards truth (*Ausrichtung auf die Wahrheit*). Religion, although not itself a component of the general

---

[27] Cf. Karl Barth, "Ideen und Einfälle zur Religionsphilosophie," in *Vorträge und kleinere Arbeiten 1909–1914* (GA IV), ed. Hans-Anton Drewes and Hinrich Stoevesandt (Zürich: TVZ, 1993), 129–138.

[28] Cf. Barth, "Ideen und Einfälle zur Religionsphilosophie," 132: *"Task / 1.* proof t[he] relation of rel[igion] to cultural consciousness (logic, ethics, aesthetics) 2. essence of religion." Cf. Wittekind, *Geschichtliche Offenbarung und die Wahrheit des Glaubens*, 166–177; Pfleiderer, *Karl Barths praktische Theologie*, 190–205.

[29] Barth, "Ideen und Einfälle zur Religionsphilosophie," 132.

[30] Cf. Barth, "Ideen und Einfälle zur Religionsphilosophie," 134.

transcendental faculty-structure of consciousness, is constitutive of it. For religion, as Barth's early reflections on the religious-philosophical foundation of theology can be summarized, is the event of the disclosedness of the reference to truth and reality of cultural consciousness in individual self-consciousness.[31]

But how does the knowledge of the idea come about, which itself is not supposed to be a component of the transcendental structure of consciousness? Barth connects the disclosedness of the idea with the constitution of the immediate self-consciousness of individuality and historicity, so that the revelation of God is the true grounding of the individual in history. Therefore, although religion is bound to individual experience (*Erlebnis*), and thus is constitutive for individual subjectivity, the substance of the experience (*Gehalt des Erlebnisses*) is the truth of God as the goal of the cultural process. The realization of the truth of God as the goal of the cultural process is bound to the disclosedness of the idea in the individual. Barth places Christology in this framework with a brief reference at the end of the sketch. Christology clarifies in the Christian religion its emergence as a "continuous becoming certain of truth and reality in the context of the living tradition of Jesus."[32] Jesus Christ is the *Urbild* of faith as directedness towards the idea. By using Christology in this way to describe the structure of faith, Barth already confers to it a reflexive function.

The young Barth further developed the idea of religion just outlined in his texts before the First World War.[33] This idea remains fundamental also for his theological turn, which becomes apparent since the beginning of the war in 1914, but it receives a different justification. What changes with the emergence of dialectical theology is not the (neo-) Kantian construction of the idea of God as a pure general good as well as the directed-

---

[31] Cf. Barth, "Ideen und Einfälle zur Religionsphilosophie," 137.

[32] Barth, "Ideen und Einfälle zur Religionsphilosophie," 137.

[33] Cf. Karl Barth, "Der christliche Glaube und die Geschichte," in *Vorträge und kleinere Arbeiten 1909–1914* (GA III), ed. Hans-Anton Drewes and Hinrich Stoevesandt (Zürich: TVZ, 1993), 155–212. Cf. on this Wittekind, *Geschichtliche Offenbarung und die Wahrheit des Glaubens*, 177–193.

ness of the subject towards the moral law, but the connection of the realization of the general good to human beings.[34] The new formulation of his theology becomes tangible in the two lectures *Die Gerechtigkeit Gottes* and *Die neue Welt der Bibel*, both from 1916.[35] Barth holds fast to his idea of God. God is the universal good and as such strictly distinct from the world.[36] But unlike his pre-war theology, Barth now holds that any human appropriation of God's will in faith is its transgression and instrumentalization for inner-worldly ends (*Zwecksetzungen*).[37] The reception and realization of God's justice by human being is now denied. However, Barth does not entirely drop his earlier thought of the realization of the kingdom of God. He redefines the realization of the good in history by assigning it solely to God. God and God's justice, that is, the historical realization of the general good, is solely "God's affair" and not that of humans, whose moral action always remains broken by egoistic motives.[38]

From Barth's detachment of the historical realization of the kingdom of God from human being and its recasting as a component of the idea of God results a redetermination of religion as faith. The concept of faith now takes the place of the earlier religious experience (*Erlebnis*) and denotes the recognition that God realizes God's kingdom in history Godself.

---

[34] Against the background of the war interpretation of his German academic teachers, Barth detaches the realization of the kingdom of God from inner-worldly instances. Thus, his own earlier conception, which tied the realization of the general good to socialism, also falls prey to criticism. For this one functions just like those of his teachers. Cf. Wittekind, *Geschichtliche Offenbarung und die Wahrheit des Glaubens*, 210–230; Pfleiderer, *Karl Barths praktische Theologie*, 249–261.

[35] Barth included both lectures in his collection of essays *Das Wort Gottes und die Theologie* of 1924. Cf. Karl Barth, "Die Gerechtigkeit Gottes," in *Das Wort Gottes und die Theologie. Gesammelte Vorträge* (7th and 8th ed. München: Kaiser, 1929), 5–17; "Die neue Welt der Bibel," in *Das Wort Gottes und die Theologie. Gesammelte Vorträge* (7th and 8th ed. München: Kaiser, 1929), 18–32.

[36] Cf. Barth, "Die Gerechtigkeit Gottes," 6: "We rejoice in justice where we think we perceive a will that is clear and constant in itself, free from the capacity for choice and fickleness [*Willkür und Wankelmut*], a will that has in itself an order that holds and cannot be bent."

[37] Cf. Barth, "Die Gerechtigkeit Gottes," 11: "Therefore the righteousness of God, which we had already seen and touched, changes under our clumsy hands into all kinds of human righteousness."

[38] Barth, "Die Gerechtigkeit Gottes," 15.

Faith is thus no longer the individual appropriation of God's salvation in Jesus Christ, but exactly the opposite, the ethical recognition of the impossibility of an appropriating human realization of God's will. In God's revelation in Jesus Christ, God has already realized the kingdom of God in history. By recognizing this, human beings at the same time recognize that the realization of God's will is impossible for them. As such an ethical self-transparency of humanity, faith is also here still the true foundation of historical individuality, which is bound to the underivable performance of faith.

In the years leading up to 1923, Barth continued to develop this new version of his theology, which incorporates elements of his pre-war theology on a new basis. In doing so, he increasingly separated the realization of the kingdom of God as the universal good from human action.[39] God alone realizes God's kingdom in history through the revelation in Jesus Christ. The new world of God cannot be derived from history. There is no continuity between God's new world and the human world and its history. Knowledge of God's revelation in Jesus Christ is disclosed to faith alone. But faith is also a component of the divine revelation.[40] Faith is bound to its performative act that arises without preconditions in human beings and, as knowledge of God, is only real as this performance. Similar to the contemporaneous writings of Paul Tillich, the revelation of God is also paradoxical for Barth. The overcoming of the world in the breakthrough of God remains unintuitable (*unanschaulich*). Unlike Tillich, however, Barth limits the revelation of God exclusively to Jesus Christ. The event of the truth and the disclosedness of the human being are determined in a Christological way. At the same time, the revelation of God, that is, the realization of the kingdom of God in history by God alone, is

---

[39] While Barth in the above-mentioned lectures from 1916 still leaves it open whether and if so, which consequences follow from faith for human action, only the second edition of the *Römerbrief* leads to a fundamental clarification. Cf. Karl Barth, *Der Römerbrief* (9th ed. Zollikon-Zürich: Evangelischer Verlag, 1954).

[40] Cf. Barth, *Der Römerbrief*, 6: "But the *resurrection* from the dead is the turning point, the 'setting in' of that point from above and the corresponding insight from below. The resurrection is the *revelation*, the discovery of Jesus as the Christ, the appearance of God and the knowledge of God in him, the entrance of the need to give glory to God and to reckon with the unknown and unintuitable [*Unanschaulichen*] in Jesus, Jesus is the end of time, as the paradox, to be counted as the victor as primal history [*Urgeschichte*]."

not only unintuitable, but in contrast to Paul Tillich, revelation is, for Barth, a special performance. Barth uses Christology to reflexively describe the structure of God's revelation and its event character (*Ereignischarakters*): Jesus Christ is the *Urbild* of faith. Now, however, Jesus Christ as *Urbild* of faith no longer functions as a representation of the realization of the kingdom of God by human beings—as in his pre-war theology—but rather as a denial of such a possibility. As revelation of God, Jesus Christ now represents the structure of faith, which can be realized by God alone and not by human beings.[41] Its substance is the (ethical) self-transparency of human beings, i.e., the recognition that the Kingdom of God, as the ultimate goal (*Ziel*) of the world, is realized by God alone and that human action in this world remains broken by egoistic motives and interests. Both dimensions of the true grounding of the individual in God's revelation represent the cross and resurrection of Jesus Christ, God's "no" to the world that is at the same time God's "yes."[42] In this way, Christology explicates the structure of faith, or God's revelation. Reality for the individual, however, becomes the revelation of God only in the performative act of faith as (ethical) self-transparency. But this revelation is bound to a particular history and not to any principle or general idea. This is what Jesus Christ stands for in Barth's theology, even if Jesus himself remains unintuitable as divine revelation.

3. The Controversy between Tillich and Barth about the Concept of Revelation

In his discussion with the dialectical theologians Barth and Gogarten, published in the *Theologische Blätter* in 1923, Tillich transferred his understanding of theology to them. From this arises the central question of his essay, namely, to show the position on which their critique is based and

---

[41] Cf. Barth, *Der Römerbrief*, 70: "Christ is the content of this knowledge: the righteousness of God itself."

[42] Cf. Barth, *Der Römerbrief*, 99: "Abraham, with his human righteousness and unrighteousness before God, is *only* 'irreverent' (1:18), *only* placed under the no, like all others. That he awakens to the awareness of this situation, that he becomes aware of the crisis and recognizes it as a divine crisis, that he chooses the fear of the Lord in this crisis, that he hears and understands the *no* of God, because it is the no of *God*, as a *yes*, that is his faith."

which makes it possible in the first place.[43] Tillich shares the epistemolog-ical-critical restrictions of the theologies of Barth and Gogarten: God is transcendent and cannot be an object of human knowledge. "Anyone who sees the relation of the unconditioned and the conditioned undialectically does not see it at all, has no conception of the violence of what is meant in the concept" (GW VII, 216). Consequently, statements about God are not only tied back to God's revelation, but are also consistently paradoxical. As human statements, all determinations of God are subject to critical nega-tion. However, according to Tillich's critique of Barth and Gogarten, every critique presupposes a standpoint that makes it possible in the first place. For this standpoint, however, it must be true that it is itself under the crit-ical "no," otherwise, the critical negation would be suspended at one point and there would be, therefore, a standpoint that is removed from criticism. The critical paradox of the dialectical theologians thus itself presupposes a positive paradox. But it is precisely this, the recognition of a positive par-adox, that both Barth and Gogarten refuse to acknowledge.[44] Thus, their dialectical theologies tend toward an undialectical supranaturalism that makes one's own point of view absolute and withdraws it from the critical "no."

Tillich's critique of the dialectical theologies of Barth and Gogarten results from his own conception of the revelation of God, as presented above with reference to his lecture *Die Überwindung des Religionsbegriffs in der Religionsphilosophie*. The disclosedness of the unconditioned in the self-relation of consciousness consists in the negation of the determinateness of consciousness, which must be presented in this as a paradoxical unity of affirmation and negation. For every statement about the paradox remains a human statement, which fundamentally misses the determination of the general substance-basis of consciousness and therefore must be negated

---

[43] Cf. Tillich, "Kritisches und positives Paradox," 216: "Therefore, I would like to venture the attempt of an argument which, while recognizing the critical negation, seeks to show the position on whose ground the negation is possible in the first place."

[44] Cf. Tillich, "Kritisches und positives Paradox," 218: The "making con-scious of the irrevocable position, which is also in the proclamation of the crisis" is "the grasping of the yes, which is the precondition of the no, it is the decline from the critical to the positive paradox." Cf. also Wittekind, "Grund- und Heil-soffenbarung," 101–2.

again.[45] This is precisely what Tillich calls the positive paradox, the subordination of the formulation of one's theology to the critical "no." By not recognizing it, the critical theology of the dialectical theologians is epistemologically not critical enough.

The starting point of Tillich's critique remains, also in his argument with Barth and Gogarten, his understanding of God's revelation as the disclosedness of the general foundational structure of consciousness in consciousness, which is precisely not supposed to be a special event. In his essay, Tillich unfolds this understanding of revelation as a connection of creation, redemption, and consummation structured in itself, and he contrasts it with the Christology-bound concept of revelation of the dialectical theologians.[46] Thus, the determinacy of God's revelation, on which the dialecticians insist, is criticized, while Tillich, in order to be able to hold on to the universality of revelation, emphasizes precisely its indeterminacy. The emergence of religion is not a particular act in consciousness, but the negation of the determinacy in the self-relation of consciousness, or the transition of consciousness from its cultural acts of determinacy to the directedness of the unconditioned. If religion consists in the disclosedness of the dimension of unconditionality already given in consciousness, and if it presents this disclosedness in its contentual statements, which must therefore necessarily have a paradoxical character, then also the revelation of God in Jesus Christ cannot be a special event, but only a symbolically powerful illustration of the apprehension of the general foundational structure of consciousness.[47]

Karl Barth objected to Tillich's interpretation of his theology and to the claim that dialectical theology must recognize that its critical paradox is based on a positive one. Tillich's claim is completely rejected by Barth

---

[45] Cf. Tillich, "Kritisches und positives Paradox," 218: "The dialectician must realize that as a dialectician he has a position among others that does not cease to be a position by any dialectical self-sublation [Selbstaufhebung], and he must be prepared, just as he is prepared to place himself under the no despite the conviction of the truth of his position, to concede to the other positions the same yes as to himself despite the no that he executes on them."

[46] Cf. Tillich, "Kritisches und positives Paradox," 219–225. "These basic ideas are now to be examined in three ways: in the relation of God and nature, of God and spirit, of God and history." (GW VII, 219) Cf. also "Religionsphilosophie," 353.

[47] Cf. Tillich, "Kritisches und positives Paradox," 221.

in his statement *Von der Paradoxie des "positiven Paradoxes."*[48] The fact that this refusal does not confirm Tillich's criticism that dialectical theology proceeds from a presupposition that is beyond criticism can be seen from the development of the history of the work of Barth's theology, which was outlined above.[49] Barth, like Tillich, also incorporated the epistemological critique of modernity into the foundation of his theology. For Barth, this theological foundation takes the form of a binding of God's revelation to Christology. However, this is exactly what Tillich's critique aimed at. How must Barth's objection to Tillich and his rejection of Tillich's demand for a recognition of a positive paradox, which is the precondition of the critique, be understood?[50]

In his remarks, Barth first refers to Tillich's foundation of theology in what Tillich calls the positive paradox. This paradox, which is supposed to form the basis of the criticism, is—according to Barth's objection—not critical enough.[51] Barth thus rejects Tillich's presuppositional construction of a general substance-basis in consciousness, which is already given in consciousness and is disclosed in religion, as uncritical metaphysics.[52] Since it remains unclear how such a principle can be known, it is merely the *"dogmatic positing* of a first *principle"* (GW VII, 232). Barth criticizes that Tillich's theological construction of God's revelation amounts to a "broad, universal steamroller of faith and revelation [*Glaubens- und Offenbarungswalze*]" through which "everything is simply included 'in' the dispute and peace of the 'positive paradox'" (GW VII, 234). This critique refers to Tillich's assertion of a general foundational structure of consciousness, which is disclosed in the revelation of God within consciousness as a negation of its determinacy. Tillich's positive paradox denotes the

---

[48] Cf. Barth, "Von der Paradoxie des 'positiven Paradoxes,'" 227: "Thus, I do not find [...] the occasion given for the solid inquiry whether the 'theology of crisis' is willing to 'recognize' the positive version of the paradox presupposed in the critical one."

[49] Not affected by this, of course, is the fact that Barth's theology is also a theological construction, which tends to make its constructional character disappear in the claimed revelation of God.

[50] Cf. Wittekind, "Grund- und Heilsoffenbarung," 101–105.

[51] Cf. Barth, "Von der Paradoxie des 'positiven Paradoxes,'" 232.

[52] Cf. Barth, "Von der Paradoxie des 'positiven Paradoxes,'" 231: "how do I recognize such an otherwise-grounded abolition?"

becoming aware (*Gewahrwerden*) of a general structure that already under-lies culture and religion, so that all the contents of consciousness partici-pate in the "yes" and "no." This brings us to the central point of Barth's critique. Since Tillich, interested in the universality of God's revelation, can understand it only as a negation of the acts of consciousness, he must reject any particularity of revelation. The consequence of this construction is that, in Tillich's theology, Christology can only appear as a powerfully symbolic representation of an already given general relationship between God and human beings.[53] Therefore, Tillich's positive paradox is not par-adoxical enough.

In his response, Barth focuses the discussion on Christology.[54] In Barth's judgment, Tillich's positive paradox, as the indeterminate dis-closedness of a general foundational structure in consciousness, is under-determined. According to Barth's proposal, the positive paradox must be christologically determined, since only in this way can the particularity of God's revelation, in contrast to other acts of consciousness, be maintained and the critique of knowledge be taken into account. Jesus Christ as God's revelation in history is the positive paradox. However, does Barth not now refer, as Tillich had asserted against Gogarten, to "a theology of the posi-tive absurdum" (GW VII, 223)? This is not the case, since Barth—just like Gogarten—uses Christology to describe the reflexive structure of re-ligion, newly determined as faith, as well as its event character. Faith is not the unintuitable (*unanschauliche*) disclosedness of an already given general structure of the God-world-relationship, but a determined performative act that arises underivably in history and represents, in an image of itself, both its underivability (*Unableitbarkeit*) and its performance-binding (*Vollzugsbindung*) character. It is exactly the particularity of religion that is represented by Jesus Christ in the Christian religion, for he exists as reve-

---

[53] Cf. Barth, "Von der Paradoxie des 'positiven Paradoxes,'" 234: Revelation is "by no means a relation to be determined by a general 'it is' and 'there is' and merely to be discovered by human, not a secret given," "but a most special *event*, opened only from God and to be known only by being known by him, an *event* from person to person, a *communication*, a gift in the strictest sense of the word, both the thing *and* the knowledge of it."

[54] Barth, "Von der Paradoxie des 'positiven Paradoxes,'" 235: "And now the place where this opposition [sc. between Barth and Tillich] comes to the fore will indeed be *Christology*."

lation of God only in the performance of faith. If one dissolves the particularity of this performative act into a general structure, then one cancels it. One then ends up with an act that one can no longer specify in what it itself consists of. Therefore, theology "must not be carried away into contesting the singular qualification of this history by revelation, or what comes to the same thing: to assert the qualification of *all* history by revelation" (GW VII, 237).

4. Foundational Revelation and Salvation Revelation; or, The Threefold Rhythm of the History of Revelation

Paul Tillich responded to Karl Barth's criticism of his approach with a short *Antwort* in the *Theologische Blätter* in 1923, defending his theology of positive paradox.[55] For the contemporary spiritual situation (*gegenwärtige Geisteslage*), that is, a modern culture based on autonomy, it is necessary, as Tillich emphasizes, to assume a general revelation of God. Since all contents of faith are subjected to doubt, the symbol of the unconditioned must be used to open up anew the meaning of the idea of God.[56] The same applies to Christology. The special revelation of God in Jesus Christ presupposes a general revelation, so that it is possible to limit the idea of revelation to Christ only at the price of a fatal isolation.

> Now, however, the spirit of Christ [*Christusgeist*], the positive paradox, is not exhausted in the empirical appearance. Even theology has never asserted the absolute contingency of the positive paradox. Rather, it has spoken of the Logos who, revealing himself in Jewish and pagan history, leads toward perfect revelation. (GW VII, 241)

If one denies, like the dialectical theologians, that the special revelation of God in Jesus Christ is linked back to a general revelation, then theology tends toward an "undialectical supranaturalism" (GW VII, 243), which, moreover, can only relate negatively to the world.

In the following years, Paul Tillich further specified his understanding of revelation, which is in the background of his argument with Barth,

---

[55] Cf. Tillich, "Antwort," 240–243.
[56] Cf. Tillich, "Antwort," 241.

but he did not modify it fundamentally. Tillich continues to hold to an understanding of revelation, which is precisely not supposed to be a particular act, and relates the revelation of God in Jesus Christ to this general breakthrough of the unconditioned in consciousness. However, Tillich now pays more attention to the historical involvement of consciousness and, thus, to its determinacy than he did in his writings from the early 1920s. This becomes visible in a differentiation of the concept of revelation, which he introduces in his 1924 Gießen lecture *Rechtfertigung und Zweifel*, and which remains constitutive for the further development of his theology.[57] Here, for the first time, Tillich makes a terminological distinction between "foundational revelation" (*Grundoffenbarung*) and "salvation revelation" (*Heilsoffenbarung*). This differentiation takes up the criticism of dialectical theology from the controversy with Barth and Gogarten from the year before.[58] In the lecture of 1924, "every theological direction," "in which revelation is conceived exclusively as salvation revelation, exclusively christologically," (GW VIII, 93) must be rejected. Tillich opposes this with a general revelation, which he now calls foundational revelation, as the basis of the revelation in Christ.[59]

What is the function of the newly introduced distinction between foundational revelation and salvation revelation? To begin with, both belong together. Every revelation is at the same time a foundational revelation and a salvation revelation, whereby the former refers to the fact that the substance-basis of consciousness is disclosed in consciousness as a negation of its determinacy and the latter refers to this consciousness, which

---

[57] Cf. Christian Danz, "Erläuterungen zu Paul Tillich 'Rechtfertigung und Zweifel,'" in Paul Tillich, *Rechtfertigung und Neues Sein*, ed. Christian Danz (Leipzig: Evangelische Verlagsanstalt, 2018), 66–111.

[58] Folkart Wittekind interprets the 1924 lecture *Rechtfertigung und Zweifel* as Tillich's answer to Karl Barth's objections. It is clear that the lecture, which takes up motifs from the 1919 draft but gives them a new thrust, refers to dialectical theology. At the same time, as Wittekind also emphasizes, the newly introduced distinction between foundational revelation and salvation revelation serves to clarify the older concept of revelation, which is retained by Tillich.

[59] Cf. Tillich, "Rechtfertigung und Zweifel," GW VIII, 93: "Revelation in Christ, the breakthrough of divine unconditionality in the face of all the work of religion, presupposes a broad basis of human religion and of divine ground-revelation."

is negated.[60] In this respect the foundational revelation is the beginning of the revelation and the salvation revelation is its inner goal. Then, in the process of the history of religion, in which religion and culture differentiate from each other, both step apart. In *Rechtfertigung und Zweifel,* Tillich merely hints at this integration of the history of religion, using as a basis the structural framework of the construction of the history of religion from the *Religionsphilosophie.*[61] That is, with the emergence of an autonomous culture, religion differentiates itself as a separate realm in culture, so that the revelation of God underlying every religion is represented in particular forms. With the formation of the God-conceptions of religion, the foundational revelation becomes ambiguous, since the breakthrough of the unconditioned in the always-historically-involved-and-determined consciousness is at the same time the negation of the determinacy of this consciousness. However, consciousness holds precisely this determinacy as a representation of the foundational revelation in the religious conceptions of God. The religious-historical construction in the *Religionsphilosophie* already functions in such a way that the process of the history of religion is built as an inner-religious protest against the religious images in which the revelation is represented, that is, as a struggle of the divine and the demonic. The inner goal of the development of the history of religion is the religion of paradox or grace, which already in the *Religionsphilosophie* cannot be derived from the history of religion but must be understood as a revelation in its own right. In the religion of paradox, and this distinguishes it from the religious-historical process, the consciousness of revelation itself becomes reflexive. That is, the representation of the disclosedness of the unconditioned in consciousness represents, at the same time, the determinacy of the consciousness that is negated, and the negation of that consciousness. Consequently, not only is an image of the

---

[60] Cf. Tillich, "Rechtfertigung und Zweifel," 97: "The foundational revelation is the liberation from the despair of doubt and emptiness of meaning. In this respect it is the beginning of the salvation revelation. And the salvation revelation is liberation from the despair of contradiction and remoteness from God."

[61] Cf. Tillich, "Religionsphilosophie," 340–349.

performance of the religious act represented in consciousness, but also the binding of this act to the performance of its negation.[62]

In *Rechtfertigung und Zweifel*, Tillich refers to the earlier religion of paradox from the *Religionsphilosophie* as salvation revelation, but he retains its older determination as a reflexive consciousness of revelation. With it, the reflexive religion, the foundational revelation is completed, since the content of the consciousness of revelation is the (foundational) revelation as a breakthrough of the unconditioned into the conditioned, or as direct-edness towards the unconditioned itself. And as in the *Religionsphilosophie*, so too in the lecture of 1924, Christology is the image of the completion of the foundational revelation in the salvation revelation. Tillich's distinc-tion between foundational revelation and salvation revelation, newly in-troduced in *Rechtfertigung und Zweifel*, builds on older motifs and holds to the fundamental conviction that God's revelation does not consist in a par-ticular act, but in the disclosedness of the substance-basis already given in consciousness. Therefore, both in the foundational revelation and in the salvation revelation, faith is "determined by intention" alone (GW VIII, 96). But as directedness towards the unconditioned, the latter, toward which faith is directed, remains itself indeterminate and indeterminable. Obviously, the unconditioned, which is always already given in conscious-ness, can only come about as a negation of the determinations produced by consciousness, but not as itself—for the unconditioned only has univer-sal validity if it is itself not determined.

Does the introduction of the distinction between foundational reve-lation and salvation revelation thus change anything at all in the systematic foundations of Tillich's theology? Against the dialectical theologians, Til-lich continues to hold on to the construction of religion as revelation of God, which is not a particular but an indetermined act itself. What changes is that Tillich ties his general understanding of revelation, the di-rectedness towards the unconditioned, more explicitly to the historically involved concrete consciousness. Although this was already the case in the writings since 1919, it is now reflected terminologically. In the middle of

---

[62] Cf. Tillich, "Religionsphilosophie," 343–4: "But the goal of the whole movement is the connection of the theocratic demand and mystical negativity with the sacramental sanctification of *a* concrete. Now, since this unity of the pre-sent and the demanded sacred cannot be made [!], but can only be experienced as a breakthrough, we speak of the religion *of grace* or of the *religion of paradox*."

the decade, the definition of religion as directedness towards the unconditioned, which was significant for the early 1920s, becomes the formula that determines the rest of his work: religion is that which unconditionally concerns human beings. Tillich introduced his new definition of God's revelation in the dogmatics lecture that began in Marburg in 1925 and continued in Dresden.[63] In connection with this new formulation, the idea of a history of revelation also receives a new weight. But even this idea is not new in Tillich's writings; it takes up motifs of his old construction of the history of religion from the *Religionsphilosophie* and connects them with the distinction between foundational revelation and salvation revelation introduced in *Rechtfertigung und Zweifel* from 1924.[64] In the dogmatics lecture, Tillich develops these considerations further in his discussion of the object of dogmatics, namely the revelation of God, into a three-stage history of revelation.

The starting point of Tillich's explanations of the concept of revelation in the dogmatics lecture remains the foundational revelation, which as revelation is at the same time the revelation of salvation.[65] Against the background of the differentiation of religion and culture, he now determines the concrete consciousness embedded in history, which is negated in the breakthrough of revelation, as a concrete path of salvation. By its turn, such a concrete path is, as it were, retained as negated by the religious consciousness and used to represent religion. Accordingly, the path to salvation becomes ambiguous and, as the breakthrough of the unconditioned into the conditioned, is both divine and demonic at the same time.[66] In the foundational revelation there is indeed a divine revelation, but this remains imperfect because of its ambivalence. The religious consciousness in the foundational revelation is not able to detach itself from the concretely determined consciousness negated in it, in which alone it can represent itself. For this, a new revelation of God is needed, which refers to

---

[63] Already the first leading sentence (*Leitsatz*) of the dogmatics lecture in 1925 introduces the new definition of the concept of revelation, which is the subject of dogmatics. "*Dogmatics is scientific speech about that which concerns us unconditionally.*" (EW XIV, 1)

[64] Cf. Tillich, "Rechtfertigung und Zweifel," 86–89.

[65] Cf. Paul Tillich, "Dogmatik-Vorlesung (Dresden 1925–1927)," in EW XIV, 37–41.

[66] Cf. Tillich, "Dogmatik-Vorlesung," 41–45.

the foundational revelation and, at the same time, uses and negates the concrete way of salvation in which it presents itself.[67] It is Tillich's older idea of reflexive revelation or religion of paradox that forms the substance of the revelation of salvation in the dogmatics lecture.

> The perfect revelation is the one in which the demonization of revelation in itself is made impossible by the fact that every claim of the path of revelation to unconditionality is excluded. But this is to enter into the concrete way of salvation, i.e., the concrete and the negation of the concrete are to be realized in the way of salvation. (EW XIV, 49)

The idea of the history of revelation and its threefold rhythm results from the outlined classification of foundational revelation and salvation revelation. Tillich distinguishes between an immediate foundational revelation, the completed revelation, in which the meaning of the foundational revelation is fulfilled as salvation revelation, and the historical realization of the salvation revelation in the "inner polarity of realization and self-sublation" (EW XIV, 49) of the concrete path, to which the salvation revelation is also necessarily bound.[68] Thus, also in the dogmatics lecture, Til-

---

[67] Tillich specifically points out the importance of this thesis in the dogmatics lecture: "It is the decisive proposition of the whole fundamental theology, because only from it arises the possibility of a truth claim of dogmatics." (EW XIV, 45)

[68] Tillich takes up this distinction from Ernst Troeltsch and transfers the differentiation between preparation, center and reception on the explication of the theological circle. Cf. Ernst Troeltsch, *Glaubenslehre. Nach Heidelberger Vorlesungen aus den Jahren 1911 und 1912* (München; Leipzig: Duncker & Humblot, 1925), 85. The three-stage history of revelation from the dogmatics lecture also takes up older considerations of Tillich, which can already be found in the *Religionsphilosophie* as well as in the discussion with Barth and Gogarten, namely the inner gradation of the concept of revelation into creation, redemption and consummation. Cf. Tillich, "Kritisches und positives Paradox," 219; "Religionsphilosophie," 353. This forms the basis of Tillich's revelation-theological version of the doctrine of the Trinity. Cf. Christian Danz, "Geschichtliche Offenbarung. Die Trinitätslehre Paul Tillichs," in *Gott und die menschliche Freiheit. Studien zum Gottesbegriff in der Neuzeit* (Neukirchen-Vluyn: Neukirchener, 2005), 102–128. Karl Barth is not the only theologian in the 1920s who uses the concept of revelation to ground the doctrine of the Trinity.

lich rejects an isolated, and therefore special revelation of God, which Friedrich Gogarten and Karl Barth claim as the starting point of theology. Such an isolated revelation, which is removed from the history of revelation, could only be a demonic one.[69] Against the demand for determinacy of the dialectical theologians, Tillich holds on to the indeterminacy of God's revelation, but now in such a way that the idea of revelation is embedded in a history of revelation. Thus, the concreteness as well as the existentiality of revelation, as signaled by its redefinition as "that which unconditionally concerns us," receive stronger weight, which leads to a distinct anthropological orientation of Tillich's theology in the following years.[70] But the systematic structure of the understanding of revelation does not change. The disclosedness in the individual consciousness of the substance-basis already laid out in consciousness is not a particular act. This disclosedness can still only be represented as negation solely in the theoretical and practical functions of consciousness, through which the unconditioned, which itself must remain undetermined, is intended (gemeint).

5. From the Revelation of God to the Method of Correlation

In confrontation with the dialectical theology of Karl Barth and Friedrich Gogarten, Paul Tillich specified his understanding of God's revelation as the basis of theology since 1924 by introducing the distinction between foundational revelation and salvation revelation, but at the same time he has maintained that revelation is not a particular act in consciousness. Tillich rejects the insistence of the dialectical theologians on the determinacy of revelation and its Christological binding. Tillich's rejection of such a Christological and soteriological narrowing of revelation, as explained in the second and third chapters, began already in his writings before the First World War. With the modern-positive theology of Adolf Schlatter and Wilhelm Lütgert, Tillich—against Albrecht Ritschl and his school—

---

[69] Cf. Tillich, "Dogmatik-Vorlesung," 49: "It is readily apparent that no isolated revelation [sc. as Friedrich Gogarten claims in his Christology (cf. EW XIX, 37)], in which this three-act is missing, could satisfy the requirement of perfect revelation. For it would lack precisely that which is decisive, namely, the negation of the immediacy of revelation, that is, the negation of its demonic nature."

[70] Cf. Fritz, Menschsein als Frage.

starts from a general revelation of God and ties the revelation of salvation in Christ back to the former. As shown, this intention is also followed by the elaboration of the understanding of revelation in the 1920s in confrontation with dialectical theology. The basis of Tillich's theology of the history of revelation, then, is the foundational revelation, which receives its completion in God's revelation of salvation. The differentiation in the concept of revelation, which was introduced in 1924 and systematically carried out in the dogmatics lecture that began a year later, remains constitutive for Tillich's subsequent work up to the *Systematic Theology*. It is only after his emigration to the United States that he drops the terms foundational revelation and salvation revelation and replaces them with other terms. These new terms then become the markers, as it were, of his late main work, namely, the correlation of human question and divine answer.[71] Tillich's method of correlation represents the result of his reflections on the concept of revelation as the basis of a modern theology in dispute with the dialectical theologians Karl Barth and Friedrich Gogarten. The replacement of the older terminology of foundational revelation and salvation revelation by the scheme of question and answer is tangible in his 1935 works *What is wrong with the "Dialectic" Theology?* and *Natural and Revealed Religion*.

When Tillich revised his dogmatics lecture during his Dresden years in 1927/28 for a planned publication by Otto Reichl Publishing house in Darmstadt, entitled *System der religiösen Erkenntnis*, he still used the distinction between foundational revelation and salvation revelation to structure the history of revelation.[72] This changes in his essay *What is wrong*

---

[71] The extensive literature on Tillich's method of correlation, since it has largely concentrated on the late *Systematic Theology*, has, as far as I can see, so far completely overlooked the systematic foundations of this method in his understanding of revelation. Cf. only John P. Clayton, *The Concept of Correlation. Paul Tillich and the Possibility of a Mediating Theology* (Berlin; New York: de Gruyter, 1980); Dirk-Martin Grube, "Kontextinvariante Wahrheit in geschichtlicher Vermittlung? Eine Analyse von Tillichs Methode der Korrelation," in *Offenbarung, absolute Wahrheit und interreligiöser Dialog. Studien zur Theologie Paul Tillichs* (Berlin; Boston: de Gruyter, 2019), 157–174.

[72] Two versions of the revision of the *Prolegomena* of the dogmatics lecture for the intended publication, which, however, did not come about, have survived from Tillich's estate: Paul Tillich, "Das System der religiösen Erkenntnis," in EW

with the "Dialectic" Theology? as well as in his lecture *Natural and Revealed Religion,* delivered at Harvard University on April 30, 1935. In both his essay on dialectical theology and his lecture, Tillich repeats, on the one hand, his critique of Barth's early 1920s claim that God's revelation is determinate, tending toward an uncritical supranaturalism.[73] But on the other hand, and in contrast to 1923, he now elaborates his critique of Barth's and Gogarten's understanding of revelation on the basis of the distinction between foundational revelation and salvation revelation introduced a year later, although Tillich now no longer uses either term.

Also in *What is wrong with the "Dialectic" Theology?*, Tillich shares the epistemological critique of dialectical theology. Because of God's transcendence, no direct statements can be made about him, but only dialectical ones. However, the insistence of the dialectical theologians on the determinacy of revelation turns into an undialectical position. This results in both the thesis of Tillich's essay, which argues that dialectical theology is not dialectical enough,[74] and in the structuring of his explanations in two parts. In the first part of his essay, he situates Barth's theology of the critical paradox within the theological-historical development of modernity and elaborates Barth's reception of epistemological criticism with reference to theology, philosophy of religion, liberal theology, and the relationship between God's kingdom and the world. Similar to his discussion with Barth and Gogarten twelve years earlier, Tillich agrees with their critical paradox,[75] but believes that this critical paradox is not critical enough in

---

XI, 79–116 (1st version), 116–174 (2nd version). Similar to the dogmatics lecture, in *Das System der religiösen Erkenntnis* Tillich introduces the distinction between foundational revelation and salvation revelation as the conclusion of the discussion of the concept of revelation. Cf. Tillich, "Das System der religiösen Erkenntnis," 173 (§ 22).

[73] Cf. Tillich, "What is wrong with the 'Dialectic' Theology?" 127; "Natural and Revealed Religion," in *Ausgewählte Texte*, ed. Christian Danz, Werner Schüßler and Erdmann Sturm (Berlin; New York 2008), 265–273.

[74] Cf. Tillich, "What is wrong with the 'Dialectic' Theology?" 127: "When I am asked, What is wrong with the 'dialectic' theology? I reply that it is not 'dialectic.'"

[75] Cf. Tillich, "What is wrong with the 'Dialectic' Theology?" 135: "Unquestionably, this [sc. the epistemic-critical moment of the critical paradox introduced by Barth] seems to me to be the truth that is preserved not only in the Barthian theology but in any theology that deserves the name."

that it is itself subordinated to epistemological criticism and thereby made dependent on one position.[76] Tillich elaborates his own view of a truly dialectical grounding of the critical paradox in the second part of his essay by contrasting Barth's alleged supranaturalistic grounding of the critical paradox with his dialectical construction of the revelation of God.

Tillich's remarks on a dialectical theology of revelation in the second part of his essay from 1935, in which he orients himself on the individual aspects from the first part, build throughout on the differentiation between a foundational revelation and a salvation revelation. What is new compared to his texts from the German period, however, is that he drops the terminology of foundational revelation and salvation revelation and replaces it with the dialectic of question and answer. Like Barth, true "dialectical thinking" denies "that what is a purely divine possibility may be interpreted as human possibility." But unlike Barth, Tillich asserts,

> that the *question* about the divine possibility is human possibility. And, further, it maintains that no question could be asked about the divine possibility unless a divine answer [sc. of foundational revelation], even if preliminary and scarcely intelligible, were not always already available.[77]

Also, for Tillich, the question about God, which is mentioned in the quotation, is possible as a human possibility only because of a revelation of God. It presupposes the foundational revelation as the disclosedness of the substance basis already laid out in consciousness. As in the writings of the 1920s, divine revelation is not a determinate act, but one that can only be represented by the functions of consciousness and the contents produced by them as their negation. The disclosedness of the consciousness of the foundational revelation, which is ambiguous throughout, comes also here to perfection (*Vollendung*) only in the revelation of salvation, i.e., in a reflexive consciousness of revelation, which is bound to a path of salvation,

---

[76] Cf. Tillich, "What is wrong with the 'Dialectic' Theology?" 136: "Does Barth's interpretation of the Christian paradox protect it from the distortion of its meaning? Or does not this interpretation directly weaken the paradox and restrict [!] the sovereign prerogative of God?"

[77] Tillich, "What is wrong with the 'Dialectic' Theology?" 137.

but one which at the same time cancels it.[78] The inner (teleological) connection of human question and divine revelatory answer, i.e., the earlier differentiation of foundational revelation and salvation revelation, forms the basis of the construction of the history of revelation, which takes the place of a natural-liberal and a supranatural-Barthian theology of revelation.[79]

Thus, the revelation-theological foundations of the later method of correlation are made clear from the history of the development of Tillich's theological work[80] His first New York dogmatics lecture, *Advanced Problems in Systematic Theology*, which began in 1936, was based on the dialectic of "question and answer, answer and question" in the development of the dogmatic material, which, as in the German dogmatics lecture, is oriented to the Trinitarian structure of the concept of revelation.[81] While the first lecture still begins with the divine answer to revelation and follows it with

---

[78] Cf. Tillich, "What is wrong with the 'Dialectic' Theology?" 138: "Thus there can be a 'fullness of time,' a moment in history when history by means of preliminary procedures [sc. the foundational revelation] has become capable of realizing the ultimate [sc. the salvation revelation]—a moment when history has become ripe for the event, which does not [!] originate from history and also is not injected into it as a foreign substance, but breaks out within it and is capable of being received in history."

[79] Cf. Tillich, "Natural and Revealed Religion," 273: "This we replace the mechanistic scheme of natural substructure and supernatural superstructure by a living interdependence between question and answer, answer and question." Cf. 271: "There is only *one* theology—it is a theology which interprets human religious experience by revelation as criticism and transformation of human religious experience." Cf. also "What is wrong with the 'Dialectic' Theology?" 140–1.

[80] Only against the background of the outlined development of the method of correlation in the history of the work, which starts from the differentiation of foundational and salvation revelation introduced in the 1920s, does Tillich's statement in the introduction of the late *Systematic Theology* become understandable. As Tillich states it, the method "is itself a theological assertion" (ST I, 8).

[81] Cf. Paul Tillich, "Advanced Problems in Systematic Theology. Courses at Union Theological Seminary, New York, 1936–1938," in EW XIX. Cf. Erdmann Sturm, "Auf dem Weg zur Methode der Korrelation. Tillichs New Yorker Vorlesungszyklus *Advanced Problems Systematic Theology* (1936–38)," in *The Method of Correlation. International Yearbook for Tillich Research*, vol. 12, ed. Christian Danz, Marc Dumas, Werner Schüßler, Mary A. Stenger and Erdmann Sturm (Berlin; Boston: de Gruyter, 2017), 45–65.

the human question, Tillich reversed this scheme in 1938 when he repeated his dogmatics in the form that he then retained in the later *Systematic Theology* and described in its introduction as the method of correlation.[82] In its background lies Tillich's old conviction, which he shares with the modern-positive theology of his teachers Schlatter and Lütgert, that already the search for God is impossible without a divine revelation. God is strictly transcendent. This is also true for the human's question about God. It does not result from any philosophical considerations, but solely from the divine foundational revelation, which already lies at the basis of the process of religion and culture as the disclosedness of consciousness.[83] Therefore, the history of religion does not coincide with the history of revelation, but the history of revelation is the basis of the history of religion, so that "in the history of religion [as well as in the history of culture] answers, mistakes, and questions which lead to the ultimate answer [sc. of the salvation revelation] and without the ultimate answer would have to remain something unasked, unintelligible, and alien."[84]

Even after his forced emigration to the United States in the 1930s, Tillich holds on to the foundation of theology in a general understanding of revelation. Against the demand of dialectical theology for the determinacy of revelation, he emphasizes its indeterminacy. Revelation of God is not a determined act in consciousness, but the disclosedness of the general basic structure of consciousness in it. But this act can only present itself as a negation of the concrete forms produced by consciousness, precisely as a transition to the directedness towards the unconditioned or, as the new formulation introduced in the mid-1920s puts it, as that which concerns us unconditionally. The unconditioned itself remains indeterminate. What changes with the transition to the United States is not the systematic grounding of theology in God's revelation, but the formulations in which

---

[82] Cf. Tillich, *Systematic Theology*, vol. I, 59–66. For the further development of the method of correlation's history of the work, cf. "The Problem of Theological Method," in *Ausgewählte Texte*, ed. Christian Danz, Werner Schüßler and Erdmann Sturm (Berlin; New York: de Gruyter, 2008), 301–312.

[83] Cf. Tillich, "Natural and Revealed Religion," 272: "the questioning for revelation presupposes revelation, and conversely: they are dependent on each other."

[84] Tillich, "What is wrong with the 'Dialectic' Theology?" 139.

Tillich now presents his theology. The level of the determined consciousness negated in the breakthrough of revelation, which, as mentioned, remains indeterminate in the interest of its generality, acquires a clearer weight with the introduction of the distinction between foundational revelation and salvation revelation since the second half of the 1920s. In the 1930s, as shown, Tillich replaces this terminology with the dialectical scheme of human question and divine revelatory answer. But even this terminological change maintains the intention of a general revelation of God in nature and culture as the basis of the search for God. Interestingly, Tillich's redescription of the terminology employed by the modern-positive theological school in the 1930s, through the dialectical relationship of "question and answer, answer and question," corresponds to the new presentation (*Neuinszenierung*) of his theological roots. Only now, as mentioned in the second chapter, does Tillich emphasize the importance of Martin Kähler for his theology while his actual academic teachers Adolf Schlatter and Wilhelm Lütgert fade into the background.[85]

---

[85] Cf. Tillich, "On the Boundary," 32.

B.

Key Issues

VI.

Absolute Faith and the God above God:
Tillich's Understanding of God

After tracing the development of Paul Tillich's theology in the context of contemporary debates in theology and philosophy of religion in the first part of this study, we will now discuss the main themes of his theology from a systematic perspective. Taking up the Trinitarian structure of his concept of revelation (creation, redemption, and consummation), we begin with the understanding of God, then turn to Christology and pneumatology. This revelation-theological structure also underlies Tillich's construction of a theology of the history of religions, with the discussion of which this systematic part is concluded and summarized.

But let us move first to Tillich's understanding of God, which is important for his thinking in several respects and was intensively perceived and received in contemporary debates.[1] What does Tillich understand by God and how does he construct the doctrine of God in his major work, the *Systematic Theology*?[2] God, according to Tillich's well-known formulation, which can be found in many places—especially in his later work—is

---

[1] In the 1960s, Tillich's doctrine of God was taken up by such diverse movements as death of God theology or pluralistic theology of religion. Cf. Gabriel Vahanian, *The Death of God. The Culture of Our Post-Christian Era* (New York: Braziller, 1961); John T. A. Robinson, *Honest to God* (Philadelphia: The Westminster Press, 1963); John Hick, *An Interpretation of Religion. Human Responses to the Transcendent* (New Haven: Yale University Press, 1989).

[2] On Tillich's doctrine of God, cf. Duane Olson, *The Depths of Life. Paul Tillich's Understanding of God* (Macon: Mercer University Press, 2019); Christian Danz, *Religion als Freiheitsbewußtsein. Eine Studie zur Theologie als Theorie der Konstitutionsbedingungen individueller Subjektivität bei Paul Tillich* (Berlin; New

that which unconditionally concerns humans beings.[3] This unconditional concern is discussed through further determinations, such as that "the being of God is being-itself" (ST I, 235). For the history of the reception of Tillich's understanding of God, however, another formulation became significant. This formulation is found in the 1952 publication, *The Courage to Be*. Here there is a discussion of a "God above God," which corresponds to what Tillich calls an absolute faith.[4] The doctrine of God in the *Systematic Theology* does not speak of such a "God above God," and so that the question arises: how does this "God above God" relate to the unconditional concern of human beings and the determination of God's being as being-itself?

Both Tillich's understanding of God as well as his doctrine of God from the *Systematic Theology* not only raise questions, but they can also only be understood against the historical background of the development of his theology, which was reconstructed in the first part of this book. The reason for this is that he intertwines different dimensions and intentions in his doctrine of God. First, the idea of God is the foundation and starting point of Tillich's theology. In its foundation, however, he takes up the epistemological critique of modernity. This is represented in his texts on the question of doubt, i.e., critical subjectivity, which is characterized by the knowledge that each of its contents is one posited by subjectivity itself. By including doubt in the foundation of theology, Tillich accommodates the modern critique of religion.[5] A second aspect is that Tillich's theology

---

York: de Gruyter, 2000), 100–175; Jörg Dierken, "Gewissheit und Zweifel. Über die religiöse Bedeutung skeptischer Reflexion," in *Theologie als Religionsphilosophie. Studien zu den problemgeschichtlichen und systematischen Voraussetzungen der Theologie Paul Tillichs*, ed. Christian Danz (Wien: LIT, 2004), 107–133.

[3] Cf. Tillich, *Systematic Theology*, vol. I, 211: "'God' is the answer to the question implied in man's finitude; he is the name for that which concerns man ultimately."

[4] Cf. Tillich, *The Courage to Be*, 175. Cf. Mary A. Stenger, "Faith (and religion)," in *The Cambridge Companion to Paul Tillich*, ed. Russel Re Manning (Cambridge: Cambridge University Press, 2009), 91–104.

[5] If one takes this seriously, then substance-metaphysical interpretations of Tillich's work are out of the question from the outset. This is true despite all allusions to such pre-critical metaphysical traditions as the *analogia entis* etc., which are undoubtedly found in Tillich's late work.

is concerned from the beginning with making possible a religious interpretation of the world as a whole. The adherence to a general (creation)
revelation of God is fundamental to the understanding of his theological
thought. In this intention, as stated in the first part of this study, motifs of
modern-positive theology can be identified, which are taken up in Tillich's
late work, even though he no longer uses the concept of a foundational
revelation. This is replaced by the human question as an element of the
correlation structure. It is against this background that Tillich's ontology
and his determination of God's being as being-itself must be read. It has
to do with the breaking up and overcoming of the soteriological narrow-
ings of twentieth-century Protestant theology. Consequently, ontology
has a very specific theological function in Tillich's theology.

For the understanding of Tillich's doctrine of God in the *Systematic
Theology*, this means above all that it has a revelation-theological foundation. God is disclosed to human being only in God's revelation. There is
no path from human beings to God.[6] It is from this framework, which
connects the doctrine of God in the *Systematic Theology* with Tillich's early
German work, that the aforementioned determinations of God as that
which unconditionally concerns human beings, the being of God as being-
itself, as well as the God above God must be understood. These concepts,
which entered the later theology, are prepared in his writings from the
German period. Only against their background his systematic construction
becomes transparent. For this reason, a look must first be taken at Tillich's
understanding of God in his texts from the period after the First World
War. In doing so, it becomes apparent that the concept of a God above
God is used here to construct the idea of God itself. The second section
discusses the doctrine of God in the *Systematic Theology*, in which Tillich
bundles his reflections on the dogmatic understanding of God. In the concluding third section, the remarks on absolute faith and the God above
God from *The Courage to Be* must be related to the doctrine of God from
Tillich's main dogmatic work. It will be shown that these considerations

---

[6] Tillich emphasizes this explicitly in *Systematic Theology*: "The ontological
structure of being implies the material for the symbols which point to the divine
life. However, this does not mean that a doctrine of God can be derived from an
ontological system. The character of the divine life is made manifest in revelation"
(ST I, 243).

move throughout on the argumentative line that is significant for his understanding of God as a whole.

1. God and Faith in Tillich's Early Work

Tillich already speaks of a God above God in his early work. He uses this formulation for the first time in his habilitation-writing *Der Begriff des Übernatürlichen, sein dialektischer Charakter und das Prinzip der Identität – dargestellt an der supranaturalistischen Theologie vor Schleiermacher*, from 1915. Here he speaks of the natural law as the "God under God" and the absolute as the "God above God" (EW IX, 474). The formulation lies in the context of Tillich's remarks on the dialectic of the supra, that is, the problem of the determination of God.[7] In his draft *Rechtfertigung und Zweifel*, written four years later, he takes up this formulation again, however, it is redefined here. As shown in the third chapter, Tillich had reworked the fundamental theoretical foundations of his theology. While the speculative relationship between the absolute and the individual spirit still forms the background of the *Habilitationsschrift*, in 1919 he relates the God above God to the religious performative act. But what does Tillich understand by this God above God in his theology after the First World War?

The epistemological-critical and systematic foundations of Tillich's theology after the war have already been discussed above, so that they do not need to be elaborated in detail again here. We will therefore limit ourselves to the elements of his construction that are constitutive for the idea of God.[8] The starting point of Tillich's reflections in *Rechtfertigung und Zweifel* is the inclusion of modernity in the foundation of theology. Modernity's critique of itself must be part of the theological system. Doubt or subjectivity as critique or negation stands for this.[9] The inclusion of doubt in the theological principle, which is what the 1919 remarks seek to address, means to include the

---

[7] Cf. Paul Tillich, "Der Begriff des Übernatürlichen, sein dialektischer Charakter und das Prinzip der Identität – dargestellt an der supranaturalistischen Theologie vor Schleiermacher," in EW IX, 439–592, here 473–4.

[8] Cf. above Chapter III.3.

[9] Cf. Tillich, "Rechtfertigung und Zweifel," EW X, 199–200: "In doubt, subjectivity is purely actualized, it has lost the object and has not yet found a new one; it is entirely with itself. That is why Cartesius is so classical in his formulation; in him subjectivity grasps itself as the basic element of the coming culture. Doubt has become an ineliminable ferment of spiritual life."

knowledge of modernity that every content of consciousness, including God, is a positing of consciousness that can be taken back again in the foundation of theology. However, one is left to wonder what does follow from this theory for the construction of the idea of God? First of all, as explained above, Tillich starts from the understanding that God is the consciousness that has been disclosed to itself as a general foundational structure. This reflexivity of consciousness, already engaged in every act of consciousness, is denoted by the concept of the unconditioned, which is further explained by the concept of meaning (*Sinn*). On the other hand, Tillich understands religion as the contingent disclosedness of this general presuppositional structure in individual consciousness. It, religion, is bound to the performance of this disclosedness, which cannot be produced by human beings. Only in this performative act is the unconditioned given in consciousness, namely, as negation of the determinacy of consciousness. Religion is consequently a performative act of reflection in consciousness, in which the unconditioned is made accessible to it as the precondition and basis of all its acts. Since the unconditioned itself is in principle unrepresentable and indeterminate, it can represent itself in consciousness only as negation of all determinate contents.

The breakthrough of the unconditioned into the conditioned, and thus the transition from cultural consciousness to the intention (*Meinen*) of the unconditioned, in which the disclosedness of consciousness consists, is called "faith" by Tillich. Faith is the affirmation of the absolute paradox, because the negation of the content posited by consciousness, that is, doubt, is the way in which consciousness is disclosed in its wholeness.[10] The certainty of faith lies in this performative act of the disclosedness of consciousness, which cannot be produced by itself. This certainty is the substance of the concept of God. But as a concept of God or conception of God in consciousness, God is always a content posited by consciousness. God has the status of a conviction (*Überzeugung*), and not that of certainty.[11] As an image of consciousness, in which the substance of the act of reflection is represented, God represents this act and its paradoxical structure. This is exactly

---

[10] Cf. Tillich, "Rechtfertigung und Zweifel," 218: "There remains only the paradoxical way out, to affirm in faith that doubt does not cancel standing in the truth."

[11] Cf. Tillich, "Rechtfertigung und Zweifel," 225: "There is thus already contained in the primary grasp of paradox, in the absolute act of faith, a moment of relativity."

what the "God above God" (EW X, 219) denotes in *Rechtfertigung und Zweifel*. In and with its content, religious consciousness refers to itself and represents itself, that is, its reflexive disclosedness. This arises in the negation of the contentual determinations posited by the acts of consciousness, since the unconditioned is not itself a determinate content, but is only represented as a negation of content. As such, the reflexivity of consciousness is at the same time the precondition of all determinate theoretical and practical determinations of reality in consciousness but is itself unrepresentable, or, as Tillich's later formulation goes, the unconditioned is ground and abyss.[12]

Thus, it is clear that Tillich uses the God above God in *Rechtfertigung und Zweifel* to designate the religious status of the thought of God as a whole. The knowledge of God is bound to God's revelation, that is, to the act of the certainty of faith. The image of the latter in consciousness represents the conception of God, which refers to the act and its reflexive structure. The God above God does not refer to a God behind the images of God, but it represents the reflexivity of religious consciousness in its relation to its contents, for which Tillich will later use the concept of symbol as a designation.[13] In the conception of God, the symbolicity of that reflexive determination is presented, which is religion as an act itself.

Tillich held on to this construction of the idea of God in his texts from the 1920s and developed it further. Thus, the metalogical conception of the *Religionsphilosophie* determines the "intention" (*Meinen*) of the unconditioned as "directedness" (*Richtung*) towards the unconditioned, but it also ties act and act-object together. "God is the object intended (*gemeinte*) in faith and, besides that, nothing" (GW I, 333). Likewise, the concept of God functions as a representation of the disclosedness of the foundational structure of consciousness in consciousness, which is bound to its performance. As the con-

---

[12] Cf. Tillich, "Religionsphilosophie," 334.
[13] Cf. Tillich, "Rechtfertigung und Zweifel," 221: "There is here, as it were, an oscillation between intuition [*Anschauung*] and concept [*Begriff*], an objectifying of the meaning [*Sinn*] to a being through intuition and a de-objectifying of the being to a meaning through the concept." In the first version of *Rechtfertigung und Zweifel* (cf. EW X, 172), Tillich, as mentioned above, uses the term symbol to designate the reflexivity of consciousness.

tent of religious consciousness, it symbolizes that reflexive structure that characterizes religion itself.[14] For the unconditioned, the reflexivity of consciousness, as a precondition and basis of all contentual determinations, is itself no content, thus neither a subject nor an object. It underlies all acts of consciousness. With the introduction of the distinction between foundational revelation and salvation revelation in 1924, nothing changes in the construction of the idea of God itself. The breakthrough of the unconditioned in consciousness, which is always concretely determined in terms of content, remains an indefinite act. However, the new differentiation of the concept of revelation and the teleological assignment of foundational revelation and salvation revelation are accompanied by an emphasis on the historically integrated consciousness. It now moves into the focus of the so-called history of revelation.[15] This results in a new formulation of the determination of God's revelation. The earlier formulation "directedness towards the unconditioned" is now replaced by the one that says revelation is "that which unconditionally concerns human beings," which is also retained by Tillich in his late work. What do these changes mean for the construction of the dogmatic doctrine of God?

Tillich's Marburg and Dresden dogmatics lectures are based on the distinction between foundational revelation and salvation revelation. This is already visible in the structure of the doctrine of God developed in these lectures. Tillich places the doctrine of creation before the doctrine of God;[16] its object is the being (*Seiende*) and its structures in the breakthrough of revelation with the exception of the fall of humanity.[17] This

---

[14] Cf. Tillich, "Religionsphilosophie," 334: "'God' is the symbol for the unconditioned; but it is a symbol just as faith as an act—not as act-ground and act-abyss—is a symbolic act. God is not only his own ground, but also his abyss."

[15] Cf. chapter V.4 above.

[16] Cf. Tillich, "Dogmatik-Vorlesung," 125–148: (*I. The being in its pure creatureliness [Urstand]*); 148–176 (II. *The unconditional being as origin of the being [The power of God: The Godhead of God and the stages of being]*). The dogmatic structure of the *Systematische Theologie* of 1913 is different. Here Tillich—in correspondence to the speculative foundation of the system in the absolute idea of truth—begins with the doctrine of God and then proceeds to the doctrine of creation. Cf. "Systematische Theologie von 1913," 328–336.

[17] Cf. Tillich, "Dogmatik-Vorlesung," 124: "The immediate being becomes a symbol of revelation, i.e., we are dealing with theological ontology. Not with

means that the doctrine of creation and the doctrine of God in the dogmatics lectures explicates the reflexive structure of the foundational revelation. While the doctrine of creation theologically describes the negation of the determinateness of consciousness in the duality of being shaken and being carried, or courage and melancholy, the dogmatic doctrine of God has to do with that which breaks through in the breakthrough of revelation. Tillich calls that which is disclosed in this performative act the "symbol of the unconditional being" (EW XIV, 149). Here, too, no being outside of consciousness is meant, but the reflexivity of consciousness, which is presupposed and already claimed in every concrete act of consciousness. And in the same way, in the dogmatics lectures, that which unconditionally concerns human beings is bound to the actual performative act of the disclosedness event in consciousness, so that it can be represented by it only as negation of the determinacy of consciousness. The consciousness that is disclosed to itself is thus directed to the unconditioned, but the objective correlate of intention is negated, since this is not an object, but the indeterminable ground and abyss of all object-positing in consciousness, which already underlies them.

Tillich's explanations of the doctrine of God in the Marburg and Dresden lectures remain oriented toward the old model of the intention (*Meinen*) of the unconditioned from *Rechtfertigung und Zweifel* of 1919. The contentual implementation of the doctrine of God, taking up the dogmatic doctrinal tradition, provides a theological description of the disclosedness of the general foundational structure of consciousness in individual consciousness. Accordingly, Tillich discusses God as a symbolic description of the apprehension of that reflexivity that is already engaged in every act of consciousness. Since this reflexivity, as the constitution of all determinations in consciousness, remains withdrawn from consciousness itself, this must also be reflected in its theological description. From this result the polar pairs of depth and clarity, seclusiveness (*Abgeschlossenheit*) and openness (*Aufgeschlossenheit*), glory and lowliness result, which Tillich uses for the material development of the doctrine of God.[18] They

---

ontology per se [...], but with mythically fulfilled ontology, with doctrine of creation." Cf. Folkart Wittekind, "Das Sein und die Frage nach Gott," in *Paul Tillichs 'Systematische Theologie'. Ein werk- und problemgeschichtlicher Kommentar*, ed. Christian Danz (Berlin; Boston: de Gruyter, 2017), 104–110.

[18] Cf. Tillich, "Dogmatik-Vorlesung," 148–158.

structure the self-referential act of the disclosedness in consciousness, which refers to itself with its contents. The religious idea of God described by dogmatics is thus an image of the reflexive structure of the performative act of faith, represented in an image of itself. However, this image produced by consciousness only corresponds to the reflexivity of the act that refers to itself when it is itself negated. Tillich thus incorporates into his dogmatic doctrine of God in the mid-1920s the substance of the formula "God above God" from *Rechtfertigung und Zweifel*, but no longer the formulation. This is now replaced by the concept of symbol, which describes the position of the religious consciousness to its contents. With this, the basic structures of Tillich's early doctrine of God are described to such an extent that we can now turn to the *Systematic Theology*.

2. The Doctrine of God in the *Systematic Theology*

If one compares the doctrine of God from the *Systematic Theology* with that of the dogmatics of the 1920s, it is noticeable that the former follows the German dogmatics in its structure. As in his German dogmatics, Tillich places the doctrine of creation before the doctrine of God.[19] Both doctrinal pieces not only form an inner unity, but they must also be understood only in this context. However, in the doctrine of creation preceding the doctrine of God in the narrower sense in the *Systematic Theology*, Tillich discusses an ontological structural theory structured in three parts: the basic ontological structure with its constituent polar elements, being and finitude, and finitude and the question of God.[20] But this ontological reformulation is not a new element, since already in the German dogmatics lectures the doctrine of creation was understood as theological ontology.[21]

---

[19] Cf. Wittekind, "Das Sein und die Frage nach Gott," 108–110.

[20] Cf. Tillich, *Systematic Theology*, vol. I, 163–210 (*I. Being and the Question of God*). Folkart Wittekind has rightly pointed out that the basic structures of the *Systematische Theologie* of 1913 shine through this structure. Cf. Wittekind, "Das Sein und die Frage nach Gott," 111.

[21] Cf. also Paul Tillich, "Eschatologie und Geschichte," in GW VI, 72–82, esp. 74–5 (*2. Theological Ontology*).

This has the function of rejecting a soteriological foundation of the doctrine of God and creation.[22] However, while the doctrine of creation and the doctrine of God in the dogmatics lectures discusses the reflexive structure of foundational revelation, Tillich, as explained in the previous chapter, has dropped this term since the 1930s and replaced it with the interrelation of question and answer. This restructuring is documented in the New York lecture *Advanced Problems in Systematic Theology* of 1936, which is based on the continuation of the distinction and assignment of foundational revelation and salvation revelation to the dialectic of question and answer, whereby Tillich begins with the revelation-theological answer and treats the human question according to it. Therefore, in contrast to the dogmatics of the 1920s, in the New York lecture he begins with the doctrine of God and only then goes into the doctrine of creation.[23] The *Systematic Theology*, on the other hand, returns to the structure of the German dogmatics lectures.

In the *Systematic Theology*, Tillich retains the revelation-theological construction from his German dogmatics. For his interlocking of the doctrine of creation and the doctrine of God, this means that it describes the reflexive structure of foundational revelation. But unlike in the dogmatics of the 1920s, Tillich separates the doctrine of creation and the doctrine of God from both Christology and pneumatology in his late major work. The doctrine of creation and of God, as well as the doctrine of Christ, are

---

[22] Cf. Tillich, "Eschatologie und Geschichte," 75: In contrast to the "one-sided turn to soteriology" that is significant for dialectical theology, it is necessary to work out the ontological foundations on which the soteriological doctrine of creation "rests and with it the entire personal and social ethics up to the most pressing problems of the day."

[23] Cf. Tillich, "Advanced Problems in Systematic Theology," 61–110 (*Part Two: God and the world*). Tillich structures the doctrine of God and Creation in four parts—different from the outline given before the lecture: I. [The meaning of the concept of God in religion and philosophy], II. [The philosophical idea of the Unconditioned and the religious idea of God], III. [The idea of God from the point of view of creation], IV. [The idea of God from the point of view of providence].

referred to as abstraction.[24] That is, the first volume of the *Systematic Theology* deals with the general disclosedness of God in the world and culture, which, since all revelation is redemptive,[25] has a soteriological dimension.

In the first part of the doctrine of creation and God, under the heading *Being and the Question of God*, Tillich discusses an ontological structural theory that is polar in structure and determines the nature of experience. The basis of the explanations is the reflexive and self-referential structure of consciousness that is now reformulated as a self-world-relation and which is constituted by the three polarities: individualization and participation, dynamics and form, and freedom and destiny. Because both the polar pairs of individuality and participation and dynamics and form depend upon concrete acts, these acts are free acts, and they therefore depend upon the final polarity of freedom and destiny. From the last polarity results the possibility of transition to the reality of finite life and its categorical forms.[26] It is decisive that the unconditioned is always already underlying this ontological structural theory, but it cannot be grasped from it; the structure expresses the ontological nature of experience but the ground of being itself is not derivable from it.[27] All concrete reality-consciousness (*Wirklichkeitsbewusstsein*) and every concrete reality-encounter (*Wirklichkeitsbegegnung*) already presupposes the disclosed reflexivity of the self-relation of consciousness as ground and abyss, that is, the unconditioned.

---

[24] Cf. Tillich, *Systematic Theology,* vol. I, 66–7: "A third part is based on the fact that the essential as well as the existential characteristics are abstractions [!] and that in reality they appear in the complex and dynamic which is called 'life.'" The German dogmatics treats the doctrine of sin within the framework of the doctrine of creation and God. Cf. "Dogmatik-Vorlesung," 177–222.

[25] Cf. Tillich, *Systematic Theology*, vol. I, 144–147 (*Revelation and Salvation*), here 144: "The history of revelation and the history of salvation are the same history. Revelation can be received only in the presence of salvation, and salvation can occur only within a correlation of revelation."

[26] Cf. Danz, *Religion als Freiheitsbewußtsein*, 13–99. In the *Systematische Theologie* of 1913, this corresponds to the transition from the intuitional to the reflexive standpoint. Cf. Tillich, "Systematische Theologie von 1913," 307–8.

[27] Cf. Tillich, *Systematic Theology*, vol. I, 174: "The question, 'What precedes the duality of self and world, of subject and object?' is a question in which reason looks into its own abyss—an abyss in which distinction and derivation disappear. Only revelation can answer this question."

This general basic structure is developed, however, only in the event (*Geschehen*) of the revelation. For the "object" of the doctrine of God in the narrower sense, which Tillich treats under the heading *The Reality of God*,[28] this means that it thematizes the unconditioned disclosed in revelation as the presupposition and foundation of the ontological structural theory. But precisely this is possible only on its ground as its negation. For the unconditioned, as that which concerns the human being unconditionally, is neither an object nor is it determined.

Tillich's material realization of the doctrine of God results from this structure. First of all, the determination of God's being as being-itself[29] takes up his thought from the German dogmatics. There Tillich designated that which is disclosed in the breakthrough of revelation with the "symbol of the unconditioned being." What is meant is the general basic structure of consciousness, which, bound to a performative act of reflexivity in the individual consciousness, is disclosed to it. This is only possible as negation of the determinations posited by consciousness, since the disclosed reflexivity is the basis and precondition of all concrete determinations. It is, therefore, neither subject nor object, neither an I nor an object, but the reflexivity of consciousness that is already claimed in these acts of determination—a reflexivity, however, that is always withdrawn from consciousness.[30] It is thus clear that Tillich's determination of God's being in the *Systematic Theology* takes up that of the unconditioned from his early work.

In his German dogmatics, as stated in the first section of this chapter, Tillich had referred to the disclosedness of the reflexivity already claimed in consciousness, which is bound to the breakthrough event, as the unconditioned being, but added, similarly to the controversy with Karl Barth in 1923,[31] that this unconditioned being is a symbol. In contrast to this, Tillich writes in the *Systematic Theology*:

---

[28] Cf. Tillich, *Systematic Theology*, vol. I, 211–289.

[29] Cf. Tillich, *Systematic Theology*, vol. I, 235. On the doctrine of God in the *Systematic Theology*, cf. Jörg Dierken, "Die Wirklichkeit Gottes," in *Paul Tillichs 'Systematische Theologie'. Ein werk- und problemgeschichtlicher Kommentar*, ed. Christian Danz (Berlin; Boston: de Gruyter, 2017), 117–141.

[30] In this sense, Tillich's statement that the image of God is always a positing or projection of consciousness, but not the reflexivity of consciousness disclosed in consciousness, is to be understood. Cf. Tillich, *Systematic Theology*, vol. I, 212.

[31] Cf. chapter VI.4 above.

The statement that God is being-itself is a nonsymbolic statement. It does not point beyond itself. It means what it says directly and properly; if we speak of the actuality of God, we first
assert that he is not God if he is not being-itself. Other asser-
tions about God can be made theologically only on this basis.
(ST I, 239)

The determination of the being of God as being-itself is a non-symbolic statement and indeed the only one. All further statements about God
are symbolic. This remark of Tillich's in the first volume of the *Systematic
Theology* as well as his commentary on it in the introduction of the second
volume ignited a broad controversy in which the most different arguments
were put forward.[32] Since this debate proceeded throughout from presuppositions of a pre-critical metaphysics of substance, which miss Tillich's
approach already in the beginning, it did not lead to a conclusive result.
How, then, must the only non-symbolic statement of Tillich's doctrine of
God be understood against the background of the development of the history of the work just outlined?

Already the placement of the non-symbolic statement at the beginning of the section on the knowledge of God makes clear that it deals with
Tillich's understanding of symbols, to which the further explanations then
also turn.[33] This means that the statement that the being of God is being-
itself, which must actually be understood and does not point beyond itself,
does not refer to a somehow given substantial being. It designates—similarly to the early German work discussed above—the reflexivity of the self-

---

[32] The starting point of the debate was the English translation of Tillich's
1928 essay on Symbol in 1940, to which Wilbur Marshall Urban responded in the
same year. Cf. Wilbur M. Urban, "A Critique of Professor Tillich's Theory of the
Religious Symbol," in *Journal of Liberal Religion* 2 (1940) 34–36. Urban refers to
Tillich's distinction between a non-symbolic and symbolic statements about God,
which is already found in the 1928 essay. Cf. Tillich, "Das religiöse Symbol," 207.
On the controversy over Tillich's so-called one non-symbolic statement, cf. Danz,
Religion als Freiheitsbewußtsein, 159–168.

[33] Cf. Tillich, *Systematic Theology*, vol. I, 238–241 (*God as Being and the
Knowledge of God*). Already in the New York dogmatics lecture of 1936, Tillich
treats his understanding of symbols in this context. Cf. "Advanced Problems in
Systematic Theology," 97–102. Tillich here takes up his reflections on the reli-
gious symbol from his 1928 essay. Cf. "Das religiöse Symbol," 196–212. Cf. Danz,
"Symbolische Form und die Erfassung des Geistes im Gottesverhältnis," 59–75.

referential consciousness, that is, the connection between consciousness and being, which is already claimed in every act of consciousness, but which is withdrawn from it.[34] The non-symbolic statement that the being of God is being-itself is, at this point, a summary description of the basic theory underlying Tillich's entire theology. Religion, on the other hand, is the underivable event of the disclosedness of this reflexivity of consciousness in the individual consciousness.

With the non-symbolic statement, Tillich takes up the construction of the idea of God in the *Systematic Theology*, the basic features of which he had already worked out in his draft *Rechtfertigung und Zweifel* of 1919. For the material elaboration of the doctrine of God, for which he uses an ontological structural theory in his main dogmatic work, this means that it, too, must be read in a self-referential way. The contentual determinations of God represent the occurrence of the transparency of consciousness as well as the binding of this transparency to its performative act in consciousness. Since the reflexivity (the unconditioned), which is already claimed in every act of consciousness, is itself in principle indeterminable, consciousness can grasp its own determinacy only as negation of the determinations posited by it. With the idea of God, also in the *Systematic Theology*, religious consciousness refers to itself and represents itself in it.[35] For this status of the idea of God and its binding to the reflexive act of faith, Tillich used the formulation "God above God" in 1919. In his main dogmatic work, as in the dogmatics lectures of the 1920s and 1930s, this determination is replaced by the concept of symbol. Even though Tillich refers to the *analogia entis*[36] in the *Systematic Theology* to explain his understanding of symbols and speaks of symbols as pointing beyond themselves, it would be a complete misunderstanding of his explanations if one wanted to understand them as referring to a being or a supernatural God behind and beyond consciousness. The religious image of God, precisely

---

[34] Cf. Folkart Wittekind, "Gottesdienst als Handlungsraum. Zur symbol-theoretischen Konstruktion des Kultes in Tillichs Religionsphilosophie," in *Das Symbol als Sprache der Religion. International Yearbook for Tillich Research*, vol. 2, ed. Christian Danz, Werner Schüßler and Erdmann Sturm (Wien: LIT, 2007), 77–100, esp. 79, note 4.

[35] For this reason, it is not yet sufficient to fix the difference between Tillich's understanding of God and theism on the determination of God as the depth of life, as Duane Olson suggests. Cf. Olson, *The Depths of Life*, 31–38.

[36] Cf. Tillich, *Systematic Theology*, vol. I, 239–40.

because it is bound to the act of the disclosedness of consciousness, that is, revelation,[37] remains self-referential. It is an image of the act of faith that represents itself in the image of God by referring to God.

3. The "God above God" in *The Courage to Be*

Tillich explicitly took up his early formula of a "God above God" in his 1952 book *The Courage to Be*, which is based on four lectures he gave from late October to early November 1950 at Yale University in New Haven as the Dwight Harrington Terry Foundation Lectures on Religion in the Light of Science and Philosophy.[38] The context of the history of the work of the lectures and their publication is the first volume of the *Systematic Theology*, which appeared in 1951. In this, as just shown, Tillich does not use this formula, while it holds a prominent position in the 1952 writing. Its convoluted course of argumentation, which leads through the history of Western philosophy and theology, its interpretations of courage and anxiety, to contemporary existentialist debates, culminates in the concept of a God above God, which corresponds to a so-called absolute faith. There has been much puzzling over this God in Tillich scholarship: is it a limit statement (*Grenzaussage*) by Tillich or an absorption of philosophical thinking about being in the tradition of a negative theology?[39]

If one places *The Courage to Be* in the context of the history of the work and understands it against this background, then it quickly becomes clear that it deals with that which Tillich called foundational revelation in his dogmatics lectures of the 1920s. This foundational revelation, as stated above in the second section of this chapter, also forms the subject of the first volume of the *Systematic Theology*. The subject of the 1952 writing is the possibility of a knowledge of God that is possible everywhere in the world. In this respect, it is not unjustified to understand *The Courage to Be* as a modern edification book for intellectuals. It is from this perspective

[37] Cf. Tillich, *Systematic Theology*, vol. I, 240.
[38] Cf. Christian Danz, "Der Mut zum Sein. Ein werkgeschichtlicher Prospekt," in Paul Tillich, *Der Mut zum Sein*. With a preface by Christian Danz (Berlin; Boston: de Gruyter, 2015), 1–14.
[39] Cf. Traugott Koch, "Die Macht zum Sein im Mut zum Sein. Tillichs Gottesverständnis in seiner 'Systematische Theologie,'" in *Paul Tillich. Studien zu einer Theologie der Moderne*, ed. Hermann Fischer (Frankfurt a.M.: Athenäum, 1989), 169–206.

that Tillich's manifold references to the philosophical and theological tradition, which he draws upon and uses to illustrate and make plausible his line of argument, must be understood. But at the core of the matter is the possibility of a religious interpretation of the world, the reflexive basic structures of which the text elaborates.

In the background of *The Courage to Be*, fundamental elements of the interpretation of modernity can be recognized—albeit in the changed terminology of the late work—that can already be encountered in the draft *Rechtfertigung und Zweifel* from 1919. This concerns, first of all, the understanding of modernity as a critique of itself, that is, doubt or critical subjectivity. This must be included, as was the demand thirty-three years earlier, in the justification of a theological principle. For in the modern age, the age of anxiety, we are aware that every norm and every truth, and thus also every idea of God, owes itself to a human positing that can be taken back again. In *The Courage to Be*, as in the early German work, doubt stands for this.[40] And now, as then, doubt cannot be overcome, but must be taken up in theology.[41] What does this mean for the understanding of God as summarized in the 1952 writing through the formula of the God above God?

Tillich discusses his understanding of God in the sixth and concluding section, *Courage and Transcendence*, of *The Courage to Be*. Already the structuring of his remarks into two parts, which turn first to the concept of faith and then to the concept of God, makes it clear that both are internally connected. Even now, faith is understood as an act of reflexivity in consciousness and, as it were, as an affirmation of the absolute paradox.[42] Faith is bound to a divine revelation, to the breakthrough of the unconditioned into the conditioned, that is, to the disclosedness of the basic structure of consciousness in the individual consciousness. The unconditioned is given only in the act of reflection, which Tillich calls faith, namely as negation of the determined consciousness. The certainty of faith consists

---

[40] Cf. Tillich, *The Courage to Be*, 102–3.

[41] Cf. Tillich, *The Courage to Be*, 161: "The answer must accept, as its precondition, the state of meaninglessness. It is not an answer if it demands the removal of this state; for that is just what cannot be done."

[42] Cf. Tillich, *The Courage to Be*, 162: "The paradox of every radical negativity, as long as it is an active negativity, is that it must affirm itself in order to be able to negate itself."

in this self-transparency. Therefore, similar to 1919, the doubt about the concrete contents of consciousness does not cancel the standing in truth. For faith as an act of reflection, described by Tillich as an attitude and state, has no "special content."[43] Rather, faith is determined solely by its intention, i.e., the disclosedness of the unconditioned in consciousness.[44] The transparency of consciousness is not a content, but rather the negation of all contentual determinations posited by consciousness.

It is therefore clear that what Tillich describes with the idea of absolute faith in *The Courage to Be* is the reflexive structure of the act of faith, which is determined solely by its intention and is possible in all contents of consciousness. This reflexive structure of the act of faith is clarified in the 1952 writing in discussion of two misforms of the religious disclosedness of religious consciousness, which Tillich calls mysticism and Protestantism. Therefore, the construction of the history of religion from the early *Religionsphilosophie* is taken up. The latter distinguished sacramentalism and theocracy as ways of historical self-apprehension and the representation of religion in contrast to culture. In *The Courage to Be*, Tillich reformulates this difference along the lines of the polarity of participation and individuation. Absolute faith, however, as well as the God above God corresponding to it, are not simply a union of mysticism and Protestantism. Rather, both are fundamentally false religious self-apprehensions and un-theological in the sense of the divine (foundational) revelation. For mysticism denies the form, that is, the contentual determinations of consciousness, but it leaves the difference of a given God and human beings and devalues the form.[45] Protestantism, on the other hand, discussed as a personal relation to God, appears in Tillich's remarks as a theocratic critique and as an isolated revelation of salvation. Such a theology, and this was already the critique in the early writings, ties the soteriological God-relationship to the revelation of God, but it assumes a God

---

[43] Tillich, *The Courage to Be*, 162.

[44] Cf. Tillich, *The Courage to Be*, 162–3: "It is simply faith, undirected, absolute. It is undefinable, since everything is dissolved by doubt and meaninglessness."

[45] Cf. Tillich, *The Courage to Be*, 163–4: "Certainly mysticism also transcends all specific contents, but not because it doubts them or has to find them meaningless; rather it deems to be preliminary. Mysticism uses the specific contents as grades, stepping on them after having used them."

who exists, as it were, before his revelation.[46] In both forms, which Tillich contrasts, the event of disclosedness in consciousness and its representation in consciousness contradict each other. God, who is bound to the act of faith or its revelation, is, as it were, placed next to this performative act as its presupposition. But every such presupposition, since it is conscious as one posited by consciousness, stands under the doubt and sinks into it.

Absolute faith as well as the "God above God" corresponding to it leads beyond these two false forms solely because it represents the reflexive structure of the act of faith to which it is related as its image. The content of the thought of God is the inner connection of act and representation in consciousness as the object of consciousness. Exactly this reflexive structure represents the God above God, the disclosedness of consciousness bound to its act, which can appear in consciousness only as negation of the functions of consciousness.

In *The Courage to Be*, Tillich describes the reflexive structure of the foundational revelation under the conditions of modernity as the absolute faith as well as the God above God. In this modernity, every concrete way of salvation is under doubt, since its relativity has become transparent.[47] Tillich counters this with the possibility of a knowledge of God that is possible everywhere in the world and thus also outside of religions and their concrete paths of salvation. For every revelation of God is itself already salvation, even if—which *The Courage to Be* only hints at—the disclosedness of God in consciousness comes to completion only in the final (salvation) revelation, that is, a revelation that has become reflexive.[48] Also

---

[46] Cf. Tillich, *The Courage to Be*, 164: "The theologians who speak so strongly and with such self-certainty about the divine-human encounter should be aware of a situation in which this encounter is prevented by radical doubt and nothing is left but absolute faith."

[47] This is already the theme of *Rechtfertigung und Zweifel* of 1919. It is taken up again by Tillich in the dogmatics lecture of the 1920s. Cf. Tillich, "Dogmatik-Vorlesung," 40–1: "It comes to the paradoxical situation that standing beyond a concrete revelation of salvation is addressed by the foundational revelation itself as salvific, that from not being able to go a way of salvation itself becomes a way of salvation."

[48] Cf. Tillich, *The Courage to Be*, 173: "It is the Church under the Cross which alone can do this, the Church which preaches the Crucified who cried to God who remained his God after the God of confidence had left him in darkness

in the writing of 1952, the act of the breakthrough of revelation remains undetermined as already in *Rechtfertigung und Zweifel*. The disclosedness of consciousness, that is, the transition from cultural consciousness and its self-criticism to the intention (*Meinen*) of the unconditioned, is not a determined act in consciousness, but this disclosedness presents itself solely as negation of the functions of consciousness.[49]

If one examines Tillich's understanding of God from the perspective of the history of the work, as done in this chapter, then one must see a high degree of continuity. This becomes clear not only in the leading concepts of his doctrine of God, such as God above God, but above all in the systematic construction of the idea of God. Since 1919 at the latest, the idea of God describes and structures the reflexive structure in which religion emerges and exists as an interpretation of the world.

---

of doubt and meaninglessness." On the relationship between the foundational revelation and salvation revelation, cf. chapter V.4 above.

[49] Cf. Tillich, *The Courage to Be*, 173: "Absolute faith, or the state of being grasped by God beyond God, is not a state which appears beside other states of the mind. It never is something separate and definite, an event which could be isolated and described. It is always a movement in, with, and under other states of the mind."

VII.

The Christian Event as Fact and Reception: Paul Tillich's Christology

In his magnum opus *Systematic Theology*, Paul Tillich starts his considerations on Jesus as the Christ with remarks about the Christian event as fact and reception. He writes: "For the event on which Christianity is based has two sides: the fact which is called 'Jesus of Nazareth' and the reception of this fact by those who received him as the Christ." (ST II, 97) The Christian event is neither the sole fact of Jesus of Nazareth, nor the sole reception of Jesus by his followers, but rather both are aspects of this same event. With his thesis, Tillich rejects both the historical Jesus and the so-called *kerygma* as the starting point of Christology.[1] Christology deals neither solely with Jesus of Nazareth, nor just simply with the interpretation given to him by his followers. The Christian faith is always both fact and reception. Tillich's meaning is clear if we take into account the methodological construction of his *Systematic Theology*, namely the so-called theological circle,[2] and also the development of his theological thinking from his early years. Tillich's late major work—its structure and its methodological foundation—can be understood only against the background of the development of his understanding of theology. So it is not surprising if we find the main structure of the *Systematic Theology* already in his 1913 draft

---

[1] The first is the starting point of Adolf von Harnack's Christology and the second is the starting point of Rudolf Bultmann. Cf. Adolf von Harnack, *Das Wesen des Christentums*, ed. Claus-Dieter Osthövener (3rd. ed. Tübingen: Mohr Siebeck, 2012); Rudolf Bultmann, *Jesus* (Tübingen: Mohr Siebeck, 1964). Cf. Christian Danz, "Der erinnerte Christus. Überlegungen zur Christologie," in *Jesus Christus – Alpha und Omega. Festschrift für Helmut Hoping*, ed. Jan-Heiner Tück and Magnus Striet (Freiburg i.Br.: Herder, 2021), 286–305.

[2] Cf. Tillich, *Systematic Theology*, vol. I, 8–11.

of a *Systematische Theologie*.[3] Like in his later work, Tillich structured the conception of the *Systematische Theologie* from 1913 in three parts, namely: intuition, reflection, and the theological standpoint.[4] In the 1920s, Tillich associated this structure with the distinction between foundational revelation and salvation revelation, which, as discussed in chapter five, he further developed during the 1930s into the interrelation of question and answer. The late *Systematic Theology* takes up the early tripartite division in the distinction of essence, existence, and life and combines it with the method of correlation.[5] Tillich's Christology and his theological circle-structure must be understood against this background. Behind this stands his conviction that the task of theology is not to give a foundation of the Christian faith, but rather to give an explanation and interpretation of the Christian message.[6] And this interpretation always has its place in the theological circle.

It is exactly this, namely the circular structure of theological thinking, that we do not find alone in the *Systematic Theology*, but also just as well in Tillich's writings before the First World War. It is also in these pre-World War writings where he denies the possibility of giving a foundation for the Christian faith through the historical Jesus. Christian certainty, as Tillich wrote in his 128 theses *Die christliche Gewißheit und der historische Jesus* from 1911, is not based on the historical Jesus.[7] Against the background of the theological debates around 1900 on the one hand, and the historical Jesus research on the other, the young Tillich works out his own understanding of Christology. As a result of these debates, he does not understand the task of Christology as a theological description of the historical Jesus. Rather, Christology has a reflexive function. This means that Christology is a description of the performative act of faith and not a description of a historical person. Jesus Christ is an image of the Christian faith from itself as an act that happens in history. In his dogmatics lectures held in

---

[3] Cf. Tillich, "Systematische Theologie von 1913," 278–434.

[4] Cf. Wittekind, "Allein durch Glauben," 39–65; Stefan Dienstbeck, *Transzendentale Strukturtheorie. Stadien der Systembildung Paul Tillichs* (Göttingen: Vandenhoeck & Ruprecht, 2011).

[5] Cf. Tillich, *Systematic Theology*, vol. I, 66–7.

[6] Cf. Tillich, *Systematic Theology*, vol. I, 10.

[7] Cf. Tillich, "Die christliche Gewißheit und der historische Jesus," 31–50. Cf. Neugebauer, *Tillichs frühe Christologie*, 192–227.

Marburg and Dresden during the 1920s, as well in his later *Systematic Theology*, Tillich calls this the "real picture" (ST II, 115).[8] But how does Jesus function for Tillich's Christology, and how is his Christology constructed? Is his Christology a Christology without Jesus?[9] And what exactly is the function of Tillich's doctrine of Christ in his *Systematic Theology*?

As has been my method in the previous sections, an answer to these questions is only possible if we look at the development of Tillich's Christology in his entire work. Against the history of his work, we can see that Tillich is elaborating a doctrine of the Christ that takes up the horizon of the problems of Christology under the conditions of modernity. More than this, he works out Christology as a theological description of the act of faith. Jesus represents—in and for faith at the same time—the reflexive structure of the act of faith and its event-character. Both aspects are also important for the contemporary Christological debates against the background of the so-called "third quest" for the historical Jesus research and global religious pluralism. This is the theme of this chapter. After the discussion in the previous chapter on the dimension of the understanding of revelation in connection with the doctrine of God, which Tillich calls creation, the task now is to discuss the doctrine of redemption in connection with Christology. It, too, forms an element of the tripartite structure of revelation. In the first part of the following considerations, we must examine the development of Tillich's Christology from the early writings until his late *Systematic Theology*. Against this background, the second part will discuss the Christology of Tillich's dogmatics. Finally, we will show the significance of his doctrine of the Christ for the Christological debates of our time.

1. The Historical Jesus and the Christian Faith; or, The Development of Tillich's Christology

In 1911, the young Tillich discussed with friends his 128 theses about *Die christliche Gewißheit und der historische Jesus*. Later, in his autobiographical sketch *On the Boundary*, he calls these theses not only very important for

---

[8] Cf. Tillich, "Dogmatik-Vorlesung," 339.

[9] Cf. Gunther Wenz, "Theologie ohne Jesus? Anmerkungen zu Paul Tillich," in *Kerygma und Dogma* 26 (1980) 128–139.

his theological development but also considers them to be radical.[10] What is the reason for this statement? In his theses from 1911, Tillich claims that the certainty of the Christian faith is independent from the historical Jesus. We find this position also in Tillich's philosophical dissertation from 1910 with the title *Die religionsgeschichtliche Konstruktion in Schellings positive Philosophie*. Here he criticizes Schelling's attempt to connect the revelation of God in Christ with empirical history.[11] For it is only a matter of intuition (*Anschauung*) in which empirical history consists for the inner history of self-consciousness, and Christian faith as well. What are the foundations and systematic basis for Tillich's position?

In the background of Tillich's 128 theses from 1911 there is, on the one hand, the contemporary historical Jesus research which leads to a difference between the historical Jesus and Christianity. Especially Johannes Weiss and other theologians from the so-called History of Religion School (*religionsgeschichtliche Schule*), like William Wrede, for example, had all shown that Jesus of Nazareth must be understood in the apocalyptic horizon of the ancient Judaism.[12] Albert Schweitzer in his famous book about the history of Jesus research from 1906 had taken up this result from historical debates of his time and declared that the historical Jesus plays no role for the Christian religion.[13] The result for the theological debates is a dissolution of the historical Jesus from Christology. Christology does not start with the Jesus of history, but rather with the Christian religion which refers itself back to Jesus—but let me explain what I mean by this. We find such a construction of Christology both by Ernst Troeltsch[14] and by the young Tillich. This is one dimension in the background of Tillich's 128

---

[10] Cf. Tillich, "On the Boundary," 33–34. Cf. Neugebauer, *Tillichs frühe Christologie*, 192–227.

[11] Cf. Tillich, "Die religionsgeschichtliche Konstruktion in Schellings positive Philosophie," 272. Cf. Neugebauer, *Tillichs frühe Christologie*, 175–189.

[12] Cf. Johannes Weiss, *Die Predigt Jesu vom Reiche Gottes* (Göttingen: Vandenhoeck & Ruprecht, 1892); William Wrede, *Das Messiasgeheimnis in den Evangelien. Zugleich ein Beitrag zum Verständnis des Markusevangeliums* (Göttingen: Vandenhoeck & Ruprecht, 1901).

[13] Cf. Albert Schweitzer, *Geschichte der Leben-Jesu-Forschung*, vol. 2 (Hamburg; München: Siebenstern, 1966), 620–630.

[14] Cf. Johann H. Claussen, *Die Jesus-Deutung von Ernst Troeltsch im Kontext der liberalen Theologie* (Tübingen: Mohr Siebeck, 1997).

theses.[15] On the other hand, there is the framework in which Tillich's Christology is understood as a conception of a speculative theology. Following Fichte and Schelling, the foundation of the theological system is for Tillich—as stated in the second chapter—the absolute truth or the absolute identity. The main principle is *spirit* that is characterized through a relation to itself. Tillich calls this principle the identity of self-consciousness, which is at the same time the principle of certainty and autonomy.[16] It is important to see that this principle means an identity of the universal and the concrete. This is the structure of the absolute spirit or the absolute truth. The concrete is true insofar and only insofar as it is a representation of the universal. If the concrete exists for itself as concrete, then the concrete stands in contradiction to the absolute truth.[17]

Against the mentioned background, Tillich constructs not only his theology and philosophy of history but also his Christology. The concrete is a medium that represents the absolute. In this sense, Jesus Christ is an image that is produced from the spirit, namely the relation between the universal and the concrete. "The autonomous version of the Christological problem has to replace the two-nature-doctrine through a doctrine about the relation between the absolute and the concrete spirit that must be viewed in Christ and realized through him." (EW VI, 45) Tillich identifies the dialectical structure of the absolute spirit and its realization in history with Jesus Christ. Only in this way does Jesus play a role in Christology— namely, as an image of the relationship between absolute and individual spirit. Certainty is the individual spirit which knows itself as the realization of the absolute spirit. But the localization of this event in history remains doubtful.[18]

In Tillich's early Christology, which we find in the 128 theses from 1911, Jesus Christ is an image of faith from itself, as an identity between

---

[15] Cf. Tillich, "Die christliche Gewißheit und der historische Jesus," 32–34 (*A. Critique of the historical evidence*).

[16] Cf. Tillich, "Die christliche Gewißheit und der historische Jesus," 43 (thesis 102): "If the proposition 'I equals I' or the identity of self-consciousness is the principle of certainty, there is no principle of cognition above the autonomy of the self-positing I [*sich selbst setzenden Ich*]."

[17] Cf. Tillich, "Die christliche Gewißheit und der historische Jesus," 41 (thesis 87).

[18] Cf. Tillich, "Die christliche Gewißheit und der historische Jesus," 42–3 (thesis 100).

the absolute and the concrete spirit. The foundation of Christian certainty is faith in this sense, and not the historical Jesus. Jesus is an element of the Christian faith: he is an image of faith, but this image of faith is produced by consciousness, or the spirit.

During and after World War One, Tillich transformed his early theology as well as his Christology, which was built within the horizon of the speculative construction of absolute truth and identity. Absoluteness is no longer a subordinate frame of the construction of history, but rather absoluteness is a part or an element of the act of self-disclosedness of the concrete existence. In his writings after the War, Tillich calls this breakthrough a metaphorical description of the revelation of God. Instead of the absolute, Tillich speaks now of the unconditioned. Religion is a performative act in human consciousness.[19] What happens in religion is that consciousness becomes aware that the unconditioned is the presupposition of all acts of consciousness. But this presupposition is not a content as such, because the unconditioned is the condition of all contents. On the one hand, this structure must be disclosed for an individual; that is to say, it is always an act of revelation—otherwise knowledge of God is not possible. On the other hand, insofar as one can talk about this breakthrough, namely the disclosedness of the unconditioned as a presupposition of all acts of consciousness, this is only possible by using cultural forms, which must at the same time be negated. Every concept of God is a human production and, therefore, both necessary and totally wrong.[20] This understanding of revelation leads also to important transformations of Tillich's Christology. The latter is now understood as a symbolic description of the reflexive structure of the religious performative act, and within another aspect, it is connected with soteriology.[21] What remains is that the doctrine of Jesus as the Christ does not start with the historical Jesus. The historical Jesus is not the foundation of the Christian faith. In contrast, Jesus as the Christ is a structural description of the faith event as a personal act in the present. This shows that Tillich's Christology describes the appropriation of faith by the individual as an act in history. Jesus the Christ is thus a

---

[19] Cf. above chapter III.3.

[20] Cf. Tillich, "Die Überwindung des Religionsbegriffs in der Religionsphilosophie," 381. Cf. above chapter VI.

[21] Cf. Wittekind, "Allein durch Glauben," 46–52.

symbolic description of the act of appropriation. In the religion of para-dox—of which Christ is the image—the content of religious consciousness is the connection between religious act and the representation of this act in consciousness. Only by representing this connection in the religious consciousness does consciousness become transparent, true, and whole.

Tillich's Christology is elaborated in the lectures on dogmatics that he gave at the University of Marburg and Dresden between 1925 and 1927. In this series, he develops a reflexive version of Christology. Clearly, the starting point is not the historical Jesus. Like in the Christological considerations before the First World War, and in the time shortly after the war, Jesus is a part or an element within the Christian faith and not a foundation of the faith, which is given independently of the faith.[22] If Christology explains the structure of the performative act of faith, then Christology must begin with the act of faith as the breakthrough of the unconditioned in the human consciousness. Since 1924, Tillich calls this salvation revelation, as differentiated from foundational revelation.[23] The latter is the disclosedness in human consciousness that the unconditioned is the presupposition of all acts of the consciousness. This general revela-tion is the condition of the salvation revelation but at the same time is always ambiguous.[24] Furthermore, the general, or the foundational, reve-lation is a part of the theological circle, namely a moment in the structural description of the Christian faith. Having this in mind, it becomes clear that Tillich goes out from the conviction that the foundational revelation has a teleological orientation to the salvation revelation.

The starting point of Tillich's Christology in his dogmatics lectures in the 1920s is neither the historical Jesus nor the faith of his followers, but rather the image of Jesus as the Christ.[25] That means an interrelation from both aspects. Already here the image of Jesus as the Christ is a "real

---

[22] Cf. Tillich, "Dogmatik-Vorlesung," 328: "The decision about the Chris-tological judgement strikes on the dogmatic level, i.e., in the sphere of faith inde-pendent [!] from the historical knowledge."

[23] To this differentiation, cf. Tillich, "Rechtfertigung und Zweifel," GW VIII, 85–100. Cf. above chapter V.4.

[24] Tillich takes this up in the *Systematic Theology* in his conception of the ambiguity of life. Cf. Paul Tillich, *Systematic Theology*, vol. III (Chicago: The Uni-versity of Chicago Press, 1963). Cf. below chapter VIII.

[25] Cf. Tillich, "Dogmatik-Vorlesung," 332–335.

picture" of the structure of the performative act of faith.[26] But what does this image symbolize? Nothing other than the reflexive structure of the religious act, as previously mentioned. Christology describes the salvation revelation. In this act, consciousness becomes aware that the representation of the disclosedness of consciousness is on the one hand necessary and on the other hand not representable. Only this reflexive structure is the content of the image of Christ that is focused on the cross. The image of Christ is an expression of the reflexive structure of the religious act or the performative act of faith. This act depends always on a concrete history because it is an act in history and therefore a concretely determined act. The breakthrough of the unconditioned in consciousness is only possible as negation of the concrete determinations of consciousness. Consequently, faith can only be realized in the dialectic of critique and formation in history.[27] The content of salvation revelation is the foundational revelation and, therefore, the negation of the content within consciousness which represents the foundational revelation in consciousness. Exactly this dialectic of critique and formation in history represents the image of the Christ in and for the Christian faith.[28]

In 1936, Tillich gave his first dogmatics lectures in New York entitled *Advanced Problems in Systematic Theology*. What is new in these lectures is not the construction of Christology as such. In his dogmatics from the 1930s Tillich also does not deal with the historical Jesus in his Christology.[29] Rather, Jesus as the Christ is an image produced from faith which is not dependent upon the historical Jesus.[30] As in his German dogmatics, Tillich connects the explication of Christology with the performative act of faith and the doctrine of man, or anthropology. So it remains that Christology is an explanation of the reflexive structure of faith. What is

---

[26] Cf. Tillich, "Dogmatik-Vorlesung," 339.

[27] Cf. Danz, "Critique and Formation. Paul Tillich's Interpretation of Protestantism," 237–244.

[28] Tillich offers a short summary of his Christology in the 1920s in his article *Christologie und Geschichtsdeutung* from 1930. Cf. Paul Tillich, "Christologie und Geschichtsdeutung," in GW VI, 83–96.

[29] Cf. Paul Tillich, "The Significance of the Historical Jesus for the Christian Faith," in EW XIX, 317–321.

[30] Cf. Tillich, "The Significance of the Historical Jesus for the Christian Faith," 319: "The content of our faith is a picture which is created by faith—namely, the picture of Jesus given in the whole New Testament."

new in the dogmatics courses given at Union Theological Seminary is two things: first, the transference of the distinction between foundational revelation and salvation revelation to the interrelation of question and answer; and second, that compared to the German dogmatics lecture, there has been a shift toward a more general structure of the human condition.[31] This becomes clear against the background of Tillich's early lectures in exile about the doctrine of man.[32] We also find here a focus on general structures of human beings in an existentialist manner. One can say that the Christological conception in the dogmatics courses from New York is an intermediate stage on the way to the Christology of the *Systematic Theology*.[33]

2. The Christology of the *Systematic Theology*

As we have seen, the task of Christology for Tillich is not to give a description of the historical Jesus. The man from Nazareth is not the founder or the foundation of the Christian religion. Rather, he is an element in—and a part of—the Christian faith. This is exactly the content of Tillich's formula in the *Systematic Theology*: that the Christian event is both "a historical fact and a subject of believing reception" (ST II, 98). This structure we find also in his Christology in the time before the First World War, but also in the dogmatics lectures in Germany in the 1920s and in New York in the 1930s. The starting point for the Christological construction in the *Systematic Theology* is that the Christian faith is an event in history and theology has the task of explaining this faith. We must now deal with the construction of Tillich's Christology in his magnum opus. First, we must explain the interrelation between fact and reception in the Christian event; second, we must consider the function of the historical Jesus for the Christian faith; and finally, we must elucidate the function of Christology as an expression of the reflexive structure of the performative act of faith.

---

[31] Cf. Tillich, "Advanced Problems in Systematic Theology," 115: "The method of our lecture is to show the correlation of the theological concepts with anthropological concepts. [...] Christology in correlation to the doctrine of man."

[32] Cf. Paul Tillich, "Frühe Vorlesungen im Exil (1934–1935)," in EW XVII.

[33] Cf. also Paul Tillich, *Existential Questions and Theological Answers. First Series: Existence and the Christ. Syllabus of Gifford Lectures 1953* (University of Aberdeen, 1953).

First: One does not obtain a correct understanding of Tillich's differentiation between the fact of the Christian event and the believing reception of this fact if, for example, the fact is understood as a presupposition. The fact of the Christian event and the believing reception of this fact are not two separate parts. Indeed, there are some phrases from Tillich that sound as if he meant a historical assumption,[34] but this is not correct. As we have seen in our overview of the development of his Christology, this is not Tillich's position. The historical fact as one aspect in the Christian event is not a presupposition of faith, rather the historical fact is a presupposition which only exists in the act of faith, with the believing reception consisting not of a separated element. The Christian event, namely the act of faith, is both fact and reception. Tillich constructs his Christology as an expression of the act of faith and this means an act of appropriation. For him, faith is a personal act. The personal dimension, i.e., that it must be performed by a human being, is represented by Jesus as the image of faith. But this act is always an act bound to the history of revelation. Its basis is the distinction between foundational revelation and salvation revelation. This means, for the image of Christ, that it describes the transition from foundational revelation to salvation revelation. Tillich's differentiation between fact and reception exemplifies this structure of the faith.

Tillich's formula of the Christian event as fact and reception is not a historical thesis but rather a systematic thesis about the beginning of Christianity. The Christian religion begins neither with Jesus (Adolf von Harnack) nor with the *kerygma* of the early Christians (Rudolf Bultmann).[35] It starts with an interrelation between Jesus and his followers, or—as we can call it within the contemporary terminology that is used in historical research—with the "remembered Jesus."[36] With the interrelation between both *factum and reception*, Tillich exemplifies the structure of faith

---

[34] Cf. Tillich, *Systematic Theology*, vol. II, 98: "If theology ignores the fact to which the name of Jesus of Nazareth points, it ignores the basic Christian assertion that Essential God-Manhood has appeared within existence and subjected itself to the conditions of existence without being conquered by them."

[35] Cf. Tillich, *Systematic Theology*, vol. II, 97: "Christianity was born, not with the birth of the man who is called 'Jesus,' but in the moment in which one of his followers was driven to say to him, 'Thou are the Christ.'"

[36] Cf. James D. G. Dunn, "Remembering Jesus. How the Quest of the Historical Jesus Lost Its Way," in *The Historical Jesus. Five Views*, ed. James K. Beilby and Paul Rodes Eddy (Downers Grove: IVP Press, 2009), 199–225.

as an act, which is bound to a concrete history. Jesus means here an image produced by faith to describe itself as a personal act of the disclosedness in the self-relation of the consciousness. Without this act, no faith is possible, and at the same time this act produces an image from itself. Christianity is what it is only through this act, namely the individual appropriation of the remembered Jesus as an image of the act of faith. This reception is an act of interpretation and new creation. In this way, there arises the continuity of the Christian religion in history. Consequently, the Christian religion would end when the reception of Jesus as the Christ ceases.[37]

Second: Tillich clearly distinguishes in his *Systematic Theology* two meanings of the concept of the historical Jesus. On the one hand, the term "historical Jesus" is defined as the result of historical research. Historical knowledge is not simply a contemporary construction, it is also always "fragmentary and hypothetical" (ST II, 107).[38] In this sense, the term "historical Jesus" is a methodological construct. Yet, there is another meaning of the term "historical Jesus" that differs from this conceptual usage. Here the term is used as "the factual element in the Christian event" (ibid.). And this is, as we have seen, very different from the first sense used in the historical research. As an element of the interrelation in which the Christian faith is composed, the term "historical Jesus" does not mean the man from Nazareth behind the sources of the New Testament. Rather, the term refers to the personal act in which faith consists, and which occurs in history. Tillich's distinction between the two meanings of the "historical Jesus" is very helpful for the Christological debates. Historical research is important for an understanding of the history of the Christian religion, its sources, and their relation to the ancient Judaism, but the historical research itself gives us no foundation for the Christian faith. The question of both historical research and Christology are not identical but are rather two independent questions that cannot be collapsed together into homogeneity. The image of faith from its own history is, so we can say, not only different from the historical image of the history, but also the image of faith is, to a

---

[37] Cf. Tillich, *Systematic Theology*, vol. II, 100: "Corresponding to this beginning, the end is the moment in which the continuity of that history in which Jesus as the Christ is the center is definitely broken."

[38] Cf. Tillich, "The Significance of the Historical Jesus for the Christian Faith," 317.

certain extent, independent from history. Undoubtedly, there are interrelations between both dimensions, but as Tillich says, faith "cannot even guarantee the name 'Jesus' in respect to him who was the Christ" (ST II, 107).

What follows from this is that faith has its own foundation not in the historical Jesus as a result of historical research, but in a historical event. This is only momentarily a paradox, because the historical event means that faith arises without historical foundations in history. Faith, and this is Tillich's thesis, has its foundation and its worth in itself. "And the inevitable answer is that faith can guarantee only its own foundation, namely, the appearance of that reality which has created the faith." (ST II, 114) There is no ground or principle through which one can give a justification of faith as a personal act which has happened in history. But does that not mean that faith is its own creator and, in this sense, consequently, only another name for sin?[39] That is not the case, because all foundations of faith are only possible through a construction that puts the theological circle as a justification of this circle. All justifications of the Christian religion are circular. So the task of theology is not to give reasons for faith, but rather to explicate the theological circle. Only in the happening, or in the event of faith, lies the justification of faith, for Christology gives no reason for faith. Against this background, the doctrine of Jesus as the Christ is not a content of faith; rather, Christology has a reflexive function for faith, namely, to give a description of the structure of the act which faith is. This is what is meant when Tillich called Jesus as the Christ the "real picture" of faith in his earlier writings.

Third: Like in his writings after the First World War, Tillich connects his Christology with Soteriology in the *Systematic Theology*.[40] This is not really surprising because the Christology is an expression of the act of faith that is at the same time salvation. Tillich called this salvation revelation in his dogmatics of the 1920s, and final revelation in the *Systematic Theology*. But what exactly does Christology express if it is a description of

---

[39] With this argument, Wolfhart Pannenberg criticizes such a construction of the Christian faith. Cf. Wolfhart Pannenberg, *Systematische Theologie*, vol. III (Göttingen: Vandenhoeck & Ruprecht, 1993), 175.

[40] Cf. Tillich, *Systematic Theology*, vol. II, 150: "Christology is a function of soteriology. The problem of soteriology creates the christological question and gives direction to the christological answer."

the act of faith? Since the late 1920s, Tillich names the reality of faith the "New Being."[41] Faith, or the "New Being" in history, is a happening in the human consciousness which finds its representation in the image of Jesus as the Christ. In this event, consciousness becomes aware of the fact that the unconditioned, as ground and abyss, is the presupposition of all acts of human consciousness—but exactly this performative act is, at the same time, the content of consciousness. The position and the negation of forms creates the content of the image of Jesus as the Christ. He represents a concrete personal life that negates his own life. Only in this act is Jesus *the* Christ, or the final revelation.[42] In this manner, Jesus as the Christ is an image of faith and the reflexive structure of the act of faith. The content of the true religion is the reflexive structure of the act of faith itself, namely, the negation of the concrete contents of consciousness. This is exactly what Tillich calls final revelation or salvation revelation, because in it there is the conquering of both demonization and profanation of religion.

Christology describes the reflexive structure of the act of faith, or the New Being. Therefore, Tillich focused his Christology on the cross and the resurrection of the Christ.[43] Cross and resurrection are on both sides of the act of faith, namely, the negation of form and the affirmation of form. In this dialectic of critique and formation (*Gestaltung*), which constitutes the act of faith as a reflexive revelation-consciousness in the disclosedness of the unconditioned, lies the realization of the true religion in history. In short, Jesus as the Christ is the real image of faith. Also in the *Systematic Theology*, Christology has a reflexive function and does not deal with a historical content or person. Rather, the doctrine of Jesus as the Christ is a theological description of the act of faith as a happening in history. To this extent, Christology has a reflexive function of a critique of religion within religion.

---

[41] Cf. Paul Tillich, "Die Gestalt der religiösen Erkenntnis," in EW XIV, 395–431, here 428–9.

[42] Cf. Tillich, *Systematic Theology*, vol. I, 134: "Jesus is the religious and theological object as the Christ and only as the Christ. And he is the Christ as the one who sacrifices what is merely 'Jesus' in him. The decisive trait in his picture is the continuous self-surrender of Jesus who is Jesus to Jesus who is the Christ."

[43] Cf. Tillich, *Systematic Theology*, vol. II, 150–165. Cf. Danz, *Religion als Freiheitsbewußtsein*, 218–272.

3. The Significance of Tillich's Christology for the Twenty-first-century Christological Debates

Paul Tillich works out his Christology as a theological description of the act of faith. Christology does not deal with the historical Jesus or the *kerygma* of the early Christians. The historical context of the problems taken up by Tillich's doctrine of the Christ are the debates in the first half of the twentieth century, especially the historical Jesus research on the one hand, and the Christological debates in Protestant theology on the other hand. In this respect, one can say that Tillich's Christology is a child of his own time. But what is the significant importance of Tillich's Christology that must be considered for twenty-first-century debates? There are two aspects of his Christological conception that are significant for a Christology in our time: the first is his starting point with the theological circle, and the second is what follows from this regarding the debates about a theology of religions. But both aspects mentioned, in contrast to Tillich, must be reformulated based on another understanding of religion. Tillich starts from a conception of religion as a breakthrough of the unconditioned in the human consciousness, whereby the unconditioned is already given in consciousness. Religion is, as explained in the first part of this book, directedness towards the unconditioned. In the interest of the generality of religion, the disclosedness of the basic dimension of consciousness, i.e., the unconditioned, is itself indeterminate. But this is a construction of a presupposition that is today not plausible in the least. In contrast to Tillich, a general concept of religion must be rejected and the construction of the concept of religion must be limited to Christianity.[44] Religion is also not an essential part of the human being, as Tillich presupposes. Rather, religion is a special form of communication in culture, which, as such, is not necessary for being human. Religion arises contingently in history and underlies an evolution in culture. So religion is a form of interpretation of the world in symbolic forms and the knowledge of religion must be a part of religion. There is no unconscious religion. Such an understanding of religion is a postulate that finds no plausibility in a pluralistic world. Based

---

[44] Cf. Christian Danz, *Gottes Geist. Eine Pneumatologie* (Tübingen: Mohr Siebeck, 2019); "Religious Diversity and the Concept of Religion. Theology and Religious Pluralism," in *Neue Zeitschrift für Systematische Theologie* 62 (2020) 101–113.

on this new understanding of religion as communication, it is possible to take up Tillich's Christology. At first, however, we must deal with his formula that the Christian event is both fact and reception, and then with the implications of this formula for a theology of religions.

Tillich presupposes in his Christology the historical Jesus research from the first half of the twentieth century. In this time, the historical research stands in the shadow of the so-called "form-history," and the general opinion is that there is no certain knowledge about the historical Jesus.[45] The further development in historical research, especially in the so-called third quest since the 1980s, leads in the end to a methodological change. On the one hand, it becomes clear that the historical Jesus is a methodological construct of historical science, and on the other hand that it is not possible to go behind the sources in a methodological way. Against this development, the historical Jesus behind the sources is no longer the aim of historical research, rather the remembered Jesus *in* the sources.[46] Memory is always a construction of the past and not merely a photographic record.[47] For the historical research on Jesus, this means that we can only find the interrelation between Jesus and his followers, i.e., the remembered Jesus, but not a Jesus for himself.[48]

---

[45] Cf. the overview about the historical Jesus research by Paul Rhodes Eddy and James K. Belby, "The Quest for the Historical Jesus: An Introduction," in *The Historical Jesus. Five Views*, ed. James K. Belby and Paul Rhodes Eddy (Downers Grove: IVP Press, 2009), 9–54; Christian Danz, *Grundprobleme der Christologie* (Tübingen: Mohr Siebeck, 2013), 13–54

[46] So, for example, James D. G. Dunn, and the New Testament scholar Jens Schröter in Germany.

[47] Cf. Jan Assmann, *Das kulturelle Gedächtnis. Schrift, Erinnerung und politische Identität in den frühen Hochkulturen* (7th. ed. München: C. H. Beck, 2013); Paul Ricœur, *Gedächtnis, Geschichte, Vergessen* (München: Wilhelm Fink, 2004).

[48] Cf. Dunn, "Remembering Jesus," 203: "The fact that Jesus made disciples is generally recognized. What has not been given sufficient recognition or weight, however, is the effect of his impact. These disciples encountered Jesus as a life-transforming experience: they followed him; [...] Why? Because they had believed Jesus and what he said and taught." Cf. Jens Schröter, "Der erinnerte Jesus als Begründer des Christentums? Bemerkungen zu James D. G. Dunns Ansatz in der Jesusforschung," in *ZNT* 20 (2007) 47–53.

As we have seen above, Tillich starts his Christology, not unlike the so-called third quest, with an interrelation between fact and believing reception. Christology deals neither with a historical Jesus that stands behind the interpretations of his followers, nor simply with these interpretations alone. Historical Jesus research is different from the task of Christology. The first deals with history, while the second deals with the actual Christian faith and explains its structure. For this reason, and as previously mentioned, Tillich distinguishes two meanings of the term "historical Jesus." In addition, for Tillich, the historical Jesus as a historical question is a construct of science, but as such is not the basis or foundation of the Christian faith. The historical Jesus as an element of faith must be understood quite differently. Jesus exists as the Christ only in and for the act of faith. So, it is not simply the remembered Jesus that constitutes faith, but solely the religious *use* of the memory of Jesus that gives rise to the Christian religion that he represents. Therefore, Tillich's Christology is important for the contemporary debates because his conception can be connected with the historical Jesus research in the horizon of the third quest and its methodological program of the remembered Jesus. His Christology allows for a theological interpretation of the remembered Jesus of historical research.

And there is yet another aspect in Tillich's Christology that is significant for contemporary debates, namely his construction of Christology as a reflexive description of the act of faith. As we have observed, this means that Jesus is only seen as the Christ *in* and *for* the act of faith. One can say that Jesus is the origin of faith *in* the Christian religion, and is not a presupposition outside of the Christian religion. From this point of view, consequences for a theology of religions follow. In contemporary debates about the theology of religions, especially in the so-called "pluralistic theology," we find the demand for a reduction of Christology. If Jesus as the Christ is the only incarnation of God in an objective historical fact, then all other religions are false and wrong. The argument is that there is no possible recognition of other religions within the framework of a traditional Christology.[49] Therefore, the doctrine of the Christ must be reduced. Jesus Christ is like other religious heroes—an appearance of the

---

[49] Cf. Hick, *An Interpretation of Religion*; Perry Schmidt-Leukel, *Religious Pluralism & Interreligious Theology. The Gifford Lectures – An Extended Edition* (Maryknoll: Orbis Books, 2017), 26–27.

absolute Real, but neither identical with the Real nor the only one who manifests the absolute. The presupposition of the pluralistic model is a general concept of religion, which reduces religious diversity.[50] Religions are equal because they are human responses to manifestations of the same indeterminate transcendence. The pluralistic model is based on an unclear understanding of the relationship between theology and religion because this model constructs the equality of religions in the dimension of theology that is different from the self-view of the religions themselves. Such a model can neither explain how religions function nor could it recognize the distinctiveness of concrete religions. For the pluralistic model all religions are fundamentally the same, namely, the transition from "self-centeredness to Reality-centeredness."[51]

Against the pluralistic model of a theology of religions, we must explain both how religions function, and also how religions legitimately differ from each other. For this task allows us to reject a general concept of religion that assumes religion is intrinsic to being human, and at the same time to explain, on a theological level, the distinctiveness of Christianity in contrast with other religions. The peculiarity of the Christian religion lies in Christology.[52] But the doctrine of the Christ is neither a content of the Christian religion, nor is Christology related to other religions. As we have seen, Jesus as the Christ is an image of the Christian faith for Tillich. With the doctrine of the Christ, the Christian religion describes in itself its distinctiveness, namely, that the individual appropriation of God is a part or an element of the understanding of God. Christology has a function for the description of religion in Christianity, and it does not refer to a historical person. Jesus as a man of history is both a part of the ancient Jewish religion and the Christian religion.[53] However, only in the latter is he the Christ. But this is the central insight of Tillich's Christology. He opens a new perspective on the contemporary debates of Christology in the age of religious pluralism that allows, on the one hand, the recognition

---

[50] Cf. Hick, *An Interpretation of Religion*, 235–236. Cf. in detail below Chapter IX.

[51] Hick, *An Interpretation of Religion*, 240.

[52] Cf. Danz, *Grundprobleme der Christologie*, 223–240.

[53] Cf. Christian Danz, *Jesus zwischen Judentum und Christentum. Eine christologische und religionstheologische Skizze* (Tübingen: Mohr Siebeck, 2020).

of other religions as religions and, on the other hand, to explain the distinctiveness of the Christian religion. But this is only possible, however, if Tillich's own understanding of religion is itself transformed.[54]

---

[54] Cf. below chapter X.

VIII.

The Divine Spirit and the Realization of the Christian Religion in History: Reflections on Paul Tillich's Pneumatology

It is well known that the third volume of the *Systematic Theology* is dedicated (alongside eschatology) to pneumatology. Here Tillich constructs the doctrine of the divine Spirit as a theory of the realization of the Christian religion in the history of religion and of culture. "The Spiritual Presence, elevating man through faith and love to the transcendent unity of unambiguous life, creates the New Being above the gap between essence and existence and consequently above the ambiguities of life" (ST III, 138–9). With this program, Tillich follows the Protestant doctrinal tradition by making a connection between pneumatology and the realization of the Christian religion in history.[1] The Holy Spirit is the individual appropriation of the salvation in Jesus Christ. At the same time, Tillich expands the doctrine of the divine Spirit by correlating it with life in its multiple dimensions. This aspect especially—the universal presence and efficacy of the Spirit, which is not only in Christ—is broadly discussed in the research literature on Tillich's pneumatology.[2] The universal dimension of the Holy

---

[1] Cf. Albrecht Ritschl, *Unterricht in der christlichen Religion* (4th. ed. Bonn: Adolph Marcus, 1890), 42 (§ 46); Kähler, *Die Wissenschaft von der christlichen Lehre von dem evangelischen Grundartikel aus im Abrisse dargestellt*, 381. Cf. Danz, *Gottes Geist*, 40–93.

[2] Cf. Nimi Wariboko and Amos Yong (eds.), *Paul Tillich and Pentecostal Theology. Spiritual Presence and Spiritual Power* (Bloomington; Indianapolis: Indiana University Press, 2015); Keith Ka-fu Chan, *Life as Spirit. A Study of Paul Tillich's Ecological Pneumatology* (Berlin; Boston: de Gruyter, 2018). On Tillich's pneumatology, cf. also Frederick J. Parrella (ed.), *Paul Tillich's Theological Legacy:*

Spirit seems to distinguish the pneumatology of the later *Systematic The-ology* from his early work on the draft of a *Systematische Theologie* from 1913. Already here we find a pneumatology as a part of the theological system. However, Tillich discussed the doctrine of the Spirit along more traditional lines, within the framework of soteriology and ecclesiology.[3] The divine Spirit is the return of the world to God. Nevertheless, we already find an elaborated pneumatology in the *Systematische Theologie* from 1913, even if Tillich does not work out here the doctrine of the Holy Spirit as a distinct part of the theological system. This is also the case in his writings from the 1920s. The dogmatics lectures that Tillich held in Marburg and Dresden leave off at Christology—only the outlines of a pneumatology survive. Additionally, the lectures on dogmatics given at Union Theological Seminary in New York between 1936 and 1938 do not work out a pneumatology as an independent part of the dogmatics. Here the Holy Spirit is understood as a part of Christology and eschatology, along the lines of the lectures from the German period. It is only the late *Systematic Theology* that he finally offers a developed pneumatology as an independent part of the theological system. Here, pneumatology is discussed in the broad horizon of life and its ambiguities. The *Systematic Theology* understands the presence of the divine Spirit as the fragmentary overcoming of these ambiguities.

It is important for Tillich's pneumatology that he connects the universal dimension with a critique of the Christological or soteriological conception of the Holy Spirit. What follows is that Tillich discusses the divine Spirit in a twofold way: on the one side, he discusses the divine Spirit in a universal dimension and, on the other side, in relation to Jesus Christ. This construction of pneumatology presupposes both the doctrine of God and Christology explained in the sixth and seventh chapters. And, like the doctrine of God and Christology, the doctrine of the Spirit forms a dimension

---

Spirit and Community. International Paul Tillich Conference, New Harmony, 17–20 June 1993 (Berlin; New York: de Gruyter, 1995); "Tillich's theology of the concrete spirit," in *The Cambridge Companion to Paul Tillich*, ed. Russel Re Manning (Cambridge: Cambridge University Press, 2009), 74–90; Christian Danz, "Die Gegenwart des göttlichen Geistes und die Zweideutigkeiten des Lebens," in *Paul Tillichs 'Systematische Theologie'. Ein werk- und problemgeschichtlicher Kommentar*, ed. Christian Danz (Berlin; Boston: de Gruyter, 2017), 227–256.

[3] Cf.Tillich, "Systematische Theologie von 1913," 364–71.

of the concept of revelation. Following the method of the preceding chapters, a brief sketch of the historical development of Tillich's work and theology is necessary, for it is only against this background that his pneumatology and its indicated peculiarity can become understandable. The *Systematic Theology* takes up the earlier, fundamental idea of the divine Spirit that is based on an understanding of religion as the awareness of human consciousness about its own presupposition. Therefore, Tillich's understanding of the Holy Spirit in his early theology will be briefly elucidated in the first section. With this background clearly detailed, the second section of this chapter deals with the pneumatology of the *Systematic Theology*. Finally, we will investigate pneumatology as the realization of Christian religion in history.

1. The Holy Spirit as the Return of the World to God

Already in his early conception of a *Systematische Theologie*, written in 1913, Tillich understands the Holy Spirit within the horizon of a universal dimension. With this, he criticizes the so-called "soteriological pneumatology," an understanding of the divine Spirit in which the Spirit is bound to Jesus Christ and his salvific work. We find this type of pneumatology not only in Martin Luther, but also in the late nineteenth-century theologies of Albrecht Ritschl and Martin Kähler, whose conceptions Tillich contradicts with the modern-positive theology of Adolf Schlatter and Wilhelm Lütgert. Already in the examination paper from 1908 about the monism, as well as in the *Systematische Theologie* from 1913, Tillich explicitly criticizes Ritschl's understanding of theology.[4] For Tillich, the principle of Protestant theology, namely, justification, is broader than the usual use.[5] That means justification is not only related to Jesus Christ, but to the cosmos as such. In this horizon Tillich construes his early pneumatology. The basis for this is the construction of the theological system that he works out in his early systematic theology.

The composition of the *Systematische Theologie* from 1913 is three-fold.[6] Not only does Tillich distinguish the whole system in three parts— i.e., fundamental theology, dogmatics, and ethics—but also every part into

---

[4] Cf. above chapter II and III.
[5] Cf. Tillich, "Systematische Theologie von 1913," 320.
[6] To Tillich's *Systematische Theologie* from 1913, cf. Wittekind, "Allein durch den Glauben," 40–46; Dienstbeck, *Transzendentale Strukturtheorie*, 223–234.

three sections. The distinction between the standpoints of intuition, re-flection, and theology from the first part of the theological system is foun-dational. The theological standpoint, as Tillich declares in the first part of his system, is the paradox. What he calls the paradox is the unity between the absolute and the relative or between intuition and reflection.[7] Tillich identifies the paradox not only with the standpoint of theology but also with religion. Therefore, just as the paradox is the unity, or better, the return of the relative to the absolute, so is religion the return of the finite to the infinite. The paradox is derivable neither from intuition nor from reflection. Rather, it is demanded by both intuition and reflection at the same time. A further aspect is also important for Tillich's understanding of religion in his early systematic theology, which is that the finite, or the reflection, can only return to the absolute if it negates or sublates itself. This means, for religion, that it introduces the return of the finite to the absolute in history through the self-sublation of the finite. In this act, the finite becomes a representation of the absolute.

The argumentation of the first part of the theological system comes to an end with the concept of the paradox as the standpoint of theology. Tillich distinguishes the paradox, or the theological principle, in three mo-ments: the absolute, the finite, and the teleological moment.[8] It becomes clear that the structure of the theological principle explains the structure of justification in a universal dimension. In the dogmatic part of the sys-tem, for instance, Tillich transfers the structure of the paradox to the dog-matical material. Like the first part, the dogmatics also have a threefold structure. The principle of theology is the paradox, or justification, and Jesus as the Christ introduces this principle into history. Therefore, the return of the standpoint of reflection to the absolute is connected with Jesus Christ. This means that the Holy Spirit is the realization of Jesus as the Christ, or the return of the finite to God. The Spirit is the "principle of the return to God" (EW IX, 365–6). Tillich explains his pneumatology in the third part of the dogmatics, which starts with the exaltation of Jesus the Christ. So, one can say that Christology describes the return of the standpoint of reflection to God in a principle manner and pneumatology in a factual manner. And here arises the question of how the Christian

---

[7] Cf. Tillich, "Systematische Theologie von 1913," 315.

[8] Cf. Tillich, "Systematische Theologie von 1913," 317–8. Cf. Danz, "The-ologie als normative Religionsphilosophie," 73–106.

religion is realized in history. The object of pneumatology is, therefore, the historical realization of the theological principle, i.e., justification. In this way, Tillich connects Christology both with the doctrine of the church and eschatology in his systematic theology. The reason for this is that Tillich relates the divine Spirit, as the principle of the return to God, with the standpoint of reflection as a whole.[9]

The *Systematische Theologie* from 1913 is an ambitious conception of modern theology. In fact, Tillich changes the foundations of his theological system during the time of the First World War. But what remains is the structure of the system. In the late *Systematic Theology*, we also find the distinction between what Tillich called in 1913 the standpoints of intuition, reflection, and theology both in the whole conception and in every part of the late system.[10] What changes in Tillich's theology after 1916 is that he transfers the earlier concept of the absolute into a description of the religious act as an act of reflection in human consciousness. Thus, the theological principle, or justification, is used to describe religion and its emergence in human beings.[11] This is not deprived of consequences for the understanding of the Holy Spirit. However, it is important to observe that we have no elaborated pneumatology from Tillich's German period. The dogmatics lectures from Marburg and Dresden are not finished because they come to an end with Christology and do not work out a pneumatology. But the structure of the doctrine of the Spirit is already visible.

First, as Tillich explains in his *Religionsphilosophie*, written in 1923 and published two years later, the Holy Spirit is a moment in the structure of the religious performative act. Here we read: "Only in the 'Holy Spirit' does the essence of the spirit come to fruition" (GW I, 329). The Holy Spirit describes an act of reflection in the human spirit, or consciousness. Second, like in the theological system from 1913, pneumatology is a part of Christology and eschatology and not an independent part of the system.

---

[9] Cf. Tillich, "Systematische Theologie von 1913," 367.

[10] Cf. Wittekind, "Das Sein und die Frage nach Gott," 93–115.

[11] We find this change of the earlier conception in Tillich's draft *Rechtfertigung und Zweifel* from 1919 and other texts since 1916. In *Rechtfertigung und Zweifel*, the justification is not, as it is the case in the *Systematische Theologie* from 1913, the superordinate frame of the absolute, but rather the justification describes the appropriation of the faith. Cf. Tillich, "Rechtfertigung und Zweifel," 128–185. Cf. above chapter III.3.

In the outlines of the dogmatics from Marburg and Dresden, pneumatology appears in the last part of the system under the headline "History of the Reception of the Perfect Revelation" (EW XIV, 238). The Holy Spirit is also referred to here as the description of the realization of faith in history or, as Tillich now calls it, in the history of revelation. Therefore, the divine Spirit is the "history of revelation as unity of overcoming and fight against the demonic" (ibd.). This leads to a third aspect. Since 1924, the distinction between foundational revelation and salvation revelation has been a fundamental structural element in Tillich's theology.[12] With the concept of foundational revelation, Tillich names the disclosedness of consciousness as the basis for all acts of consciousness. Tillich construes a teleological connection between the foundational revelation and the salvation revelation, so that the former is related to latter. Since the foundational revelation is ambiguous, the salvation revelation is unambiguous. This is so because in the latter one finds the disclosedness of consciousness as a consciousness that is at the same time the negation of its contentual representation. Therefore, salvation history is the way from the universal foundational revelation to the concrete salvation revelation. Pneumatology presupposes both.[13] With this is connected a double explanation of the Holy Spirit: it describes both the foundational revelation and the salvation revelation. But there is also a further important aspect, which is that the divine Spirit delineates the realization of the Christian faith in history. As the religious appropriation that finds its expression in the image of the Christ, the Holy Spirit symbolizes the historical fulfilment of meaning and an orientation toward the transcendent fulfilment. That means that the presence of the Holy Spirit is at the same time the knowledge about the enduring difference between the human spirit and the divine Spirit in history.[14]

---

[12] Tillich introduces this distinction in his article *Rechtfertigung und Zweifel* from 1924. Cf. GW VIII, 85–100. He takes up this differentiation in the distinction between natural and revealed religion in the 1930s. This distinction is as we have seen in chapter V also the basis for the so-called method of correlation in the *Systematic Theology*. Cf. above chapter V.

[13] Cf. Tillich, "Dogmatik-Vorlesung," 49–50.

[14] Cf. Tillich, "Eschatologie und Geschichte," 72–82. In this sense, it is not true when Jean Richard asserts that in the theology of the early Tillich there is no

After his emigration to the United States, Tillich held lectures on dogmatics at Union Theological Seminary in New York in 1936. Just like in his early systematic theology, we find here, once again, an elaborated pneumatology. But here, too, the doctrine of the Holy Spirit is not an independent part of the theological system. Like in his German dogmatics, Tillich discusses the divine Spirit in Christology and eschatology. Under the heading "Christology and the doctrine of man's eschatological nature" (EW XIX, 197), one part of his pneumatology appears in the first subsection on "Christology and the reality of a new being."[15] Faith, as Tillich declared, "is a product of the spirit, and generally speaking is the new being in existence in its preparatory and in its receptive stage as well as in its full appearance" (EW XIX, 201). The divine Spirit describes, therefore, the realization of the Christian faith in history. And in the dogmatics from 1936, the divine Spirit also remains transcendent.[16] In the dogmatics lectures on *Advanced Problems in Systematic Theology*, we see that Tillich discusses the individual-related elements of the traditional doctrine of the Holy Spirit in his Christology. The history-related elements of the traditional doctrine, like the doctrine of the church, he transfers into the eschatology.[17] Here he explains the relation between salvation-history and world-history. Even though Tillich does not use the term Spirit in the eschatological part of his dogmatics, what he describes is the realization of

---

difference between the human and the divine Spirit. Cf. Jean Richard, "The Hidden Community of the Kairos and the Spiritual Community: Toward a New Understanding of the Correlation in the Work of Paul Tillich," in *Paul Tillich's Theological Legacy: Spirit and Community. International Paul Tillich Conference, New Harmony, 17–20 June 1993*, ed. Frederick J. Parrella (Berlin; New York: de Gruyter, 1995), 43–64, here 60: "In Tillich's early philosophy, the spirit is at the same time human and divine: finite on account of rational thought, infinite on account of the rational being, the living substance. In Volume III, on the contrary, both dimensions are distinguished; the divine Spirit symbolizes the transcendence of the spirit."

[15] Cf. Tillich, "Advanced Problems in Systematic Theology," 197–202.

[16] Cf. Tillich, "Advanced Problems in Systematic Theology," 202: "the transcendent dynamics which is not identical with our spirit—or mind."

[17] Cf. Tillich, "Advanced Problems in Systematic Theology," 202: "The new being in existence is the salvation of existence. The application of this category to history and nature, to the church and community belongs to the Kingdom of God and history."

the Christian religion in history. In other words, he is describing salvation.[18]

Tillich's first lectures on dogmatics in New York follows the structure
of his German dogmatics, but there is also a further development. Tillich
now explains the theological material based on a new formulation of the
distinction between foundational revelation and salvation revelation. He
structures the material under the correlation of what he calls theological
answer and anthropological question. That means he transfers the methodological circle into the explanation of the dogmatics. In the following
years, Tillich changes this conception, and he begins with the question and
goes on to the answer.[19] But more important for our questions on the Holy
Spirit is that he introduces the pneumatology as an independent part of
the dogmatics in the lecture-cycle from 1940/41 until 1941/42. Now the
theological system has five parts, just like the later *Systematic Theology*. For
the first time, Tillich mentions this new structure of the system in his in-
augural-lecture at the Union Theological Seminary on September 25,
1940, with the title *Philosophy and Theology*.[20]

2. The Divine Spirit in the *Systematic Theology*

In the *Systematic Theology*, we find Tillich's final conception of the divine
Spirit. It is important to note that his magnum opus takes up the whole
development of pneumatology since his early draft from 1913. In the *Systematic Theology*, Tillich also uses the divine Spirit for a description of the
realization of the Christian Religion in history. First we must deal with
the structure of the Holy Spirit, and then, in the next section, with the
realization of Christianity in history.

---

[18] Cf. Tillich, "Advanced Problems in Systematic Theology," 245–277. "Redemption is the actual overcoming of the contradictions between essence and existence upon which world history is based." (EW XIX, 261) It is worth to note
that the fourth part of the lecture *Advanced Problems in Systematic Theology* was
originally written for the Universal Christian Council for Life and Work, realized
in Oxford, 1936. Cf. Erdmann Sturm, "Historische Einleitung," in EW XIX,
XV-XX, here XIX.

[19] Cf. Sturm, "Historische Einleitung," XXI–LVII.

[20] Cf. Paul Tillich, "Philosophy and Theology," in *Religion in Life* 10 (1941)
21–30, also in MW IV, 279–288, here 286.

The divine Spirit is related to the human consciousness or spirit, but both are not identical. The human spirit appears in the *Systematic Theology* as a dimension of life[21] and is defined as "the actualization of power and meaning in unity" (ST III, 111). The human self-relation—as Tillich's determination must be understood—is a conscious self-actualization in meaning (*Sinn*).[22] All concrete acts of the self are determinations in the horizon of meaning. Tillich correlates the divine Spirit with the already disclosed or conscious self-consciousness. The divine Spirit is also the "fruition" of the human spirit like in his early *Religionsphilosophie*. The methodological basis of the determination of the divine Spirit is the human spirit, without deriving or explaining, however, the former from the latter.[23] The Spirit of God is thus not an external, substantial entity that is somehow added to the human spirit. Tillich explicitly rejects such an understanding of the Spirit of God as a dualistic, supranaturalistic misunderstanding. This misunderstanding is replaced by an event of reflexivity in the self-relation of consciousness and is described terminologically as ecstasy.

> The spirit, a dimension of finite life, is driven into a successful self-transcendence; it is grasped by something ultimate and unconditional. It is still the human spirit; it remains what it is, but at the same time, it goes out of itself under the impact of the divine Spirit. (ST III, 112)

In Tillich's pneumatology, the divine Spirit exclusively signifies an event of reflection in the human spirit, namely, the breakthrough of the unconditioned in the self-relation of consciousness as the negation of the

---

[21] On the vitalistic groundwork of the dimension of the Spirit in its ambiguous realization, cf. Tillich, *Systematic Theology*, vol. III, 11–110.

[22] Cf. Tillich, *Systematic Theology*, vol. III, 111: "Man, in experiencing himself as man [sc. having a reflexive knowledge of himself in the act of his self-determination], is conscious of being determined in his nature by spirit as a dimension of his life." On the foundations of Tillich's concept of religion based on a theory of meaning, cf. Barth, "Die sinntheoretischen Grundlagen des Religionsbegriffs," 89–123. Cf. also above chapter III.3.

[23] Cf. Tillich, *Systematic Theology*, vol. III, 111: "This immediate experience [sc. the self-apprehension of the human as spirit] makes it possible to speak symbolically of God as Spirit and of the divine Spirit."

concrete determinations of consciousness.[24] This alone is designated by the divine Spirit to the effect that its status is that of a symbolic self-interpretation of the human spirit, which has become transparent to itself.[25] But, like in Tillich's earlier pneumatology, the divine Spirit is not identical with the human spirit.

If one were to ask what makes up the core of the pneumatologically delineated religion, then one is referred to the paradox of the self-relation, as being self-disclosed and yet withdrawn from oneself. The spirit, in its reflexive relation to itself, becomes aware that it must, as the ground and abyss of all determination in this action, already presuppose itself. The self-disclosedness of the human spirit in its reflexive constitution as equiprimordiality of ground and abyss represents the systematic content of the symbol of the divine Spirit. This self-disclosedness is not only the criterion against which all experiences of the Spirit must be measured,[26] but it also represents the content of that which Tillich calls the transcendent unity of unambiguous life.[27]

In Tillich's pneumatology, the divine Spirit functions as a symbolic self-description of the human spirit which has become self-aware in the reflexive structure of its self-relation. Therefore, the ambiguities of life are fragmentarily overcome. In the *Systematic Theology*, Tillich designates this reflexive self-disclosedness as the transcendent unity of unambiguous life.

> Therefore, the creation of unambiguous life brings about the re-union of these elements in life processes in which actual being is the true expression of potential being, an expression, however, which is not immediate, as in "dreaming innocence," but which

---

[24] Tillich discusses the self-reflexive structure of pneumatology in section *b) Structure and ecstasy*. Cf. Tillich, *Systematic Theology*, vol. III, 114–120.

[25] The basic symbol theory of pneumatology is discussed in section *c) The media of the Spiritual Presence*. Cf. Tillich, *Systematic Theology*, vol. III, 120–128.

[26] Cf. Tillich, *Systematic Theology*, vol. III, 120: "The criterion which must be used to decide whether an extraordinary state of mind is ecstasy, created by the Spiritual Presence, or subjective intoxication is the manifestation of creativity [sc., at the same time to be withdrawn from the self-transparency of the spirit as the ground of all symbolic activity] in the former and the lack [sc. since the spirit posits itself as the ground of all that is determined] of it in the latter."

[27] Cf. Tillich, *Systematic Theology*, vol. III, 129–30.

is realized only after estrangement, contest, and decision. (ST III, 129)

Regarding content, the statements on the transcendent unity of un-ambiguous life take up the *ordo salutis* of the old Lutheran dogmatics and reformulate it by means of the guiding concepts of hope and love.[28] How-ever, how must Tillich's statement, that in the reflexive self-disclosedness of the human spirit the ambiguities of life are fragmentarily overcome, be understood?

The ambiguities of life in the dimension of the spirit are rooted in the paradoxical structure of human self-relation. The human spirit can only grasp itself as a contradiction to itself. Its self-positing in the act of relating itself to itself is thus already antinomically constituted. For religion—the dimension of the self-transcendence of life in the sphere of the spirit—this means that the intention (*Meinen*) of, or the directedness towards, the ab-solute is simultaneously its transgression.[29] In this way, Tillich takes up his early conception of sin into the *Systematic Theology*. In what then does the overcoming of the ambiguities of life in the dimension of the spirit consist? It is clear that it cannot mean an overcoming of the paradoxical structure of the self-relation, for that would be tantamount to abolishing the dimen-sion of the human spirit itself. Thus, Tillich consistently rejects such an understanding of the presence of the divine Spirit in the human spirit.[30] The presence of the divine Spirit means neither intoxication nor the de-scent to a subhuman dimension. Yet, if the fragmentary overcoming of the ambiguities of life cannot consist in the elimination of the paradoxical structure of the self-relation—the subject-object divide—then all that re-mains is to understand it as the event of the becoming-evident of the par-adoxical structure of the self-relation. Only such an interpretation can be suggested from the vantage point of Tillich's conception of religion as de-veloped in the *Systematic Theology*. Religion, performed as the self-tran-scendence of life in the dimension of the spirit, is not an empirical set of

---

[28] Cf. Tillich, *Systematic Theology*, vol. III, 130–138.

[29] Cf. Tillich, *Systematic Theology*, vol. III, 97–8: "Out of this situation reli-gion arises as a special function of the spirit. The self-transcendence of life under the dimension of spirit cannot become alive without finite realities which are transcended. Thus there is a dialectical problem in self-transcendence in that something is transcended and at the same time not transcended."

[30] Cf. Tillich, *Systematic Theology*, vol. III, 100 and 119.

facts.[31] It means nothing but an act of reflection in consciousness, which becomes aware of itself as being the ground and the abyss of the infinite process of the interpretation of meaning.

On the basis of these statements on the fragmentary overcoming of the ambiguities of life in the dimension of the human spirit—in the sense of a reflexive disclosedness of the spirit as an inexorable component of human life—a new light is cast on Tillich's more specific determination of the transcendent unity of unambiguous life as faith and love. Faith represents the underivable act of self-disclosedness in the self-relation of consciousness, while love represents the realization of this event of reflection.[32] Faith and love are the two sides of the religious act in human consciousness. Both are bound to the revelation of God, whose subjective side they describe. Consciousness becomes aware that the absolute is the presupposition of all acts of the consciousness and all concrete things for the consciousness. However, the absolute is always withdrawn from consciousness, for the unconditioned is at the same time ground and abyss of meaning. Therefore, faith is on the one side the actual unity between God and human beings, but on the other side the knowledge that God remains transcendent to humanity. Love as connected with faith is the "state of being taken by the Spiritual Presence into the transcendent unity of unambiguous life" (ST III, 134). That means the realization of the transcendent unity through the believer. Only for this reason does love in the sense of agape, as distinct from faith, characterize "the divine life itself" (ST III, 138). Unity with God in the presence of the divine Spirit is possible in history only as the knowledge that in history such a unity is not possible. But exactly this presupposes the religious act in history which is connected with the orientation to the transcendent fulfillment. Tillich calls this act, which is an act of reflection in the human spirit, "Spiritual Presence."[33]

---

[31] Cf. Tillich, *Systematic Theology*, vol. III, 87.

[32] Cf. Tillich, *Systematic Theology*, vol. III, 129: "The two points of view determining the two terms can be distinguished in the following way: faith is the state of being *grasped* by the transcendent unity of unambiguous life – it embodies love as the state of being *taken into* that transcendent unity."

[33] Cf. Tillich, *Systematic Theology*, vol. III, 107–8.

3. The Divine Spirit and the Realization
of the Christian Religion in History

Tillich's statements on the divine Spirit in terms of symbol theory in the *Systematic Theology* already indicate that pneumatology is integrated in history from the outset. The description of the self-disclosedness of the spirit by means of the symbol of the divine Spirit, or Spiritual Presence, is taken over from the history of the Christian religions. The historical mediacy of religious self-interpretation is a component of pneumatology. All symbolic forms in which human self-transparency presents itself are, in terms of their contents, already determined by history.[34] The methodological circle of religious self-interpretation, only real as interpretation, and in that respect always already determined by a concrete history, is the theme of Christology as reflection on history.[35] Faith's image of Christ represents the actual moment of the self-disclosedness of human consciousness in its historical embeddedness. But this is only one aspect of Tillich's pneumatology. A further aspect is also important.

In the *Systematic Theology*, the basis of pneumatology as the description of the realization of the Christian religion is also the differentiation between what Tillich earlier calls foundational revelation and salvation revelation. As a result, the divine Spirit receives a double thematization. On the one side, as the manifestation of the Spiritual Presence in humankind and, on the other side, in Jesus Christ as the New Being in history. What matters here is that this differentiation is also a structuring part of the theological circle. When Tillich speaks of the Spiritual Presence which is "manifest in all history" (ST III, 139), he does not mean an objective matter. Rather, the differentiation is a differentiation in the view of the faith. It is faith in its own steps on the way to itself, which Tillich has in mind with the distinction between foundational revelation and salvation revelation. In this sense, the starting point of the construction of the his-

---

[34] Cf. Tillich, *Systematic Theology*, vol. III, 100: "The content of personal religious life is always taken from the religious life of a social group. Even the silent language of prayer is formed by tradition."

[35] Tillich had already summed up his history of philosophy oriented to Christology in the Dresden dogmatics lectures by means of the formula "center of history." Cf. Tillich, "Dogmatik-Vorlesung," 370–373; "Christologie und Geschichtsdeutung," 83–96. Cf. also above chapter VII.

tory of religion is the contemporary reality of the faith. The history of religion is, in this sense, an explication of the theological circle. The differentiation between a time of preparation of the Spiritual Presence in Jesus
Christ and a time of reception of the Spiritual Presence in Jesus Christ
results from the center of history, namely, the methodological circle in the
construction of history.[36] From this follows that the foundational revelation has an inward teleology to the salvation revelation.

The Spiritual Presence in humankind is, for the Christian faith, the
beginning of the faith and its own history. But this presence is both ambiguous and fragmentary.[37] What Tillich means is an awareness of the absolute as the presupposition of consciousness, which is the basis for the
history of religion. Tillich construes this history as a struggle between the
divine and the demonic.[38] The reason for this is that the awareness of consciousness must be presented. But, at the same time, every concrete
presentation of the absolute is wrong because it holds on to the disclosedness as something specific and determined and thus misses it. In this
way, the history of religion, based on the foundational revelation or the
human question, finds its solution and its inward telos in Jesus Christ, the
salvation revelation. He, Jesus Christ, is the center of history and the appearance of the transcendent unity in history. "Christ's self-sacrificial love
is the center of the Gospels as well as of their apostolic interpretation" (ST
III, 145). The image of the Christ, presented by the Gospels, is the "real-
picture" of faith. But Christ is such an image only insofar as he, as a concrete person, negates himself as a concrete person on the cross. Therefore,
Christ represents in and for the Christian faith the symbolic structure of
the faith as a symbolic consciousness. In Jesus as the Christ, the Spiritual
Presence comes to a presentation that corresponds to the symbolic structure of consciousness. Without a concrete image, it is not possible to describe the Spiritual Presence, but every image is, at the same time, wrong
and must be negated. This dialectic is the content of the event of Jesus as
the Christ. In him, the tension between profanization and demonization
that underlies the history of religion is overcome. Only because of this Jesus as the Christ is, as the center of history, at the same time the criterion

---

[36] Thus, Tillich incorporates his idea of a history of revelation from the 1920s
into the pneumatology of the late *Systematic Theology*.
[37] Cf. Tillich, *Systematic Theology*, vol. III, 138–141.
[38] Cf. Tillich, *Systematic Theology*, vol. III, 141–144.

to evaluate the religion or manifestations of the Spirit. "The divine Spirit was present in Jesus as the Christ without distortion. In him the New Being appeared as the criterion of all Spiritual experience in past and future" (ST III, 145).

The function of Tillich's Spirit-Christology set against the background of the history of religion is to connect the universal dimension of the Spiritual Presence in the world with Jesus Christ as "the keystone in the arch of Spiritual manifestations in history" (ST III, 147). Jesus Christ is not an "isolated event" (ibd.), he is rooted in a universal history of revelation.

> The event "Jesus as the Christ" is unique but not isolated; it is dependent on the past and future, as they are dependent on it. It is the qualitative center in a process which proceeds from an indefinite past into an indefinite future which we call, symbolically, the beginning and the end of history. (ibd.)

The inward telos of the manifestations of the divine Spirit notwithstanding, Jesus as the Christ is only for the Christian faith. For the Christian faith, the Christ is not only the center of history but also the telos of history. Also, the reception of the transcendent unity of unambiguous life in Jesus as the Christ underlies the tension between profanization and demonization. The history of the Christian religion is both revelation and (merely human) religion. All that is mere religion in Christianity must be every time overcome through the presence of the divine Spirit. So the Spirit of God is present in the whole world, but it is not a part of the world or derived from the world.

As we have seen, what Tillich describes in the pneumatology of the *Systematic Theology* is the historical realization of the Christian religion. Like in his early dogmatics from the German period and the first period in exile, the content of the doctrine of the divine Spirit is the appropriation of the salvation in history. But only here, in the third volume of the *Systematic Theology*, do we find a concrete description of the Christian religion both in history and in its historical development. Parts one and two of the theological system—which we have discussed in chapters VI and VII respectively—give a presentation of the structure of the religious act. The doctrine of God as well as the doctrine of the Christ are isolated presentations of the structural elements of the Christian religion as a revelation

of God. In this sense, both volumes are abstract, as Tillich explicitly mentioned.[39] Only pneumatology and eschatology give a full image of the
Christian religion in history and of the Christian understanding of the
world and nature as well as history. Precisely because of this feature, pneumatology indeed constitutes the central and most important part of the
whole *Systematic Theology*.

---

[39] Cf. Tillich, *Systematic Theology*, vol. I, 66–7. Cf. Danz, *Religion als Freiheitsbewußtsein*, 275–412.

IX.

Christianity and the Encounter of Religions: Paul Tillich and the Quest for a Theology of Religions

The social development of the last thirty years has given more attention to religious pluralism within theology in the United States and in Europe.[1] In Germany, a wide religious theological debate resulted from the Anglo-American discussion. The reasons for this new attention to religious plurality are manifold. What is important is that the question of the diversity of religions is understood as a theological task.[2] That means to give a theological or religious interpretation of the diversity of religions. But these debates are problematic because many approaches are inclined toward a negation of religious diversity. This is a consequence of the underlying general concept of religion or God. A difficulty, or a contradiction, is connected with both: namely, that on the one hand it grants the pluralism of religions, but on the other hand it reduces this very pluralism by its assertion that all religions are based on the same God. However, if that is the case, then there is only one religion in many guises. Therefore, the basic problem of a theology of religions consists in connecting the absoluteness and peculiarity of one's own religion with an acknowledgement of the absoluteness and peculiarity of other religions. Hence it is not so much the so-called tripartite scheme of exclusivism, inclusivism, and pluralism,

---

[1] Cf. Christian Danz, *Einführung in die Theologie der Religionen* (Wien: LIT, 2005); Paul F. Knitter, *Introducing Theologies of Religions* (Maryknoll: Orbis Books, 2002); Schmidt-Leukel, *Religious Pluralism & Interreligious Theology*.

[2] Cf. Hick, *An Interpretation of Religions*, 1–2; Schmidt-Leukel, *Religious Pluralism & Interreligious Theology*, 1.

which categorizes the relation between one religion to another, that constitutes the difficulties of a theology of religions. Rather, it is the concept of religion and the question as to how theology is related to religion. For theology and religion are not the same thing, but strictly distinct. Taking up this problem, one must ask whether and how Tillich's theology deals with the mentioned problems of a theology of religions.[3] Certainly, he does not speak about a theology of religions. Rather, Tillich uses the older term "theology of the history of religions."[4]

Thus, in the first part of this chapter, we must briefly deal with an analysis of the contemporary debate on the theology of religions as well as the difficulties that confront us in its represented models. I take the discussion about the tripartite scheme for granted and will not try to integrate Tillich into one of these systems.[5] In a second part, we must work out the thoughts of Tillich's theology of religions as developed in his Bampton Lectures, entitled *Christianity and the Encounter of the World Religions,*[6] and in his last lecture, *The Significance of the History of Religions for the Systematic Theologian.* Finally, in the third part of this chapter, I will offer, against

---

[3] On Tillich's theology of religions, cf. Robison B. James, *Tillich and World Religions. Encountering Other Faiths Today* (Macon: Mercer University Press, 2003); Dirk-Martin Grube, *Offenbarung, absolute Wahrheit und interreligiöser Dialog* (Berlin; Boston: de Gruyter, 2019); Sabrina Söchtig, *Absolute Wahrheit und Religion. Der Wahrheitsbegriff des frühen Tillich und seine Beurteilung außerchristlicher Religionen* (Berlin; Boston: de Gruyter, 2020); Olson, *The Depths of Life*, 83–98.

[4] Cf. Paul Tillich, "The Significance of the History of Religions for the Systematic Theologian," in *Ausgewählte Texte*, ed. Christian Danz, Werner Schüßler and Erdmann Sturm (Berlin; New York: de Gruyter, 2008), 456–465, here 459. With the catchword "theology of the history of religions," Tillich follows Ernst Troeltsch. Cf. Ernst Troeltsch, "Über historische und dogmatische Methode in der Theologie," in *Zur religiösen Lage, Religionsphilosophie und Ethik* (Gesammelte Schriften, vol. 2) (2nd. ed. Tübingen: Mohr Siebeck, 1922), 729–753, here 738.

[5] Cf. James, *Tillich and World Religions*, 52–54. Cf. also Drew Collins, *The Unique and Universal Christ. Refiguring the Theology of Religions* (Waco: Baylor University Press, 2021).

[6] Cf. Paul Tillich, "Christianity and the Encounter of the World Religions," in *Ausgewählte Texte*, ed. Christian Danz, Werner Schüßler and Erdmann Sturm (Berlin; New York: de Gruyter, 2008), 419–453; *The Encounter of Religions and Quasi-Religions* (Lewiston; Queenston; Lampeter: E. Mellen Press, 1990).

the background of Tillich's theology of religions, an outline of an alternative proposal for a theology of religions.

1. The Contemporary Debates in Theology of Religions

The contemporary debate about the theology of religions primarily discusses three points of departure: the pluralistic model of a theology of religions,[7] forms of a new, "mutual inclusivism,"[8] and the so-called "comparative theology."[9] In the following section, I will sketch these models and their difficulties.

John Hick was the first to newly determine the attitude of Christianity to non-Christian religions by overcoming the claims of Christianity's superiority and acknowledging the validity of non-Christian religions.[10] The main thought of his pluralistic model is a theory of religious experience that is connected with a categorial differentiation. For Hick, we "have to distinguish between the Real *an sich* and the Real as variously experienced-and-thought by different human communities."[11] Religions must be understood as human responses to the manifestation of the "Real an sich." To the latter, no historical religion has full access. All religions have only symbols and images from the absolute, but no one has a privileged access. Therefore, from the perspective of the "Real *an sich*," all great (for Hick)

---

[7] Cf. John Hick and Paul F. Knitter (eds.), *The Myth of Christian Uniqueness. Toward a Pluralistic Theology of Religions* (Maryknoll: Orbis Books, 1987); Hick, *An Interpretation of Religion.*

[8] Cf. S. Mark Heim, *The Depth of Riches. A Trinitarian Theology of Religious Ends* (Grand Rapids, Michigan: Eerdmans, 2001); *Salvations. Truth and Difference in Religions* (Maryknoll: Orbis Books, 1995); Reinhold Bernhardt, "Protestantische Religionstheologie auf trinitätstheologischem Grund," in *Theologie der Religionen. Positionen und Perspektiven evangelischer Theologie*, ed. Christian Danz and Ulrich H. J. Körtner (Neukirchen-Vluyn: Neukirchener, 2005), 107–120; *Ende des Dialogs? Die Begegnung der Religionen und ihre theologische Reflexion* (Zürich: TVZ, 2005).

[9] John J. Thatamanil, *The Immanent Divine. God, Creation, and the Human Predicament. An East-West Conversation* (Minneapolis: Fortress Press, 2006). Cf. Knitter, *Introducing Theologies of Religions*, 202–215.

[10] Cf. Hick, *An Interpretation of Religion*; *God has many Names* (Philadelphia: Westminster Press, 1982).

[11] Hick, *An Interpretation of Religion*, 236.

world religions are equally valid. Yet, for Hick, their differences and diversities do not result from the manifestation of the "Real *an sich*," but from their own answers to this revelation, which are influenced by the prevailing culture.[12]

Different objections to the pluralistic model have been raised. Foremost it is the question of how Hick's model is able to acknowledge religious difference.[13] Differences become insignificant in his model because all religions have the same structure. Religion is there where a shift happens between "self-centredness to Reality-centredness."[14] But this actually means that, as a matter of fact, there is only one religion with different faces in all religions. As a result, the pluralistic justification of religious pluralism leads to an annihilating of religious diversity. Accordingly, this means that the pluralistic approach is monistic. The reason for this is the construction of a transcendent absolute *beyond* the religious gods of the religions. Only through the relation to the absolute are the religions of the humankind equal. But the absolute or the "Real *an sich*" is a construction from the theology of religions. It is not the view of the particular religion. The particular religions are in relation to their own religious gods, but not in relation to a general absolute beyond their own gods. Therefore, the

---

[12] Cf. Hick, *An Interpretation of Religion*, 239–40: "Using this distinction between the Real *an sich* and the Real as humanly thought-and-experienced, I want to explore the pluralistic hypothesis that the great world faiths embody different perceptions and conceptions of, and correspondingly different responses to, the Real from within the major variant ways of being human; and that within each of them the transformation of human existence from self-centredness to Reality-centredness is taking place."

[13] Cf. Reinhard Leuze, "Gott und das Ding an sich – Probleme der pluralistischen Religionstheorie," in *Neue Zeitschrift für Systematische Theologie* 39 (1997) 42–64; Hans G. Kippenberg and Kocku von Stuckrad, "Religionswissenschaftliche Überlegungen zum religiösen Pluralismus in Deutschland. Eine Öffnung der Perspektiven," in *Multikulturalität im vereinten Europa. Historische und juristische Aspekte*, ed. Hartmut Lehmann (Göttingen: Wallstein, 2003), 145–162, here 149–50; Andreas Grünschloß, *Der eigene und der fremde Glaube. Studien zur interreligiösen Fremdwahrnehmung in Islam, Hinduismus, Buddhismus und Christentum* (Tübingen: Mohr Siebeck, 1999); Reinhold Bernhardt, *Der Absolutheitsanspruch des Christentums. Von der Aufklärung bis zur Pluralistischen Religionstheologie* (Gütersloh: Gerd Mohn, 1990).

[14] Hick, *An Interpretation of Religion*, 240. Cf. also 32–55.

question arises: How must the relation between the theology of religions and the concrete religion be understood? The pluralistic theology of religions levels the difference between theology and religion by substituting the pluralistic construction of religion with religion and claiming it as its truth. Thus, it is necessary to develop Hick's model further. Two thoughts are important for these further conceptions: on the one hand, the positive acknowledgement of non-Christian religions and, on the other hand, the consideration that religions may not be best understood as answers to a "Real *an sich*" beyond the religious gods, but rather from the perspective of the particular religion itself. More precisely, what follows from these reflections is the model of a mutual inclusivism.[15]

Mutual inclusivism indicates a whole network of different religious points of view in an interreligious dialogue. The task of a Christian theology of religions is, then, to describe its relation to other religions by means of interpretations of the Christian religion itself. For this task, the doctrine of the Trinity is used insofar as it connects the general revelation of God with the special revelation of Jesus as the Christ.[16] In this sense, the personal revelation of the Christ is for the Christian religion, whereas the impersonal dimension of the Holy Spirit for other religions.[17] This model of mutual inclusivism also wants to contribute to a recognition of other religions, but from the point of view of one's own religion. The difficulty that we might see in mutual inclusivism consists in the question of how to avoid a relationship of dependence of non-Christian religions as a result of describing Christianity's relationship to other religions in terms of a Christian doctrine of the Trinity. If the Trinity is the frame in which all different religions are rooted, how is it possible that the triune God re-

---

[15] Cf. Heim, *The Depth of Riches*; Bernhardt, *Der Absolutheitsanspruch des Christentums*; "Protestantische Religionstheologie auf trinitätstheologischem Grund," 107–120.

[16] Cf. S. Mark Heim, "The Depth of the Riches: Trinity and Religious Ends," in *Theology and the Religions. A Dialogue*, ed. Viggo Mortensen (Grand Rapids; Cambridge: Eerdmans, 2003), 387–402, here 387: "My contention is that Trinity provides the framework for Christian affirmation and interpretation of the religious ends of other traditions, and that in the process of investigating this we gain a deeper insight into the nature of salvation, the Christian religious end."

[17] Cf. Bernhardt, *Ende des Dialogs?*, 219–225; *Monotheismus und Trinität. Gotteslehre im Kontext der Religionstheologie* (Zürich: TVZ, 2023).

vealed in other religions different contents when compared to Christianity? What follows is that all other religions are forms of an anonymous Christianity and are in no way independent religions.[18] It is the same God who is manifesting in the diverse religions. This model, too, works with a unity *behind* the concrete religions and religious gods. But it is also not clear in what relation the theology of religions and the recognition of religious pluralism stands with the concrete Christian religion and the view of the world in Christianity.

Over the last years, all the difficulties of the pluralistic model, as well as those of the new model of inclusivism, have resulted in a change of basis for the theology of religions, and a bidding farewell to the global theories connected with them in the three-fold system of exclusivism, inclusivism, and pluralism as well as mutual inclusivism. Since the 1990s, especially in the United States, comparative theologies have been conceived as alternatives to the previous theology of religions.[19] All of them want to emphasize the differences between religions more strongly, and instead of dealing with religions as a whole, they turn to discussions of special religious problems.

Comparative theologians are not content to think generally about the meaning of religious diversity for Christian faith. Instead they wish to engage specific texts, motifs, and claims of particular traditions not only to understand better these traditions but also to determine the truth of theological matters through conversation and collaboration.[20]

---

[18] Cf. Karl Rahner, "Die anonymen Christen," in *Schriften zur Theologie*, vol. 6 (Einsiedeln; Zürich; Köln: Benziger, 1965), 545–554.

[19] Cf. Robert C. Neville, *Behind the Masks of God. An Essay Toward Comparative Theology* (New York: State University of New York Press, 1991); Francis X. Clooney, "Comparative Theology. A Review of Recent Books (1989–1995)," in *Theological Studies* 56 (1995) 521–550; *Theology after Vedanta. An Experiment in Comparative Theology* (Albany; New York: State University of New York Press, 1996); James L. Fredericks, "A Universal Religious Experience? Comparative Theology as Alternative to a Theology of Religions," in *Horizons* 22 (1995) 67–87; *Faith among Faiths. Christian Theology and Non-Christian Religions* (New York: Paulist Press, 1999).

[20] Thatamanil, *The Immanent Divine*, 3. Cf. also Fredericks, "A Universal Religious Experience?" 83.

And in fact, that represents a step further in comparative theology, since, by not making general judgments in a theology of religions, the differences between religious traditions can be better perceived than in the previous theology of religions.

Nevertheless, the problem of a comparative theology consists in two aspects in particular. Firstly, it is not really clear how it is possible to compare elements from different religions.[21] This presupposes not only a concept of religion, but also that the element of the other religion that is taken for comparison is religion. Secondly, it remains unclear how it could be possible to understand concrete elements from a religion without the whole symbolic system of a religion. Furthermore, comparative theology works with a universal concept of religion too, but it does not offer any theoretical explanation for this concept of religion. On the other hand, comparative theology does not explain how theology and religion relate to each other.

In summary, we can say that the contemporary debate is characterized by three problems: first of all, the pluralistic model does not seem capable of perceiving the independence and special qualities of religions; secondly, mutual inclusivism seems to dissolve the independence of other religions and thereby to absorb them; thirdly, comparative theology seems to have no answer to the question as to how religions must be compared. The fundamental problem of these diverse conceptions of a theology of religions is, as we have seen, the concept of religion which is used for the connection between Christianity and non-Christian religions.

2. Paul Tillich's Theology of the History of Religions

Throughout his academic career, Paul Tillich constantly worked on the problems of the history of religions for a modern theology. Already his philosophical dissertation on the philosophy of religion of Schelling, from 1910, was an answer to Ernst Troeltsch and the problem of the absoluteness of Christianity vis-à-vis the history of religion.[22] As we have seen in

---

[21] Following Robert C. Neville, John J. Thatamanil constructs so-called comparative categories. Cf. Thatamanil, *The Immanent Divine*, 12–18; cf. Robert C. Neville, *Normative Cultures* (Albany: State University of New York Press, 1995), 74–81.

[22] Cf. Tillich, "Die religionsgeschichtliche Konstruktion in Schellings positiver Philosophie," 156–272.

CHRISTIANITY AND THE ENCOUNTER OF RELIGIONS

the second chapter, Tillich works out in his early writings a new justification of the absoluteness of Christianity on the basis of a philosophy of history. Central motifs from this early conception of theology are taken up in his later works like the *Systematic Theology* and his lectures *Christianity and the Encounter of World Religions*. In in his 1963 Bampton Lectures, Tillich gave a detailed description of the problem of the encounter of Christianity with the non-Christian religions in the secular age. These lectures develop a theory of a modern history of religions. Tillich connects the analysis of the encounter of religions with considerations from the philosophy of religion and the theory of modernization, which should reflect the transformation of religion in modern age.

Similarly, in the Bampton Lectures, the basis for Tillich's theological considerations about the encounter of Christianity with non-Christian religions is the concept of religion and the differentiation between what he calls in the 1920s foundational revelation and salvation revelation. All aspects which he discusses in the lectures are dependent upon this foundation. Religion, as he explains in the first lecture, must be understood as "the state of being grasped by an ultimate concern" (AT, 421). That means here too an act of reflexivity in the human consciousness, namely, the awareness that the unconditional or depth dimension of consciousness is the presupposition of all cultural and religious acts. So the unconditioned underlies both culture and religion. This is a theological construction of a presupposition that has the function of enabling a religious interpretation of the world. Like in his other writings, Tillich gives no determination of religion with regard to contents, but he rather defines religion as an act of reflection in consciousness: Religion is directedness towards the unconditioned. And this act of reflection in consciousness, with which the knowledge of God is connected, is neither a determined act nor an act produced by human beings. Rather, this act arises from itself in human consciousness. Therefore, all knowledge of God is bound to a revelation of God. But the revelation of God is not limited—as in dialectical theology—to the revelation in Jesus Christ.[23] Tillich aims at a universal revelation of God. For this intention, he uses the concept of being, especially in

---

[23] Cf. Tillich, "The Significance of the History of Religions for the Systematic Theology," 458: "Both sides [sc. the neo-orthodox theology and the theology without God] are reductionistic, and both are inclined to eliminate everything from Christianity except the figure of Jesus from Nazareth."

his late theology.[24] His determination of God as being-itself is likewise a theological construction that aims at criticizing theological approaches that starts with God's revelation in Jesus Christ.

Since 1924, Tillich calls this universal revelation "foundational revelation." In his late work he takes this idea up in his method of correlation.[25] Here the foundational revelation appears as the question-side in the correlation. The earlier salvation revelation is reformulated with the theological answer and the final revelation. Between both revelations is a relation. The foundational revelation is ambiguous and directed towards the unambiguous revelation of salvation. In this way, Tillich constructs an inward teleological development from the universal, foundational revelation to the salvation revelation. Against the backdrop of the relation between foundational revelation and salvation revelation, Tillich constructs not only his theology, but he also transfers this scheme to the history of culture and the history of religions.[26] This is the case in the Bampton Lectures too, as well as in the last lecture about *The Significance of the History of Religions for the Systematic Theology*. In both lectures, Tillich works with this differentiation. His determination of Christianity and the relations between the Christian religion and non-Christian religions stems from this underlying structure. Therefore, it is not surprising when, in his investigations, Tillich starts from a universal revelation that already underlies all religions.[27]

There are three important aspects in Tillich's theology of the history of religions, which are all consequences from the underlying concept of religion. At first, we have to name the principle of a dialectical union of rejection and acceptance. For Tillich, the encounter of Christianity and other religions is characterized by complexity.[28] There is no uniform attitude of Christianity in the encounter with other religions. Not only the historical religions themselves, but also their encounters are highly complex. It follows that it is not possible to reduce the relation of Christianity

---

[24] Cf. above chapter VI.

[25] Cf. above chapter V.5.

[26] So already in the early *Religionsphilosophie*. Cf. Tillich, "Religionsphilosophie," 340–349.

[27] Cf. Tillich, "The Significance of the History of Religions for the Systematic Theology," 456: "First, one must say that revelatory experiences are universally human."

[28] Cf. Tillich, "Christianity and the Encounter of the World Religions," 430.

to the non-Christian religions to one attitude. Moreover, the encounter of religions is subject to historical change. Tillich does not understand this changing as the development from exclusivism to pluralism, as John Hick does, but as a dialectical relation of rejection and acceptance.[29] This relation is reflected within Christianity itself, and in its theology. The principle of judgment is also a dialectical union of reciprocal rejection and acceptance that stands in the place of a total rejection of non-Christian religions by Christianity and of the hopeless effort of making distinctions between value or worth among religions.[30] On this methodological basis, Tillich determines the relation between Christianity and non-Christian religions as a dialectical union of mutual rejection and acceptance.

Tillich's principle is a reformulation of his concept of foundational revelation. Every religion, and not only Christianity, is based on a revelation of God, namely the awareness that the unconditional dimension of consciousness is the presupposition of all acts of the human consciousness. It is a universal structure and, therefore, this structure underlies all religions. But this insight must be pictured in religion and this is only possible by using concrete cultural images. At the same time, the necessary images are always wrong, because the unconditioned is the presupposition of all concrete images but, as a presupposition, it is not itself a concrete image or content. Therefore, religions are always both revelation and (human) religion. What follows is that in every religion there is both a religious criticism of religion and the directedness towards the salvation revelation. But just like the foundational revelation is not produced by human beings, also the salvation revelation is not derivable. Exactly this is the content of the principle of a "dialectical union of acceptance and rejection" (AT, 430) that determines the attitude of Christianity towards non-Christian religions. We see as well that Tillich's formulation of a "principle of conditional exclusiveness" (ibid.) constitutes only an alternative formulation of this matter.

Tillich connects acknowledgement or recognition of other, strange religions with a critical reflection on Christianity itself. This point now names the second aspect of Tillich's theology of the history of religions,

---

[29] Cf. Tillich, "Christianity and the Encounter of the World Religions," 430.
[30] Cf. Tillich, "Christianity and the Encounter of the World Religions," 429–30.

that is, the construction of the history of religions. His theology of religions starts from the point of view of the Christian religion and moves on to an encounter with other religions. For the structuring of the encounter of religions, Tillich develops a typology of forms of religions on the basis of judgment of non-Christian religions on the part of Christianity as a dialogue.

> Such an attempt is perhaps the most difficult one in the comparative study of religions, but if successful it is the most fruitful for the understanding of the seemingly incomprehensible jungle which the history of religion presents to the investigating mind. (AT, 438)

Religious types result from the concept of religion and represent its internal building components.[31] Tillich speaks about types, and this shows that it is not possible to construct either a real, objective history of religion, or a gradual, higher development of the history of religion.[32]

But another aspect is also important, that is, the potential comparison of religions by means of these types. Tillich's typology of the ethical and mystical elements (formerly the theocratic and sacramental elements), which are contained in every religious act, aims at the recognition of what is proper within other religions, and what is other in one's own religion.

> If the Christian theologian discusses with the Buddhist priest the relation of the mystical and the ethical elements in both religions and, for instance, defends the priority of the ethical over the mystical, he discusses at the same time within himself the

---

[31] Cf. Tillich, "Christianity and the Encounter of the World Religions," 439: "While specific religions, as well as specific cultures, do grow and die, the forces which brought them into being, the type-determining elements, belong to the nature of the holy and with it to the nature of man, and with it to the nature of the universe and the revelatory self-manifestation of the divine." Cf. also "Religionsphilosophie," 340–349.

[32] Cf. Tillich, "Christianity and the Encounter of the World Religions," 439. "In terms of this method, for example, it would be impossible to call Christianity the absolute religion, as Hegel did, for Christianity is characterized in each historical period by the predominance of different elements out of the whole of elements and the polarities which constitute the religious realm."

relationship of the two in Christianity. This produces (as I can witness) both seriousness and anxiety. (AT, 439)

In every historical religion there are the same religious elements. But they are in every religion in different predominance. In this way, the dialogue with Buddhism is at the same time a dialogue with Christianity itself. While in the Buddhist religion the mystical element is predominant, in Christianity the predominant is the ethical or prophetic element. But given that religions are always changing in history, it is possible to assume that the mystical element in Christianity could also become predominant.

The third aspect of Tillich's theology of the history of religions is what he calls Christianity's judgment of itself in light of its encounter with the world religions.[33] This aspect is likewise a consequence of the concept of religion as the basis for the construction of the history of religion. As we have seen, Tillich understands all religions, including Christianity, both as revelation and (human) religion. Therefore, in all historical religions there is an inner-religious critique of religion. This critique aims at the salvation revelation—or, as Tillich names this revelation in the late *Systematic Theology*, final revelation. For Christianity, the final revelation—namely, Jesus as the Christ, the New Being in history—is the criterion to judge itself. But Jesus as the Christ is not a contentual criterion. And moreover, the revelation of salvation is not bound to Jesus Christ either, because it denotes a general structure.[34] For the understanding of Tillich's construction of the history of religions, it is important to have this in mind. Both revelations—that is, foundational revelation and salvation revelation—describe an act of reflexivity in the human consciousness and not a content. Jesus as the Christ is the "real picture" (ST II, 115) of the Christian faith.[35] What this image pictured is "a personal life, the image of which, as it impressed itself on his followers, shows no break in his relation to God and no claim for himself in his particularity. What is particular in him is that he crucified the particular in himself for the sake of the universal" (AT, 447). In Jesus as the Christ, it is expressed that, on the one hand,

---

[33] Cf. Tillich, "Christianity and the Encounter of the World Religions," 446–453.

[34] As we have seen, this is already the case in Tillich's early work. Cf. Tillich, "Dogmatik-Vorlesung," 51–55.

[35] Cf. above chapter VII.

it is necessary to depict the religious insight as the prerequisite of the unconditioned and that, on the other hand, every image misses this disclosedness and therefore has to be negated again. In this way, Jesus as the Christ represents in and for the Christian religion the symbolical use of symbols. And only insofar as this image represents how to use images in religion is Jesus as the Christ the final revelation and the criterion for judging religion as well as the telos of the history of religion.

What is it that follows from this construction for the history of religions and for Christianity among the religions? Tillich names the telos of the history of religions the "Religion of the Concrete Spirit" (AT, 461). Against the backdrop of the considerations about the relation between foundational revelation and salvation revelation, we can say that the religion of the concrete spirit describes the salvation revelation in every concrete historical religion as a possible telos of their own history.[36] Tillich thus incorporates his early idea of a reflexive revelation from the 1920s into his theology of the history of religions. The concrete religious symbols here are used as representations of the general structure of consciousness which, however, must at the same time be negated. Without religious forms such as myth and cult, there is no possible religion, but both are equivocal because the unconditioned is not a content. For Tillich, religion is not a particular form in culture. Rather religion is the general basis of all culture and religion. Therefore, every true religion is at the same time a fight against religion.[37] But this too must be represented in religion. Apart from concrete images, such a representation is not possible. Therefore, true religion in history is always an indication that the existence of religion in history is an expression of something that should not be in history. That is to say, true religion must express that there must be no religion.

---

[36] Tillich rejects the possibility that the history of religions leads to common religion. Cf. Tillich, "Christianity and the Encounter of the World Religions," 453.

[37] Cf. Tillich, "Christianity and the Encounter of the World Religions," 452: "In the fight of God against religion the fighter for God is in the paradoxical situation that he has to use religion in order to fight religion." Cf. also "The Significance of the History of Religions for the Systematic Theology," 461.

3. Religious Pluralism and the Diversity of the Understandings of Religion

For Tillich, religion refers to the foundational function of human consciousness. Religion is the disclosedness of consciousness, in which one becomes aware that consciousness itself is the basis of each and every cultural act of human consciousness. At the same time, religion arises in the individual consciousness not as a human production, but rather out of itself. Religion as an act of reflexivity in the human consciousness is revelation. Therefore, the basis of all religions is revelation. All religious contents represent religion in this sense, but they do not refer to objects beyond human consciousness. For religion, understood in this sense, is a part of the general structure of the human consciousness and, as such, it is universal. Religious contents describe this act of reflexivity. Tillich works in his theology of the history of religions with a universal concept of religion. That is the reason why we find in all historical religions the same structure and the same elements, namely the sacramental or the mystical and the ethical element. From this it follows that all religions can be acknowledged as religions. All historical religions, including Christianity, presupposes a divine revelation—or has as its presupposition a divine revelation. And we also find in every historical religion an inner religious critique of religion. Religions realize themselves in history as critique of religion. The aim of this process is not a common religion, but what Tillich calls the religion of the concrete spirit. In this respect, the goal of each individual religion is to form a reflexive religious self-understanding, that is, one for which the religious contents are a symbolic expression of the general foundational or unconditional structure that underlies consciousness.

Against this backdrop, Tillich understands in his theology of the history of religions the non-Christian religions as religions from a Christian point of view. The relationship between Christianity and non-Christian religions, the encounter between them is very complex and in no way uniform. Tillich applies his principle of a dialectical union of reciprocal rejection and acceptance in order to describe the complexity of such an encounter. As mentioned above, the basis for this principle is the relationship between the foundational revelation and the salvation revelation. In this way, Tillich is able to recognize non-Christian religions as religions by assigning to them the same value he assigns to Christianity. But this tolerant attitude to other religions is based on a concept of religion which ultimately reduces the diversity of religions. Like in the contemporary debate in theology of religions, Tillich too works with a general concept of religion. Thus, the starting point of the investigation is the diversity of religions, but, in the end, the use of a general concept dissolves this diversity. As a matter of fact, Tillich's theology of the history of religions is different to the later pluralistic model of a theology of religions. In contrast to John Hick, Tillich does not work with a transcendent absolute beyond the historical religions. Tillich's God above God is very different from Hick's "Real *an sich.*" The God above God does not refer to a transcendent entity behind the gods of the religions. Rather, God's transcendence has a function for religion, that is, the formula of God above God describes the religious critique of religious contents. In this way, Tillich's formula describes the reflexive structure of the religious consciousness and not a metaphysical substance or something else. As we have seen in chapter six, the formula God above God is a consequence of Tillich's concept of religion. But for Tillich, too, it is a question of a universal religious structure.

Such constructions of religion that we find by Tillich and similarly in the later theology of religions are not very helpful for a contemporary theology in a pluralistic age insofar as they make use of a universal concept of religion that underlies all particular religions. Such a universal concept of religion dissolves the diversity of religions. All religions are the expression of the same structure. So, in the end, there are not many different religions, but only one religion based on the basic structure of consciousness. The concreteness and peculiarity of historical religions is only a surface and without meaning. Therefore, if theology is really to arrive at an acknowledgment of the diversity of religions, it must give up all general conceptions of religion as well as the construction of an absolute behind historical religions. Only in this way it is possible to recognize that the different religions have also a different understanding of religion. There is no common understanding of religion in the historical religions. They all have their own interpretations of what religion is. Therefore, it is very difficult and misleading to transfer the concept of religion to other non-Christian religions[38] because the general concept of religion stems from the modern Protestant Christianity.[39] So it is not surprising that the concept of religion includes differentiations which are unknown to other religions.

How are we supposed to deal then with the plurality of religions in Christian theology? Theology has the task to interpret the Christian religion.[40] Theology develops a concept of religion, but this concept refers only to Christianity. The concept of religion has a function for the description of Christianity as religion. Therefore, it is not possible to transfer the concept of religion to other religions. What is the consequence of this position for the task of a theology of religions? First, it cannot be the task of a theology of religions to give a foundation of Christianity or of other religions. Theology gives an interpretation of the Christian religion, but not a justification of the Christian religion.[41] Second, theology refers only to the Christian religion and not to other religions. Christianity as religion is self-related. This means that all contents of the Christian religion do not refer to other religions or the world as whole. The contents of the Christian religion, like God, Jesus Christ, or the Holy Spirit, are expressions of Christianity as religion. Therefore, other religions do not appear in the Christian religion at all. Third, for the theological investigation of religious pluralism, it follows from the mentioned two aspects that it is the task of theology to ask how religion must be understood in other religions. If theology takes into due consideration that in different religions religion is always understood in a different manner, then it is possible to work out a pluralism-open theology.[42] What comes into view is both the peculiarity and the absoluteness of the concrete, particular religions. Absoluteness is

---

[38] On the problem of transferring the concept of religion—which depends on modern Christianity—to other religions or even to ancient Christianity, cf. Brent Nongbri, *Before Religion. A History of a Modern Concept* (New Haven; London: Yale University Press, 2013).

[39] Cf. Jonathan Z. Smith, "Religion, Religions, Religious," in *Relation Religion. Essays in the Study of Religion* (Chicago; London: The University of Chicago Press, 2004), 179–196.

[40] For a detailed elaboration, see below chapter X.

[41] Cf. Tillich, *Systematic Theology*, vol. I, 10.

[42] Cf. Danz, "Religious Diversity and the Concept of Religion," 101–113; "Nochmals: Monistischer Pluralismus oder pluralismusoffene Theologie? Eine Duplik auf Perry Schmidt-Leukel," in *Theologische Rundschau* 86 (2021) 106–119.

not a religious content, but an expression of the self-relation of every religion. Therefore, every religion is, as religion, particular as well as absolute. But the condition for such a vision of religious pluralism implies giving up the idea of a general concept of religion.

X.

Epilogue:
Paul Tillich and the Contemporary
Theological Debates

As we have seen in the *Prologue*, Paul Tillich elaborates his theology against the backdrop of the theological discussions in Germany around 1900. Already in his early writings, he starts from a concept of religion as the basis of a modern theology. But the concept of religion acquires a new determination. In the context of the so-called modern-positive theology, Tillich takes up the philosophies of Fichte and Schelling and formulates an understanding of religion that is not based on the faculties of human consciousness or spirit, as in the theology of Schleiermacher. Rather, religion is related to the consciousness as such, namely, the self-relation of consciousness. Tillich's statement that God, and not a religious a priori, is the basis of religion must be understood in this sense. But such a structural determination of religion or, as Tillich names it, the religious principle, is connected with the faculties of consciousness. The religious principle can be realized only through the faculties of consciousness, i.e., thinking, acting, and feeling. Religion and culture are already connected in this way in the philosophical dissertation on Schelling's philosophy of religion. With this we find the basic structure of Tillich's whole theology already in his early writings.

In the investigations offered in the first part of this book on the emergence and shaping of Tillich's theology before and after the First World War, as well as the elaboration of his dogmatics in the 1920s, it was made clear that the basis and foundation of his theology is the concept of religion. But religion is based on the revelation of God. For Tillich, every knowledge of God is bound to a revelation. Since God is strictly transcendent, there is no way to God from the human being. Still the *Systematic*

Theology is based on this insight, and it is the result of the development of considerations that we already find in his writings around 1900. Evidently, there are some important transformations in the construction of Tillich's theology. Especially the principle of the theological system—Tillich names it the theological principle—underlies a change first in the theology after the First World War and second in the end of the 1920s. But at the same time, the structure of the theological system remains relatively stable.[1] The *Systematische Theologie* from 1913 divides the theological system into the three parts of fundamental theology, dogmatics, and ethics, and then bases this structure on the distinction of three standpoints. These are intuition or the absolute standpoint, reflection or the relative standpoint, and paradox or the theological standpoint. In the dogmatic part of the system, Tillich divides the dogmatic material into three parts: creation, redemption, and consummation. This structuring is taken up by the dogmatics lecture of the 1920s, the New York lectures from the 1930s, and in the late *Systematic Theology*. However, in the mid-1920s, Tillich introduced the distinction between foundational revelation and salvation revelation into the structure of his system, from which the method of correlation emerged since his exile in the mid-1930s. How this distinction is reflected in the doctrine of God in the *Systematic Theology*, its Christology and pneumatology, and finally in Tillich's theology of the history of religions, was elaborated in the second part of this book. In this way, Tillich elaborates a theology that provides the possibility of a religious interpretation of modern culture. And therein lies not only the significance of his theology, but also its most important contribution.

Tillich's *Systematic Theology* is without doubt one of the main works of Protestant theology in the twentieth century. In this concluding chapter, however, we must raise the question not only of the contribution of his work to contemporary theological debates, but also of the limits of Tillich's theology in the context of the twenty-first century. First, I will give a brief overview of Tillich's theology, and then I will turn to a further development of his theology based on a changed conception of religion and theology compared to that of Tillich.

---

[1] Cf. Danz, *Religion als Freiheitsbewußtsein*; Dienstbeck, *Transzendentale Strukturtheorie*.

1. The Contribution of Tillich's Theology for Contemporary Theology

Like other theologians of his generation, Tillich dissolves an understanding of religion as an independent faculty in the structure of human consciousness. As we have seen, religion is, for him, a performative act in consciousness. Religion is the disclosedness of the unconditioned in the individual consciousness as directedness towards the unconditioned. Since it is not a determined act, this disclosedness can present itself in consciousness only as the negation of particular consciousness. It follows from this construction of religion that religion is not an independent part or an independent form in culture. A religion that understands itself as a separated area in culture is a mistaken form of religion. Over against this position, Tillich starts from the conviction that religion is the awareness of the foundation of all cultural acts, and such an aware consciousness is possible in all cultural forms. But this means that the general structure of consciousness remains the basis and the frame of the conception of religion as well as culture. Like the dialectical theologians, Tillich understands the emergence of religion in human beings as the revelation of God, but unlike Karl Barth and Friedrich Gogarten, he integrates religion in the frame of human consciousness.[2] Furthermore, Tillich rejects a restriction of the revelation of God in Jesus Christ. For him, God's revelation is also found in nature and culture. With this conviction, Tillich follows the modern-positive theology of his teachers Adolf Schlatter and Wilhelm Lütgert. The late *Systematic Theology* takes this up in the ontology that Tillich had developed since the late 1920s. The notion of being functions to criticize soteriological conceptions of theology as usually constructed in the German-speaking Protestant theologies of the twentieth century. Therefore, Tillich's ontology has a theological function that is quite different from traditional ontologies. The concept of being describes a structural presupposition for a religious interpretation of the cultural world. This is so because religion is for Tillich nothing other than the human disclosedness that the unconditioned is the presupposition of all concrete acts of the consciousness. Being, too, is always being *for* a consciousness, and not an instance that would lie beyond human consciousness. If we have in mind

---

[2] Cf. above chapter V.

this structural function of Tillich's ontology for his theology, then numerous controversial topics and misinterpretations of his theology are overcome—for example, the controversies about his so-called one "nonsymbolic statement" (ST I, 238), elaborated in the first volume of the *Systematic Theology*.[3]

What is the contribution of Tillich's theology to contemporary theological debates in the twenty-first century? There are three aspects in which we can see the contribution and importance of Tillich's work. Tillich develops a theology for his own time and brings, as we have seen, religion and culture into a close connection. Religion—so his well-known formulation says—is the substance of culture and culture is the form of religion.[4] This is the first important aspect that has been discussed in this book. Second, we must mention the theological circle. Especially in the *Systematic Theology*, the circle-structure of theology plays a central role,[5] but this is the case in his whole work. Already in the theological debates around 1900, it is clearly impossible to give an objective or neutral justification of the Christian religion. In Ernst Troeltsch's considerations about the methodological structure of the determination of the essence of Christianity, as well as in his famous book on the absoluteness of Christianity and the history of religions, we find this as a result of the debates in the nineteenth century.[6] Like his contemporaries, Tillich takes up this methodological insight. But in contrast to Troeltsch, Tillich transfers this methodological circle to the theological explanation of the Christian religion. We find this transference in the well-known formula of Jesus the Christ as "the center of history" from the 1920s.[7] The formula is an explication of the methodological circle in the construction of history. Every history starts from the present itself and what is of importance here. But

---

[3] Cf. above chapter VI.2.

[4] Cf. Tillich, "Religionsphilosophie," 320. Cf. Christian Danz and Werner Schüßler (eds.), *Paul Tillichs Theologie der Kultur. Aspekte – Probleme – Perspektiven* (Berlin; Boston: de Gruyter, 2011).

[5] Cf. Tillich, *Systematic Theology*, vol. I, 8–11.

[6] Cf. Ernst Troeltsch, "Was heißt 'Wesen des Christentums'?" in *Zur religiösen Lage, Religionsphilosophie und Ethik* (Gesammelte Schriften, vol. 2) (2nd. ed. Tübingen: Mohr Siebeck, 1922), 386–451; *Die Absolutheit des Christentums und die Religionsgeschichte (1902/1912)*.

[7] Cf. Tillich, "Christologie und Geschichtsdeutung," 83–96.

at the same time every construction of history depends on a particular history.[8] Christology is the theological reflection on the construction of history in theology, or as Tillich calls it, an interpretation of the meaning (*Sinn*) of history. What follows from the circle-structure is that all statements of religion and the history of religions are statements in the Christian religion.

Third, the theological circle carries with it certain consequences for the understanding of theology. To begin with, theology does not have the function of giving a justification for the Christian religion. Rather theology gives an explanation of the Christian religion and its symbolic forms. If Tillich speaks about the history of religions, then he describes structural moments in the constitution of the Christian religion or the Christian faith. It is by no means an objective view of the history of religions. Theology constructs its own point of view and its historical self-transparency.[9]

All three mentioned aspects are, therefore, also important for contemporary theology. But at the same time, it is not possible to continue Tillich's theoretical construction of religion. This means that his concept of religion is, on the one hand, a strength and, on the other hand, a weakness. Especially in the debates in the second half of the twentieth century, many theologians take up Tillich's universal understanding of religion.[10] However, this is no longer possible today. The reason for this is that Tillich's concept of religion is based on a model of unity. Religion is the

---

[8] Cf. Tillich, *Systematic Theology*, vol. III, 300–306.

[9] In this sense, Tillich had already constructed the philosophy of history in 1913 on the basis of his speculative theology. Cf. Tillich, "Das Problem der Geschichte," 98: "If, however, the philosophy of history constructs nothing else but itself, so it is armed against this doubt, because, in this case, to look for another principle would mean as much as to consider the historical consideration of the world as overcome. With this, however, the philosophy of history would have given up itself."

[10] In the theological debates in Germany in the second half of the twentieth century, many theologians like Wolfhart Pannenberg, Jürgen Moltmann, and others construct a universal understanding of God's revelation against Karl Barth's restriction of the revelation of God to Jesus Christ. For such theological constructions, Tillich's theology in many ways lies in the background. So far, however, the reception of Tillich's theology in post-World War II German-speaking theology has not been adequately addressed.

awareness that all acts of consciousness presuppose the absolute as its condition. With this claim it is posited that religion represents the unity of the culture that lies under the several cultural differences. This also concerns the contrast between religion and culture. From the conception of religion, it follows not only that every human being is religious, but also that religion cannot be an autonomous form in culture. Both aspects are connected and have consequences for the construction of religion. Given that religion is the insight of the presupposition of the absolute as the condition of both religion and culture, then a non-religious human being is impossible. But such an understanding of religion has no plausibility in a pluralistic culture because it implies that a non-religious human self-understanding is an inadequate self-understanding. Only in religion could human self-understanding come to its truth. At the same time, this concept of religion leads to an abolishment of religion as an independent, autonomous form in culture. This is the consequence of the universal dimension of Tillich's concept of religion. Religion for him is not a particular cultural form. Rather, religion is a moment in all cultural life and cultural forms. Therefore, true religion is realized in history and culture only as an indication that religion should not exist as a special form of culture. But exactly this, that is, that religion should not be a particular cultural form, must be represented in culture. Only for this reason, according to Tillich, does religion exist in history.

Such an understanding of religion as proposed by Tillich should not be continued in contemporary times. Against the background of an awareness of religious and cultural pluralism, theology must work out another understanding of religion. The reason for this is that Tillich's concept of religion dissolves religious diversity in a monistic manner.[11] In all religions the same event occurs, namely, the act of reflection in human consciousness, or the awareness that the unconditioned is the precondition of all acts of consciousness. In order to take up Tillich's intention in contemporary theology, the concept of religion must be defined in a new and different way. What follows from this is also a new and different understanding of theology.

---

[11] Cf. chapter IX.

2. Religion as Communication

In the *Prologue* of this book, it was explained that, on the one hand, the concept of religion has been the methodological basis of Protestant theology since the time of the Enlightenment. On the other hand, the theology in the beginning of the 20th century criticizes the notion of religion as the foundation of theology. But the theological critique of religion must be understood as a critique of the constructions of religion as a faculty in the general structure of human consciousness, and not as a critique of religion as such. The meaning of the critique of religion, therefore, must be understood as a new determination of the concept of religion. Religion arises without a precondition, like a religious a priori, in human beings or culture because religion is an actual act which is bound to its realization. This critique of anthropological notions of religion, which we find also in Tillich, must be taken up. But in contrast to him we must also dissolve a construction of consciousness on the basis of the unconditioned. Religion is not a necessary element of human beings. Rather, religion is a contingent form which results from the process of differentiation within culture. For an explanation of the concept of religion it is necessary to integrate the criticism of religion as an element that is given in the structure of human consciousness. Thus, we follow both the notion of religion as the basis of nineteenth-century theology and the theological critique of the notion of religion in early twentieth-century theology. But at the same time, theology must give up the construction of a universal notion of religion. There is no general concept of religion.[12] Therefore, the concept of religion in theology must be restricted to Christianity. The concept of religion for Christianity only functions to explain Christianity as religion. Theology must resign from transfering the notion of religion within Christianity onto other religions. Other religions have an independent understanding of religion that is different from the Christian understanding. Only in this way it is possible for theology to recognize both other religions and non-religious self-understandings as legitimate. But what is religion for Christianity?

---

[12] Cf. Nongbri, *Before Religion*; Smith, "Religion, Religions, Religious," 179–196.

Religion is an independent form of communication that exists in culture and understands itself as religion.[13] As such, religion is a result of the process of differentiation within culture. A foundation of religion with recourse to presuppositions outside of religion, like God or a religious subject, is not possible. Both God and a religious subject are always elements of the Christian religion. Here we can see the result of the theological development since the Enlightenment. A definition of religion cannot begin either with the concept of God or a religious subject, neither can it begin with a religious a priori. As Tillich has shown, all determinations of religion are circular.[14] Thus a theory of religion can only explain religion, but not justify it. Against this backdrop of the theological development since the Enlightenment, religion must be constructed as an event of communication. Religion emerges as such, namely, as religion—in the religious use of communication through the participants of the communication. In this sense, religion is always bound to the use of communication through human beings and the religious meaning (*Sinn*) of the communication that they participate in. In this proposal to give a new determination of religion, the starting point is neither a religious subject nor a religious content for both are elements of religion as communication. We find a religious subject and religious contents only within the Christian religion, and neither are presuppositions for a foundation of religion. Rather, the religious subject and the religious content must be replaced through the triadic structure of the event of religion. In the first place, the Christian religion always depends on Christian-religious communication, which is already given as a particular form in culture. Second, without appropriation of the Christian-religious communication through human beings, Christianity as religion could never exist. And finally, religion must be articulated in symbolic forms through human beings. Without religious representations religion is not visible and therefore not cognizable. It is important to note that the

---

[13] To the notion of religion cf. Danz, *Gottes Geist; Jesus von Nazareth zwischen Judentum und Christentum*; Folkart Wittekind, *Theologie religiöser Rede. Ein systematischer Grundriss* (Tübingen: Mohr Siebeck, 2018), 29–55.

[14] Cf. Tillich, *Systematic Theology*, vol. I, 9: "The theological concepts of both idealists and naturalists are rooted in a 'mystical a priori,' an awareness of something that transcends the cleavage between subject and object. And if in the course of a 'scientific' procedure this a priori is discovered, its discovery is possible only because it was present from the very beginning. This is the circle which no religious philosopher can escape."

Christian religion only emerges in interrelation of all three elements. To reduce religion to one of the elements is not possible, neither is a deduction of religion possible from any one element.

The emergence of the Christian religion always presupposes the tradition of Christianity, namely, the narratives of the remembered Jesus the Christ as its own sphere of communication within culture. Religion, as Rudolf Otto emphasizes, always begins with itself, i.e., it already presupposes itself as religion.[15] In contrast to Otto, religion is not an a priori element in the structure of human consciousness, but rather a form of communication which is given in culture. There is no religious a priori. The latter one is a construction which always depends on the history of religions. Apart from religion as an independent form of communication, there is no religious a priori. In this way, the Christian religion presupposes the Christian-religious tradition. That does not mean that a determined faith or something else is presupposed. What is assumed is only the transmission of the Christian-religious communication, or the remembered Jesus as the Christ. Apart from it, the Christian religion cannot arise. Alone, the tradition of Christianity that is passed in history is, as such, not yet religion; it is only an indication towards religion. The reason for this is that the tradition of Christianity, for example, the Bible, is always able to be used by humans within a non-religious sense, for example, in a historical, aesthetical, political, or other context. Thus, the Christian religion presupposes on the one side a determined tradition, namely the remembered Jesus as the Christ, but on the other side it is impossible to derive actual religion from this tradition. Therefore, within the emergence of religion there is a necessary second element, namely, the understanding and appropriation of the remembered Jesus as the Christ through human beings as religion. Without individual appropriation of Christian-religious communication and one's own understanding of the communication as religion, the Christian religion is not possible. The personal use of the remembered Jesus as the Christ as a religious use is a necessary condition for the Christian religion. Religion is always bound to the individual use of the religious communication as religious communication. And only if this happens, can we say that there is religion. This is necessary insofar as it is impossible to recognize religion by contents such as God or Jesus. All con-

---

[15] Cf. Otto, *Das Heilige*, 163.

tents of religious communication can also be used in a non-religious manner. Thus, religious contents are on the one hand necessary and, on the other, they are not enough to recognize religion.

However, for the emergence of the Christian religion as religion, a third element is still necessary. Just as understanding is not possible without representation, so the individual appropriation of the remembered Jesus as the Christ must also be articulated in symbolic forms within the communication. Without articulation, representation, and embodiment of the Christian-religious communication, the Christian religion is not visible in culture. And if we do not see the Christian religion in culture, we cannot speak of religion, nor can the Christian religion be transmitted if it is not visible. Therefore, an inward religion without symbolic forms is only a postulate.[16] No one could recognize such an inward religion as religion. Thus, only if the appropriated religious communication is represented is the Christian religion constituted as a proper form of communication in culture.

The Christian religion as religion has an inner triadic structure. As religion, the Christian-religious communication emerges only in the interrelation of all three elements, namely, its *dependence* on religious communication, its *appropriation* and *articulation* in symbols. With this understanding of religion, which replaces Tillich's construction of religion in the structure of human consciousness, there are some interconnected consequences. First of all, the Christian religion is self-related; it refers only to itself as Christian-religious communication. All Christian contents are expressions and representations of Christianity as religion. This does not mean that the contents lose their normal or cultural significance, but rather that all contents are expressions of the Christian religion. They intend only religion and nothing else. In this way religion is absolute, that is, self-related. Thus, absoluteness is an expression of the self-relation of the Christian religion as communication and not a determination with regard toward its contents. Second, the contents of the Christian religion, like God, Jesus Christ, the Holy Spirit, and so on, are elements of the Christian religion and not preconditions of religion that are given as presuppositions outside of religion. They have a reflexive function for the Christian religion and do not refer to contents. Rather, they are both the expression and

---

[16] Cf. Thomas Luckmann, *Die unsichtbare Religion* (Frankfurt a.M.: Suhrkamp, 1991).

reflection of religion within the Christian religion. With its contents, the Christian religion describes in and for religion how Christianity as religion emerges and functions. Thus God, Christ, and the Holy Spirit are not objects outside the Christian religion. Third, the knowledge of religion is an essential element of the Christian religion itself. The believer must know that they practice religion when they are performing religion. Without the knowledge to practice religion, Christianity as religion cannot exist. For this reason, an unknown or implicit Christian religion, or an anonymous Christianity, is not possible.[17] Such constructions are postulates that aim at claiming universality for the Christian religion, but such constructions are not helpful. No one can verify such postulates. Religion must be visible, and the Christian-religious communication must be intended as religion.

With this, I have given a notion of religion which is able to be the basis for theology in the age of religious and cultural pluralism. However, not only the notion of religion must acquire a new determination, but also the understanding of theology.

3. Systematic Theology as the Science of the Christian Religion

Tillich gives systematic theology the task of explaining the Christian message. "The 'scientific' theologian wants to be more than a philosopher of religion. He wants to interpret the Christian message generally with the help of his method" (ST I, 10). Theology does not justify the Christian religion. This is not possible because every theology or theory of religion already presupposes the Christian religion. Without the Christian religion that already exists in culture as a proper form of communication, theology also could not exist. So systematic theology can only explain the circle-structure of the Christian religion. Tillich's methodological insight, which he calls the theological circle, should be taken up in a new determination of the task of systematic theology. But in contrast to Tillich, it is not the goal of systematic theology to give an explanation of the world as a whole. For him, this explanation is a consequence of the concept of religion. Under the conditions of a pluralistic culture, such a construction is no longer plausible or convincing. As suggested above, if we transform the notion of

---

[17] This is the thesis of Rahner, "Die anonymen Christen," 545–554.

religion then another understanding of theology follows as well. As for Tillich, the concept of religion is a construction of theology, but this very concept of religion must nevertheless be restricted to the Christian religion as a religion. Systematic theology is, as proposed here, a *Wissenschaft*—science—of the Christian religion.

The task of systematic theology is to describe the Christian religion. But theology is not itself religion. Theology is a science and as such it is self-differentiated from religion. Therefore, systematic theology is neither faith nor religion in another form, nor is it the truth of religion. Both claims destroy the character of science for theology. Systematic theology does not have any special knowledge that other sciences do not have, nor does it have any special presuppositions that are accessible only to it or to a faith. The only thing that theology as a science can do is to construct as complete an image as possible of the Christian religion and its transparent functioning as a religion. Otherwise, systematic theology could not know its object. There is no other way for a science to know its object than to construct it. But theology constructs the Christian religion from and in the perspective of the believers, or participants.[18] Only here lies the difference between theology and other religious studies, like sociology of religion, psychology of religion, and so on. Systematic theology describes the Christian religion from the perspective that believers have of their religion. This alone distinguishes theology from other religious studies. Nevertheless, they all can only construct religion because no science has an immediate access to its object. So, theology constructs the Christian religion as a self-transparent form of communication.

To reiterate, the object of theology is the Christian religion, where religion is understood as a triadic event of communication. Christian religion arises only in the triadic interrelation of dependence from Christian-religious tradition, its appropriation and symbolic articulation and embodiment. Without understanding and symbolic articulation, the Christian religion cannot arise in culture. If religion must be understood as an event, or a happening of communication, then faith is the reality of the Christian religion. Faith, therefore, describes the fact that Christian-religious communication is successful. With that we have overcome the differentiation or the opposition between religion and faith that was made by German

---

[18] Cf. Tillich, *Systematic Theology*, vol. I, 22: "The theologian [...] is not detached from his object but is involved in it."

Protestant theology in the twentieth century. The concept of faith designates the reality of the Christian religion in the history which is bound to the Christian-religious communication. But just like the concept of religion, the concept of faith is also a construct of theology that is built up in it as science.

Unlike for Tillich, systematic theology does not give an explication of the world in general, but only how the world is given in and for the Christian-religious communication.[19] In another contrast to Tillich, religion is a proper cultural form that stands side by side other cultural forms. Neither systematic theology nor the Christian religion have the one true view on human beings or of the world. Thus, there is no universal interpretation like what Tillich proposed. Just as systematic theology relates itself only to the Christian religion, it also follows a transformation of the project of a theology of culture. However, it remains a theology of culture, but in a different form than that of Tillich. For him theology has the task of giving a foundation or a justification of culture. Tillich is concerned with endowing the differentiated and fragmented modern culture with a new, deeper unity. But this is, under the conditions of a pluralistic culture, no longer possible. Theology cannot give a foundation of culture or cultural pluralism—this is not the task of systematic theology. It describes the Christian religion as communication. As such, it exists only as a self-description that on the one side goes back to the remembered Jesus as the Christ and his media, like the Bible, sacraments, images, and so on. On the other side, it is always possible for Christian-religious communication to use cultural forms as an expression of religion. And also, it is possible to use religious contents in a non-religious cultural meaning. The reason for this is that religion does not depend on contents but only on the religious use of contents in communication. If cultural forms are used in religion, then they lose their cultural meaning. They are in religion used as expressions of religion. Against the mentioned background, the structure and task of a theology of culture must be changed: it analyses the transference from cultural forms in the Christian religion and from religious symbolic forms into culture. In this way, systematic theology as a theology of culture describes the change of the self-descriptions of the Christian religion in its own time.

---

[19] Cf. Christian Danz, "Theology of Nature. Reflections on the Dogmatic Doctrine of Creation," in *HTS Teologiese Studies/Theological Studies* 77, no. 3 (2021) 1–7.

Paul Tillich's theology is, like all theology, an expression of its own time. But times are changing, and this is also true for systematic theology. If systematic theology would like to give a description of the Christian religion in the twenty-first century, then it must find a new form. Otherwise, systematic theology has nothing to say today. Therefore, it remains true what Tillich formulates: "Theology moves back and forth between two poles, the eternal truth of its foundation and the temporal situation in which the eternal truth must be received" (ST I, 3).

Bibliography

WORKS OF PAUL TILLICH

Tillich, Paul. "Wissen und Meinen. Zu Fichtes 150. Geburtstag am 19. Mai 1912," in *Neue Preußische Zeitung*, Nr. 232 (1912) 2, reprinted in EW XXI, 9–14

_____. "Renaissance und Reformation. Zur Einführung in die Bibliothek Warburg," in *Theologische Blätter* 32 (1922) 265–267, reprinted in GW XIII, 137–140.

_____. "Barths 'Römerbrief,'" in *Vossische Zeitung*, no. 513 (1922) 1, reprinted in EW XXI, 68–9.

_____. "Religiöse Gestalten," in *Vossische Zeitung*, no. 52 (1926) 1–2, reprinted in EW XXI, 131–134.

_____. Editor. *Kairos. Zur Geisteslage und Geisteswerdung*. Darmstadt: Reichl, 1926.

_____. Editor. *Protestantismus als Kritik und Gestaltung. Zweites Buch des Kairos-Kreises*. Darmstadt: Reichl, 1929.

_____. "What is wrong with the 'Dialectic' Theology?" in *The Journal of Religion* 15 (1935) 127–145.

_____. "On the Boundary," in *The Interpretation of History*. New York; London: Charles Scribner's Sons, 1936, 3–73.

_____. "Philosophy and Theology," in *Religion in Life* 10 (1941) 21–30, reprinted in MW IV, 279–288.

_____. *Systematic Theology*. Volume One. Chicago: The University of Chicago Press, 1951.

_____. *Existential Questions and Theological Answers. First Series: Existence and the Christ. Syllabus of Gifford Lectures 1953*. University of Aberdeen, 1953.

_____. *Systematische Theologie*. Volume One. Second Edition. Stuttgart: Evangelisches Verlagswerk, 1956.

_____. *Systematic Theology*. Volume Two. Chicago: The University of Chicago Press, 1957.

_____. *Christianity and the Encounter of the World Religions*. New York; London: Columbia University Press 1961.

_____. *Systematic Theology*. Volume Three. Chicago: The University of Chicago Press, 1963.

_____. "Foreword," in Martin Kähler, *The So-Called Historical Jesus and the His-toric Biblical Christ*. Edited and translated by Carl E. Braaten. Philadelphia: Fortress Press, 1964, IX–X.

_____. *What is Religion?* Edited by James L. Adams, translated by William B. Grenn. New York: Harper & Row, 1969.

_____. *Perspectives on the 19ᵗʰ and 20ᵗʰ Century Protestant Theology*. Edited by Carl E. Braaten. New York; Evanston; London: Harper & Row, 1976.

_____. *The Encounter of Religions and Quasi-Religions*. Lewiston; Queenston; Lampeter: E. Mellen Press, 1990.

_____. "Dialektische Theologie," in *Religion und Politik. Internationales Jahrbuch für die Tillich-Forschung*. Volume Four. Edited by Christian Danz, Werner Schüßler and Erdmann Sturm. Wien: LIT, 2009, 149–174.

_____. *The Courage to Be*. Third Edition. New Haven; London: Yale University Press, 2014.

_____. "Mystik und Schuldbewußtsein in Schellings philosophischer Entwick-lung," in GW I, 11–108.

_____. "Das System der Wissenschaften nach gegenständen und Methoden," in GW I, 109–293.

_____. "Religionsphilosophie," in GW I, 295–364.

_____. "Die Überwindung des Religionsbegriffs in der Religionsphilosophie," in GW I, 367–388.

_____. "Das religiöse Symbol," in GW V, 196–212.

_____. "Das Dämonische. Ein Beitrag zur Sinndeutung der Geschichte," in GW VI, 42–71.

_____. "Eschatologie und Geschichte," in GW VI, 72–82.

_____. "Christologie und Geschichtsdeutung," in GW VI, 83–96.

_____."Kritisches und positives Paradox. Eine Auseinandersetzung mit Karl Barth und Friedrich Gogarten," in GW VII, 216–225.

_____. "Antwort," in GW VII, 240–243.

_____. "Die Idee der Offenbarung," in GW VIII, 31–39.

_____. "Rechtfertigung und Zweifel," in GW VIII, 85–100.

_____. "Autobiographische Betrachtungen," in GW XII, 58–77.

_____. "Der Religionsphilosoph Rudolf Otto," in GW XII, 179–183.

_____. "Die Kategorie des 'Heiligen' bei Rudolf Otto," in GW XII, 184–186.

_____. "Karl Barth," in GW XII, 187–193.

_____. "Die christliche Gewißheit und der historische Jesus," in EW VI, 31–61.

_____. "Fichtes Religionsphilosophie in ihrem Verhältnis zum Johannesevange-lium (1906)," in EW IX, 1–19.

_____. "Welche Bedeutung hat der Gegensatz von monistischer und dualisti-scher Weltanschauung für die christliche Religion? (1908)," in EW IX, 20–153.

_____. "Die religionsgeschichtliche Konstruktion in Schellings positiver Philosophie, ihre Voraussetzungen und Prinzipien," in EW IX, 154–272.

_____. "Systematische Theologie von 1913," in EW IX, 273–434.

_____. "Der Begriff des Übernatürlichen, sein dialektischer Charakter und das Prinzip der Identität – dargestellt an der supranaturalistischen Theologie vor Schleiermacher," in EW IX, 439–592.

_____. "Gott und das Absolute bei Schelling," in EW X, 9–54.

_____. "Das Problem der Geschichte," in EW X, 85–100.

_____. "Theodicee," in EW X, 101–113.

_____. "Der Begriff des christlichen Volkes. Habilitationsvortrag," in EW X, 114–126.

_____. "Die prinzipiellen Grundlagen und die nächsten Aufgaben unserer Bewegung," in EW X, 237–249.

_____. "Das System der religiösen Erkenntnis," in EW XI, 79–174.

_____. "Dogmatik-Vorlesung (Dresden 1925–1927)," in EW XIV.

_____. "Die Gestalt der religiösen Erkenntnis," in EW XIV, 395–431.

_____. "Frühe Vorlesungen im Exil (1934–1935)," in EW XVII.

_____. "Advanced Problems in Systematic Theology. Courses at Union Theological Seminary, New York, 1936–1938," in EW XIX.

_____. "The Significance of the Historical Jesus for the Christian Faith," in EW XIX, 317–321.

_____. "Vorträge und Studien der Bibliothek Warburg," in EW XXI, 359–363.

_____. "Schelling und die Anfänge des existentialistischen Protestes," in MW I, 391–402.

_____. "Religiöser Stil und religiöser Stoff in der bildenden Kunst," in MW II, 88–99.

_____. "Über die Idee einer Theologie der Kultur," in *Ausgewählte Texte*. Edited by Christian Danz, Werner Schüßler and Erdmann Sturm. Berlin; New York: de Gruyter, 2008, 26–41.

_____. "Kairos," in *Ausgewählte Texte*. Edited by Christian Danz, Werner Schüßler, and Erdmann Sturm. Berlin; New York: de Gruyter, 2008, 43–62.

_____. "Natural and Revealed Religion," in *Ausgewählte Texte*. Edited by Christian Danz, Werner Schüßler, and Erdmann Sturm. Berlin; New York: de Gruyter, 2008, 265–273.

_____. "The Problem of Theological Method," in *Ausgewählte Texte*. Edited by Christian Danz, Werner Schüßler, and Erdmann Sturm. Berlin; New York: de Gruyter, 2008, 301–312.

_____. "Christianity and the Encounter of the World Religions," in *Ausgewählte Texte*. Edited by Christian Danz, Werner Schüßler, and Erdmann Sturm. Berlin; New York: de Gruyter, 2008, 419–453.

_____. "The Significance of the History of Religions for the Systematic Theologian," in *Ausgewählte Texte*. Edited by Christian Danz, Werner Schüßler, and Erdmann Sturm. Berlin; New York: de Gruyter, 2008, 456–465.

UNPUBLISHED WORKS OF PAUL TILLICH
Tillich, Paul. "Die Absolutheit des Christentums und die Religionsgeschichte in Schelling's positiver Philosophie," in Tillich, Paul, 1886–1965, Collector. Harvard Divinity School Library, Harvard University, Cambridge, Massachusetts (bMS 649/101[2]).
_____. "Hauptprobleme der Geschichtsphilosophie," in The Wilhelm and Marion H. Pauck Manuscript Collection, Wright Library, Princeton Theological Seminary, Box 42.

SECONDARY SOURCES
Althaus, Paul. "Theologie des Glaubens," in *Theologische Aufsätze*. Gütersloh: Bertelsmann, 1929, 74–118.
Assel, Heinrich. *Der andere Aufbruch. Die Lutherrenaissance – Ursprünge, Aporien und Wege: Karl Holl, Emanuel Hirsch, Rudolf Hermann (1910–1935)*. Göttingen: Vandenhoeck & Ruprecht, 1994.
Assmann, Jan. *Das kulturelle Gedächtnis. Schrift, Erinnerung und politische Identität in den frühen Hochkulturen*. Seventh Edition. München: C. H. Beck, 2013.
Barth, Karl. *Das Wort Gottes und die Theologie. Gesammelte Vorträge*. München: Kaiser, 1924.
_____. "Die Gerechtigkeit Gottes," in *Das Wort Gottes und die Theologie. Gesammelte Vorträge*. Seventh and Eighth Edition. München: Kaiser, 1929, 5–17.
_____. "Die neue Welt der Bibel," in *Das Wort Gottes und die Theologie. Gesammelte Vorträge*. Seven and Eighth Edition. München: Kaiser, 1929, 18–32.
_____. *Der Römerbrief.* Nineth Edition. Zollikon-Zürich: Evangelischer Verlag, 1954.
_____. *Die kirchliche Dogmatik*. Volume One. Zürich: TVZ, 1964.
_____. "Rezension der Zeitschrift für wissenschaftliche Theologie, 51. Jahrgang, 1. und 2. Heft," in *Vorträge und kleinere Arbeiten 1905–1909* (GA III). Edited by Hans-Anton Drewes and Hinrich Stoevesandt, Zürich: TVZ 1992.
_____. "Ideen und Einfälle zur Religionsphilosophie," in *Vorträge und kleinere Arbeiten 1909–1914* (GA IV). Edited by Hans-Anton Drewes and Hinrich Stoevesandt. Zürich: TVZ, 1993, 129–138.
_____. "Der christliche Glaube und die Geschichte," in *Vorträge und kleinere Arbeiten 1909–1914* (GA IV). Edited by Hans-Anton Drewes and Hinrich Stoevesandt. Zürich, TVZ, 1993, 155–212.

_____. "Von der Paradoxie des 'positiven Paradoxes'. Antworten und Fragen an Paul Tillich," in GW VII, 226–239.

Barth, Ulrich. "Theoriedimensionen des Religionsbegriffs. Die Binnenrelevanz der sogenannten Außenperspektive," in *Religion in der Moderne*. Tübingen: Mohr Siebeck, 2003, 29–87.

_____. "Die sinntheoretischen Grundlagen des Religionsbegriffs. Problemgeschichtliche Hintergründe zum frühen Tillich," in *Religion in der Moderne*. Tübingen: Mohr Siedbeck, 2003, 89–123.

_____. "Religionsphilosophisches und geschichtsmethodologisches Apriori: Ernst Troeltschs Auseinandersetzung mit Kant," in *Gott als Projekt der Vernunft*. Tübingen: Mohr Siebeck, 2005, 359–394.

_____. "Religion und Sinn," in *Religion – Kultur – Gesellschaft. Der frühe Tillich im Spiegel neuer Texte (1919–1920)*. Edited by Christian Danz and Werner Schüßler. Wien: LIT, 2008, 197–213.

Bayly, Christopher A. *Birth of the Modern World. Global Connections and Comparisons*. Oxford: Blackwell, 2004.

Beiser, Frederick C. *The Genesis of Neo-Kantianism, 1796–1880*. Oxford: Oxford University Press, 2014.

Bergunder, Michael. "'Religion' and 'Science' Within a Global Religious History," in *Aries* 16, no. 1 (2016) 86–141.

Bernhardt, Reinhold. *Der Absolutheitsanspruch des Christentums. Von der Aufklärung bis zur Pluralistischen Religionstheologie*. Gütersloh: Gerd Mohn, 1990.

_____. *Ende des Dialogs? Die Begegnung der Religionen und ihre theologische Reflexion*. Zürich: TVZ, 2005.

_____. "Protestantische Religionstheologie auf trinitätstheologischem Grund," in *Theologie der Religionen. Positionen und Perspektiven evangelischer Theologie*. Edited by Christian Danz and Ulrich H. J. Körtner. Neukirchen-Vluyn: Neukirchener, 2005, 107–120.

_____. *Monotheismus und Trinität. Gotteslehre im Kontext der Religionstheologie*. Zürich: TVZ, 2023.

Beyer, Peter. *Religion in Global Society*. London; New York: Routledge, 2006.

Boss, Marc. *Au commencement la liberté. La religion de Kant réinventée par Fichte, Schelling et Tillich*. Genf: Labor et Fides, 2014.

Brandt, Hermann. "Konstanz und Wandel in der Theologie Paul Tillichs: im Licht der wiedergefundenen Thesen zu seiner Lizentiaten-Dissertation," in *Zeitschrift für Theologie und Kirche* 75 (1978) 361–74.

Bultmann, Rudolf. "Die liberale Theologie und die jüngste theologische Bewegung," in *Glaube und Verstehen*, Volume One. Tübingen: Mohr Siebeck, 1958, 1–25.

_____. "Der Begriff der Offenbarung im Neuen Testament," in *Glaube und Verstehen*, Volume Three. Tübingen: Mohr Siebeck, 1960, 1–34.

_____. *Jesus*. Tübingen: Mohr Siebeck, 1964.

Brunstäd, Friedrich. *Die Idee der Religion. Prinzipien der Religionsphilosophie.* Halle: Niemeyer, 1922.

Cassedy, Steven. "What Is the Meaning of Meaning in Paul Tillich's Theology?" in *The Harvard Theological Review* 111, no. 3 (2018) 307–32.

_____. *What Do We Mean When We Talk about Meaning?* New York: Oxford University Press, 2022.

Cassirer, Ernst. *Philosophie der symbolischen Formen.* Three Volumes. Ninth Edition. Darmstadt: Wissenschaftliche Buchgesellschaft, 1994.

Chan, Keith Ka-fu. *Life as Spirit. A Study of Paul Tillich's Ecological Pneumatology.* Berlin; Boston: de Gruyter, 2018.

Chapman, Mark. *Ernst Troeltsch and Liberal Theology. Religion and Cultural Synthesis in Wilhelmine Germany.* Oxford: Oxford University Press, 2001.

Claussen, Johann H. *Die Jesus-Deutung von Ernst Troeltsch im Kontext der liberalen Theologie.* Tübingen: Mohr Siebeck, 1997.

Clayton, John P. *The Concept of Correlation. Paul Tillich and the Possibility of a Mediating Theology.* Berlin; New York: de Gruyter, 1980.

Clooney, Francis X. "Comparative Theology. A Review of Recent Books (1989–1995)," in *Theological Studies* 56 (1995) 521–550.

_____. *Theology after Vedanta. An Experiment in Comparative Theology.* Albany; New York: State University of New York Press, 1996.

Cohen, Hermann. *Der Begriff der Religion im System der Philosophie.* Edited by Andrea Poma. Hildesheim; Zürich; New York: Olms, 1996.

Collins, Drew. *The Unique and Universal Christ. Refiguring the Theology of Religions.* Waco: Baylor University Press, 2021.

Danz, Christian. *Religion als Freiheitsbewußtsein. Eine Studie zur Theologie als Theorie der Konstitutionsbedingungen individueller Subjektivität bei Paul Tillich.* Berlin; NewYork: de Gruyter, 2000.

_____. "Theologie als normative Religionsphilosophie. Voraussetzungen und Implikationen des Theologiebegriffs Paul Tillichs" in *Theologie als Religionsphilosophie. Studien zu den problemgeschichtlichen und systematischen Voraussetzungen der Theologie Paul Tillichs.* Edited by Christian Danz. Wien: LIT, 2004, 73–106.

_____. *Gott und die menschliche Freiheit. Studien zum Gottesbegriff in der Neuzeit.* Neukirchen-Vluyn: Neukirchener, 2005.

_____. "Das Werden Gottes im Bewusstsein der Menschheit. Der Begriff des Mythos bei Schelling," in *Gott und die menschliche Freiheit. Studien zum Gottesbegriff in der Neuzeit.* Neukirchen-Vluyn: Neukirchener, 2005, 28–44.

_____. "Die geschichtsphilosophische Grundlegung der Theologie bei Ernst Troeltsch," in *Gott und die menschliche Freiheit. Studien zum Gottesbegriff in der Neuzeit.* Neukirchen-Vluyn: Neukirchener, 2005, 69–87.

_____. "Glaube als Evident-Werden Gottes. Die Überwindung des Historismus bei Friedrich Gogarten," in *Gott und die menschliche Freiheit. Studien zum Gottesbegriff in der Neuzeit*. Neukirchen-Vluyn: Neukirchener, 2005, 88–101.

_____. "Geschichtliche Offenbarung. Die Trinitätslehre Paul Tillichs," in *Gott und die menschliche Freiheit. Studien zum Gottesbegriff in der Neuzeit*. Neukirchen-Vluyn: Neukirchener, 2005, 102–128.

_____. *Einführung in die Theologie der Religionen*. Wien: LIT, 2005.

_____. "Symbolische Form und die Erfassung des Geistes im Gottesverhältnis. Anmerkungen zur Genese des Symbolbegriffs von Paul Tillich," in *Das Symbol als Sprache der Religion. International Yearbook for Tillich Research*, Volume Two. Edited by Christian Danz, Werner Schüßler and Erdmann Sturm. Wien: LIT, 2007, 59–75.

_____. "Ursprungsphilosophie und Theologiebegriff. Heinrich Barth im Kontext der dialektischen Theologie Karl Barths," in *Existenz. Facetten, Genese, Umfeld eines zentralen Begriffs bei Heinrich Barth*. Edited by Harald Schwaetzer and Christian Graf. Regensburg: Roderer, 2007, 104–122.

_____. "Religion der konkreten Existenz. Heideggers Religionsphilosophie im Kontext von Ernst Troeltsch und Paul Tillich," in *Kerygma und Dogma 55* (2009) 325–341.

_____. "Theologischer Neuidealismus. Zur Rezeption der Geschichtsphilosophie Fichtes bei Friedrich Gogarten, Paul Tillich und Emanuel Hirsch," in *Wissen, Freiheit, Geschichte. Die Philosophie Fichtes im 19. und 20. Jahrhundert. Beiträge des sechsten internationalen Kongresses der Johann-Gottlieb-Fichte-Gesellschaft in Halle (Saale) vom 3.–7. Oktober 2006*, Volume Two (Fichte-Studien, Volume Thirtysix). Edited by Jürgen Stolzenberg and Oliver-Pierre Rudolph. Amsterdam; New York: Rodopi, 2012, 199–215.

_____. *Einführung in die Theologie Martin Luthers*. Darmstadt: Wissenschaftliche Buchgesellschaft, 2013.

_____. *Grundprobleme der Christologie*. Tübingen: Mohr Siebeck, 2013.

_____. "Der Mut zum Sein. Ein werkgeschichtlicher Prospekt," in Paul Tillich, *Der Mut zum Sein*. With a preface by Christian Danz. Berlin; Boston: de Gruyter, 2015, 1–14.

_____. "Die politische Macht des mythischen Denkens. Paul Tillich und Ernst Cassirer über die Ambivalenz des Mythos," in *Die Macht des Mythos. Das Mythosverständis Paul Tillichs im Kontext*. Edited by Christian Danz and Werner Schüßler. Berlin; Boston: de Gruyter, 2015, 119–141.

_____. "Die Gegenwart des göttlichen Geistes und die Zweideutigkeiten des Lebens," in *Paul Tillichs 'Systematische Theologie'. Ein werk- und problemgeschichtlicher Kommentar*. Edited by Christian Danz. Berlin; Boston: de Gruyter, 2017, 227–256.

_____. "Textgeschichtliche Einleitung zur deutschen Übersetzung der Systema-
tischen Theologie," in Paul Tillich, *Systematische Theologie*. Volumes One
and Two. Ninth Edition. Edited by Christian Danz. Berlin; Boston: de
Gruyter, 2017, XV–LXV.

_____. "'Anxiety is finitude, experienced as one's own finitude.' Werkgeschicht-
liche Anmerkungen zu Paul Tillichs Ontologie der Angst in *Der Mut zum
Sein*," in *International Yearbook for Tillich Research*, Volume Thirteen. Edited by Christian Danz, Marc Dumas, Werner Schüßler, Mary Ann Stenger and Erdmann Sturm. Berlin; Boston: de Gruyter, 2018, 25–46.

_____. "Critique and Formation. Paul Tillich's Interpretation of Protestantism,"
in *The Courage to Be. International Yearbook for Tillich Research*. Volume
Thirteen. Edited by Christian Danz, Marc Dumas, Werner Schüßler,
Mary Ann Stenger and Erdmann Sturm. Berlin; Boston: de Gruyter 2018,
237–244.

_____. "Das Dämonische. Zu einer Deutungsfigur der modernen Kultur bei
Georg Simmel, Georg Lukács, Leo Löwenthal und Paul Tillich," in *Das
Dämonische. Kontextuelle Studien zu einer Schlüsselkategorie Paul Tillichs*. Edited by Christian Danz and Werner Schüßler. Berlin; Boston: de Gruyter,
2018, 147–184.

_____. "Erläuterungen zu Paul Tillich 'Rechtfertigung und Zweifel,'" in Paul
Tillich, *Rechtfertigung und Neues Sein*. Edited and commentary by Christian Danz. Leipzig: Evangelische Verlagsanstalt, 2018, 66–111.

_____. *Gottes Geist. Eine Pneumatologie*. Tübingen: Mohr Siebeck, 2019.

_____. *Jesus von Nazareth zwischen Judentum und Christentum. Eine christologische
und religionstheologische Skizze*. Tübingen: Mohr Siebeck, 2020.

_____. "Religious Diversity and the Concept of Religion. Theology and Religi-
ous Pluralism," in *Neue Zeitschrift für systematische Theologie und Religionsphilosophie* 62 (2020) 101–113.

_____. "Der erinnerte Christus. Überlegungen zur Christologie," in *Jesus Chris-
tus – Alpha und Omega. Festschrift für Helmut Hoping*. Edited by Jan-Heiner
Tück and Magnus Striet. Freiburg in Breisgau: Herder, 2021, 286–305.

_____. "Nochmals: Monistischer Pluralismus oder pluralismusoffene Theologie?
Eine Duplik auf Perry Schmidt-Leukel," in *Theologische Rundschau* 86
(2021) 106–119.

_____. "Theology of Nature. Reflections on the Dogmatic Doctrine of Crea-
tion," in *Hervormde teologiese studies* 77, no 3 (2021) 1–7.

_____ and Werner Schüßler (eds.). *Paul Tillichs Theologie der Kultur. Aspekte –
Probleme – Perspektiven*. Berlin; Boston: de Gruyter, 2011.

Dienstbeck, Stefan. *Transzendentale Strukturtheorie. Stadien der Systembildung
Paul Tillichs*. Göttingen: Vandenhoeck & Ruprecht, 2011.

Dierken, Jörg. "Gewissheit und Zweifel. Über die religiöse Bedeutung skeptischer Reflexion," in *Theologie als Religionsphilosophie. Studien zu den problemgeschichtlichen und systematischen Voraussetzungen der Theologie Paul Tillichs*. Edited by Christian Danz. Wien: LIT, 2004, 107–133.

_____. "Die Wirklichkeit Gottes," in *Paul Tillichs 'Systematische Theologie'. Ein werk- und problemgeschichtlicher Kommentar*. Edited by Christian Danz. Berlin; Boston: de Gruyter, 2017, 117–141.

Dorrien, Gary J. *In a Post-Hegelian Spirit. Philosophical Theology as Idealistic Discontent*. Waco: Baylor University Press, 2020.

Dunn, James D. G. "Remembering Jesus. How the Quest of the Historical Jesus Lost Its Way," in *The Historical Jesus. Five Views*. Edited by James K. Beilby and Paul Rodes Eddy. Downers Grove: IVP Press, 2009, 199–225.

Eddy, Paul Rhodes and James K. Belby. "The Quest for the Historical Jesus: An Introduction," in *The Historical Jesus. Five Views*. Edited by James K. Belby. Downers Grove: IVP Press, 2009, 9–54.

Fehrenbach, Frank and Cornelia Zumbusch. *Aby Warburg und die Natur. Epistemik, Ästhetik, Kulturtheorie*. Berlin; Boston: de Gruyter, 2019.

Fischer, Hermann. "Theologie des Positiven und kritischen Paradoxes. Paul Tillich und Karl Barth im Streit um die Wirklichkeit," in *Neue Zeitschrift für systematische Theologie und Religionsphilosophie* 31 (1989) 195–212.

_____. *Systematische Theologie. Konzeptionen und Probleme im 20. Jahrhundert*. Stuttgart; Berlin; Köln: Kohlhammer, 1992.

Fredericks, James L. "A Universal Religious Experience? Comparative Theology as Alternative to a Theology of Religions," in *Horizons* 22 (1995) 67–87.

_____. *Faith among Faiths. Christian Theology and Non-Christian Religions*. New York: Paulist Press, 1999.

Fritz, Martin. *Menschsein als Frage. Paul Tillichs Weg zur anthropologischen Fundierung der Theologie*. Berlin; Boston: de Gruyter, 2024 (pending publication).

Goering, D. Timothy. *Friedrich Gogarten (1887–1967). Religionsrebell im Jahrhundert der Weltkriege*. Berlin; Boston: de Gruyter, 2017.

Gogarten, Friedrich. "Zur Geisteslage des Theologen," in GW VII, 244–246.

Gombrich, Ernst H. *Aby Warburg. Eine intellektuelle Biographie*. Hamburg: Philo Fine Arts, 2006.

Graf, Friedrich W. *Der heilige Zeitgeist. Studien zur Ideengeschichte der protestantischen Theologie in der Weimarer Republik*. Tübingen: Mohr Siebeck, 2011.

_____. "Zur Publikationsgeschichte von Paul Tillichs 'Systematic Theology.' Two Parts," in *The Journal for the History of Modern Theology* 23 (2016) 192–217; 24 (2017) 51–121.

_____ and Alf Christophersen. "Neukantianismus, Fichte- und Schellingrenaissance. Paul Tillich und sein philosophischer Lehrer Fritz Medicus," in *The Journal for the History of Modern Theology* 11 (2004) 52–78.

Grube, Dirk-Martin. *Offenbarung, absolute Wahrheit und interreligiöser Dialog. Studien zur Theologie Paul Tillichs*. Berlin; Boston: de Gruyter, 2019.

Grünschloß, Andreas. *Der eigene und der fremde Glaube. Studien zur interreligiösen Fremdwahrnehmung in Islam, Hinduismus, Buddhismus und Christentum*. Tübingen: Mohr Siebeck, 1999.

Harnack, Adolf von. *Das Wesen des Christentums*. Third Edition. Edited by Claus-Dieter Osthövener. Tübingen: Mohr Siebeck, 2012.

Harrison, Peter. "'Science' and 'Religion': Constructing the Boundaries," in *The Journal of Religion* 86 (2006) 86–106.

Heidegger, Martin. *Phänomenologie des religiösen Lebens* (Gesamtausgabe. II. Abteilung: Vorlesungen, Volume Sixty). Frankfurt a.M.: Klostermann, 1995.

_____. "'Das Heilige' (Vorarbeiten zur Rezension von Rudolf Otto, Das Heilige, 1917)," in *Phänomenologie des religiösen Lebens* (Gesamtausgabe. II. Abteilung: Vorlesungen, Volume Sixty). Frankfurt a.M.: Klostermann, 1995, 332–334.

Heim, Karl. *Das Gewißheitsproblem in der systematischen Theologie bis zu Schleiermacher*. Leipzig: J. C. Hinrichs, 1911.

_____. *Glaubensgewißheit. Eine Untersuchung über die Lebensfrage der Religion*. Leipzig: J. C. Hinrichs, 1916.

_____. "Ottos Kategorie des Heiligen und der Absolutheitsanspruch des Christusglaubens," in *Zeitschrift für Theologie und Kirche* 28 (1920) 14–41.

Heim, S. Mark. *Salvations. Truth and Difference in Religions*. Maryknoll: Orbis Books, 1995.

_____. *The Depth of Riches: A Trinitarian Theology of Religious Ends*. Grand Rapids; Michigan: Eerdmans, 2001.

_____. "The Depth of the Riches: Trinity and Religious Ends," in *Theology and the Religions. A Dialogue*. Edited by Viggo Mortensen. Grand Rapids; Cambridge: Eerdmans, 2003, 387–402.

Heinemann, Lars Christian. *Sinn – Geist – Symbol. Eine systematisch-genetische Rekonstruktion der frühen Symboltheorie Paul Tillichs*. Boston; Berlin: de Gruyter, 2017.

Herrmann, Christian. "Bücherschau," in *Kairos. Zur Geisteslage und Geisteswerdung*. Edited by Paul Tillich. Darmstadt: Reichl, 1926, 467–483.

Hermann, Rudolf. "Zur Grundlegung der Religionsphilosophie," in *Zeitschrift für Systematische Theologie* 1 (1923) 92–106.

Hick, John. *God Has Many Names*. Philadelphia: Westminster Press, 1982.

_____. *An Interpretation of Religion: Human Responses to the Transcendent*. New Haven: Yale University Press, 1989.

_____ and Paul F. Knitter. Editors. *The Myth of Christian Uniqueness. Toward a Pluralistic Theology of Religions*. Maryknoll: Orbis Books, 1987.

Hönes, Hans C. "Spielraum der Rationalität," in *Aby Warburg und die Natur*. Edited by Frank Fehrenbach and Cornelia Zumbusch. Berlin; Boston: de Gruyter, 2019, 33–48.

Jaeschke, Walter. "'Um 1800' – Religionsphilosophie in der Sattelzeit der Moderne," in *Philosophisch-theologische Streitsachen. Pantheismusstreit – Atheismusstreit – Theismusstreit*. Edited by Georg Essen and Christian Danz. Darmstadt: Wissenschaftliche Buchgesellschaft, 2012, 7–92.

James, Robison B. *Tillich and World Religions. Encountering other Faiths Today*. Macon: Mercer University Press, 2003.

Jung, Matthias. *Das Denken des Seins und der Glaube an Gott. Zum Verhältnis von Philosophie und Theologie bei Martin Heidegger*. Würzburg: Königshausen & Neumann, 1990.

Kany, Roland. *Die religionsgeschichtliche Forschung an der Kulturwissenschaftlichen Bibliothek Warburg*. Bamberg: Wendel, 1989.

Kähler, Martin. *Die Wissenschaft der christlichen Lehre von dem evangelischen Grundartikel aus im Abrisse dargestellt*. Leipzig: Deichert'sche Verlagsbuchhandlung, 1905.

Kippenberg, Hans G. *Die Entdeckung der Religionsgeschichte. Religionswissenschaft und Moderne*. München: C. H. Beck, 1997.

_____ and Kocku von Stuckrad. "Religionswissenschaftliche Überlegungen zum religiösen Pluralismus in Deutschland. Eine Öffnung der Perspektiven," in *Multikulturalität im vereinten Europa. Historische und juristische Aspekte*. Edited by Hartmut Lehmann. Göttingen: Wallstein, 2003, 145–162.

Knitter, Paul F. *Introducing Theologies of Religions*. Maryknoll: Orbis Books, 2002.

Knuth, Anton. *Der Protestantismus als moderne Religion. Historisch-systematische Rekonstruktion der religionsphilosophischen Theologie Kurt Leeses (1887–1965)*. Frankfurt a.M.: Peter Lang, 2005.

Koch, Traugott. "Die Macht zum Sein im Mut zum Sein. Tillichs Gottesverständnis in seiner 'Systematische Theologie,'" in *Paul Tillich. Studien zu einer Theologie der Moderne*. Edited by Hermann Fischer. Frankfurt a.M.: Athenäum, 1989, 169–206.

Lauster, Jörg, Peter Schüz, Roderich Barth, and Christian Danz. Editors. *Rudolf Otto. Theologie – Religionsphilosophie –Religionsgeschichte*. Berlin; Boston: de Gruyter, 2014.

Leuze, Reinhard. "Gott und das Ding an sich – Probleme der pluralistischen Religionstheorie," in *Neue Zeitschrift für Systematische Theologie und Religionsphilosophie* 39 (1997) 42–64.

Luckmann, Thomas. *Die unsichtbare Religion*. Frankfurt a.M.: Suhrkamp, 1991.

Lütgert, Wilhelm. *Die Methode des dogmatischen Beweises in ihrer Entwicklung unter dem Einfluß Schleiermachers*. Gütersloh: Bertelsmann, 1892.

_____. *Die johanneische Christologie*. Gütersloh: Bertelsmann, 1899.

_____. *Gottes Sohn und Gottes Geist. Vorträge zur Christologie und zur Lehre vom Geist Gottes.* Leipzig: Deichert'sche Verlagsbuchhandlung, 1905.

_____. *Die Religion des Deutschen Idealismus und ihr Ende.* Three Volumes Gütersloh: Bertelsmann, 1923–1925.

_____. *Schöpfung und Offenbarung. Eine Theologie des ersten Artikels.* Gütersloh: Gütersloher Verlagshaus Mohn, 1934.

McCormack, Bruce L. *Karl Barth's Critically Realistic Dialectical Theology: Its Genesis and Development, 1909–1936.* Oxford: Oxford University Press, 1995.

McEwan, Dorthea. "Making a Reception for Warburg: Fritz Saxl and Warburg's Book Heidnisch-Antike Weissagung in Wort und Bild zu Luthers Zeiten," in *Art History as Cultural History. Warburg's Projects.* Edited by Richard Woodfield. Abingdon: Routledge, 2001, 93–120.

_____. *Fritz Saxl – Eine Biographie. Aby Warburgs Bibliothekar und erster Direktor des Londoner Warburg Instituts.* Wien; Köln; Weimar: Böhlau, 2012.

Medicus, Fritz. *J. G. Fichte. Dreizehn Vorlesungen gehalten an der Universität Halle.* Berlin: Reuther & Reichard, 1905.

_____. "Review of F. W. J. Schelling, Werke, Auswahl in drei Bänden [...]" Edited by Otto Weiss," in *Kant-Studien* 13 (1908) 317–328.

_____. "Neufichteanismus" in *Die Religion in Geschichte und Gegenwart.* Volume Four. Second Edition. Tübingen: Mohr Siebeck, 1930, 498–9.

Meyer, Thomas. *Ernst Cassirer.* Hamburg: Ellert & Richter, 2006.

Mühling, Andreas. *Karl Ludwig Schmidt. "Und Wissenschaft ist Leben."* Berlin; New York: de Gruyter, 1997.

Neugebauer, Georg. *Tillichs frühe Christologie. Eine Untersuchung zu Offenbarung und Geschichte bei Paul Tillich vor dem Hintergrund seiner Schellingrezeption.* Berlin; New York: de Gruyter, 2007.

_____. "Die religionsphilosophischen Grundlagen der Kulturtheologie Tillichs vor dem Hintergrund seiner Schelling- und Husserlrezeption," in *Paul Tillichs Theologie der Kultur. Aspekte – Probleme – Perspektiven.* Edited by Christian Danz and Werner Schüßler. Berlin; Boston: de Gruyter, 2011, 38–63.

_____. "Freiheit als philosophisches Prinzip – Die Fichte-Interpretation des frühen Tillich," in *Wissen, Freiheit, Geschichte. Die Philosophie Fichtes im 19. und 20. Jahrhundert. Beiträge des sechsten internationalen Kongresses der Johann-Gottlieb-Fichte-Gesellschaft in Halle (Saale) vom 3.–7. Oktober 2006,* Volume Two (Fichte-Studien, Volume Thirtysix). Edited by Jürgen Stolzenberg and Oliver-Pierre Rudolph. Amsterdam; New York: Rodopi, 2012, 181–198.

Neville, Robert C. *Behind the Masks of God. An Essay Toward Comparative Theology.* New York: State University of New York Press, 1991.

_____. *Normative Cultures.* Albany: State University of New York Press, 1995.

Nongbri, Brent. *Before Religion. A History of a Modern Concept*. New Haven; London: Yale University Press, 2013.

Olson, Duane. *The Depths of Life. Paul Tillich's Understanding of God*. Macon: Mercer University Press, 2019.

Otto, Rudolf. "Darwinismus von heute und Theologie," in *Theologische Rundschau* 5 (1902) 483–496.

_____. "Die mechanische Lebenstheorie und die Theologie," in *Zeitschrift für Theologie und Kirche* 13 (1903) 179–213.

_____. *Kantisch-Fries'sche Religionsphilosophie und ihre Anwendung auf die Theologie. Zur Einleitung in die Glaubenslehre für Studenten der Theologie*. Tübingen: Mohr Siebeck, 1909.

_____. "Mythus und Religion in Wundts Völkerpsychologie," in *Theologische Rundschau* 13 (1910) 251–75.

_____. *Das Heilige. Über das Irrationale in der Idee des Göttlichen und sein Verhältnis zum Rationalen*. Seventh Edition. Breslau: Trewendt & Garnier, 1922.

Pannenberg, Wolfhart. *Systematische Theologie*. Volume Three. Göttingen: Vandenhoeck & Ruprecht, 1993.

_____. *Problemgeschichte der neueren evangelischen Theologie in Deutschland. Von Schleiermacher bis zu Barth und Tillich*. Göttingen: Vandenhoeck & Ruprecht, 1997.

Parrella, Frederick J. Editor. *Paul Tillich's Theological Legacy: Spirit and Community. International Paul Tillich Conference, New Harmony, 17–20 June 1993*. Berlin; New York: de Gruyter, 1995.

_____. "Tillich's theology of the concrete spirit," in *The Cambridge Companion to Paul Tillich*. Edited by Russel Re Manning. Cambridge: Cambridge University Press, 2009, 74–90.

Pfleiderer, Georg. *Theologie als Wirklichkeitswissenschaft. Studien zum Religionsbegriff bei Georg Wobbermin, Rudolf Otto, Heinrich Scholz und Max Scheler*. Tübingen: Mohr, 1992.

_____. *Karl Barths praktische Theologie. Zu Genese und Kontext eines paradigmatischen Entwurfs systematischer Theologie im 20. Jahrhundert*. Tübingen: Mohr Siebeck, 2000.

_____ and Harald Matern. *Die Religion der Bürger. Der Religionsbegriff in der protestantischen Theologie vom Vormärz bis zum Ersten Weltkrieg*. Tübingen: Mohr Siebeck, 2021.

Rahner, Karl. "Die anonymen Christen," in *Schriften zur Theologie*. Volume Six. Einsiedeln; Zürich; Köln: Benziger, 1965, 545–554.

Richard, Jean. "The Hidden Community of the Kairos and the Spiritual Community: Toward a New Understanding of the Correlation in the Work of Paul Tillich," in *Paul Tillich's Theological Legacy: Spirit and Community. International Paul Tillich Conference, New Harmony, 17–20 June 1993*. Edited by Frederick J. Parrella. Berlin; New York: de Gruyter, 1995, 43–64.

Ricœur, Paul. *Gedächtnis, Geschichte, Vergessen*. München: Wilhelm Fink, 2004.

Rieger, Klaus-Dieter. *Heiliger Geist und Wirklichkeit. Erich Schaeders Pneumatologie und die Kritik Karl Barths*. Berlin, Boston: de Gruyter, 2017.

Ritschl, Albrecht. *Unterricht in der christlichen Religion*. Fourth Edition. Bonn: Adolph Marcus, 1890.

Robinson, John T. A. *Honest to God*. Philadelphia: The Westminster Press, 1963.

Saxl, Fritz. "Bericht über die Bibliothek Warburg für das Jahr 1921," in Tilmann von Stockhausen, *Die Kulturwissenschaftliche Bibliothek Warburg. Architektur, Einrichtung und Organisation*. Hamburg: Dölling & Galitz, 1992, 124–132.

_____. "Die Kulturwissenschaftliche Bibliothek Warburg in Hamburg [1930]," in Dorothea McEwan, *Fritz Saxl – Eine Biografie. Aby Warburgs Bibliothekar und erster Direktor des Londoner Warburg Institutes*. Wien; Köln; Weimar: Böhlau, 2012, 265–270.

Shearn, Samuel A. *Pastor Tillich: The Justification of the Doubter*. Oxford: University Press 2022.

Schlatter, Adolf. *Die philosophische Arbeit seit Cartesius. Ihr ethischer und religiöser Ertrag* Gütersloh. Stuttgart: Calwer, 1906.

_____. *Das christliche Dogma*. Second Edition. Stuttgart: Calwer, 1923.

_____. "Habilitationsrede zum Zusammenhang von Dogma und Geschichte," in *Das Verhältnis von Theologie und Philosophie II. Die Berner Vorlesung (1883): Wesen und Quellen der Gotteserkenntnis*. Edited by Harald Seubert and Werner Neuer. Stuttgart: Calwer, 2019, 249–258.

_____. "Wesen und Quellen der Gotteserkenntnis. Berner Vorlesung im Sommersemester 1883," in *Das Verhältnis von Theologie und Philosophie II. Die Berner Vorlesung (1883): Wesen und Quellen der Gotteserkenntnis*. Edited by Harald Seubert and Werner Neuer. Stuttgart: Calwer, 2019, 67–247.

Schleiermacher, Friedrich. *On Religion. Speeches to its Cultured Despisers*. Edited and translated by Richard Crouter. Cambridge: Cambridge University Press, 1996.

_____. *The Christian Faith*. Two Volumes. Louisville: Westminster John Knox Press, 2016.

Schmidt-Leukel, Perry. *Religious Pluralism & Interreligious Theology. The Gifford Lectures – An Extended Edition*. Maryknoll: Orbis Books, 2017.

Schröter, Jens. "Der erinnerte Jesus als Begründer des Christentums? Bemerkungen zu James D. G. Dunns Ansatz in der Jesusforschung," in *Zeitschrift für Neues Testament* 20 (2007) 47–53.

Schröter, Marianne. *Aufklärung durch Historisierung. Johann Salomo Semlers Hermeneutik des Christentums*. Berlin; Boston: de Gruyter, 2012.

Schüßler, Werner. "Paul Tillich und Karl Barth. Ihre erste Begegnung in den zwanziger Jahren," in *Was uns unbedingt angeht.*" *Studien zur Theologie und Philosophie Paul Tillichs.* Second Edition. Münster: LIT, 2004, 119–130.

Schütte, Hans Walter. *Religion und Christentum in der Theologie Rudolf Ottos.* Berlin: de Gruyter, 1969.

Schüz, Peter. *Mysterium tremendum. Zum Verhältnis von Angst und Religion nach Rudolf Otto.* Tübingen: Mohr Siebeck, 2016.

Schweitzer, Albert. *Geschichte der Leben-Jesu-Forschung*, Volume Two. Hamburg; München: Siebenstern, 1966.

Schwöbel, Christoph. "Die Idee der Religion und die Wirklichkeit der Religionen," in *Religion und Religionen im Deutschen Idealismus. Schleiermacher – Hegel – Schelling.* Edited by Friedrich Hermanni, Burkhard Nonnenmacher and Friederike Schick. Tübingen: Mohr Siebeck, 2015, 449–475.

Semler, Johann S. *Versuch einer Anleitung zu nützliche Fleisse in der ganzen Gottesgelehrsamkeit für angehende Studiosos Theologiä.* Halle: Gebauer, 1757.

Smith, Jonathan Z. "Religion, Religions, Religious," in *Relating Religion. Essays in the Study of Religion.* Chicago; London: The University of Chicago Press, 2004, 179–196.

Stenger, Mary A. "Faith (and religion)," in *The Cambridge Companion to Paul Tillich.* Edited by Russel Re Manning. Cambridge: Cambridge University Press, 2009, 91–104.

_____. "Tillich's American Theology on the Boundary between Native and Alien Land," in *Paul Tillich im Exil.* Edited by Christian Danz and Werner Schüßler. Berlin; Boston: de Gruyter, 2017, 229–249.

Sturm, Erdmann. "Auf dem Weg zur Methode der Korrelation. Tillichs New Yorker Vorlesungszyklus *Advanced Problems Systematic Theology* (1936–38)," in *The Method of Correlation. International Yearbook for Tillich Research.* Volume Twelve. Edited by Christian Danz, Marc Dumas, Werner Schüßler, Mary Ann Stenger and Erdmann Sturm. Berlin; Boston: de Gruyter, 2017, 45–65.

Söchtig, Sabrina. *Absolute Wahrheit und Religion. Der Wahrheitsbegriff des frühen Tillich und seine Beurteilung außerchristlicher Religionen.* Berlin; Boston: de Gruyter, 2020.

Thatamanil, John J. *The Immanent Divine. God, Creation, and the Human Predicament. An East-West Conversation.* Minneapolis: Fortress Press, 2006.

Track, Joachim. "Paul Tillich und die Dialektische Theologie," in *Paul Tillich. Studien zu einer Theologie der Moderne.* Edited by Hermann Fischer. Frankfurt a.M.: Athenäum, 1989, 138–166.

Troeltsch, Ernst. "Das Historische in Kants Religionsphilosophie. Zugleich ein Beitrag zu den Untersuchungen über Kants Philosophie der Geschichte," in *Kant-Studien* 9 (1904) 21–154.

_____. *Psychologie und Erkenntnistheorie in der Religionswissenschaft. Eine Untersuchung über die Bedeutung der Kantischen Religionslehre für die heutige Religionswissenschaft.* Second Edition. Tübingen: Mohr Siebeck, 1922.

_____. "Die christliche Weltanschauung und ihre Gegenströmungen," in *Zur religiösen Lage, Religionsphilosophie und Ethik.* Gesammelte Schriften, Volume Two. Second Edition. Tübingen: Mohr Siebeck, 1922, 227–327.

_____. "Empirismus und Platonismus in der Religionsphilosophie. Zur Erinnerung an William James," in *Zur religiösen Lage, Religionsphilosophie und Ethik.* Gesammelte Schriften, Volume Two. Second Edition. Tübingen: Mohr Siebeck, 1922, 364–385.

_____. "Was heißt 'Wesen des Christentums'"? in *Zur religiösen Lage, Religionsphilosophie und Ethik.* Gesammelte Schriften, Volume Two. Second Edition. Tübingen: Mohr Siebeck, 1922, 386–451.

_____. "Wesen der Religion und der Religionswissenschaft," in *Zur religiösen Lage, Religionsphilosophie und Ethik.* Gesammelte Schriften, Volume Two. Second Edition. Tübingen: Mohr Siebeck, 1922, 452–494.

_____. "Über historische und dogmatische Methode in der Theologie," in *Zur religiösen Lage, Religionsphilosophie und Ethik.* Gesammelte Schriften, Volume Two. Second Edition. Tübingen: Mohr Siebeck, 1922, 729–753.

_____. "Zur Frage des religiösen Apriori. Eine Erwiderung auf die Bemerkungen von Paul Spieß," in *Zur religiösen Lage, Religionsphilosophie und Ethik.* Gesammelte Schriften, Volume Two. Second Edition. Tübingen: Mohr Siebeck, 1922, 754–768.

_____. *Glaubenslehre. Nach Heidelberger Vorlesungen aus den Jahren 1911 und 1912.* München; Leipzig: Duncker & Humblot, 1925.

_____. *Die Absolutheit des Christentums und die Religionsgeschichte (1902/1912). Mit den Thesen von 1901 und den handschriftlichen Zusätzen.* KGA, Volume Five. Edited by Trutz Rendtorff and Stefan Pautler. Berlin; New York: de Gruyter, 1998.

_____. "Ethik und Geschichtsphilosophie," in *Fünf Vorträge zu Religion und Geschichtsphilosophie für England und Schottland.* KGA, Volume Seventeen. Berlin; New York, 2006, 68–104.

_____. "Die Selbständigkeit der Religion," in *Schriften zur Theologie und Religionsphilosophie (1888–1902).* KGA, Volume One. Berlin; New York: de Gruyter, 2009, 364–534.

_____. "Zur Religionsphilosophie. Rudolf Otto: Das Heilige," in *Rezensionen und Kritiken (1915–1923).* KGA, Volume Thirteen. Berlin; New York, 2010, 412–425.

Trugenberger, Julius. *Neuhegelianisches Kulturluthertum. Friedrich Brundstäd (1883–1944).* Berlin; Boston: de Gruyter, 2021.

Urban, Wilbur M. "A Critique of Professor Tillich's Theory of the Religious Symbol," in *Journal of Liberal Religion* 2 (1940) 34–36.

Vahanian, Gabriel. *The Death of God. The Culture of Our Post-Christian Era.* New York: Braziller, 1961.

Veauthier, Frank Werner. "Das religiöse Apriori. Zur Ambivalenz von E. Troeltschs Analyse des Vernunftelementes in der Religion," in *Kant-Studien* 78 (1987) 42–63.

Vignoli, Tito. *Mythos und Wissenschaft.* Leipzig: Brockhaus, 1880.

Villhauer, Bernd. *Aby Warburgs Theorie der Kultur.* Berlin: Akademie Verlag, 2002.

Vischer, Friedrich Theodor. "Das Symbol," in *Philosophische Aufsätze. Eduard Zeller zu seinem fünfzigjährigen Doctor-Jubiläum gewidmet.* Leipzig: Fues's Verlag, 1887, 151–193.

Warburg, Aby. *Heidnisch-antike Weissagung in Wort und Bild zu Luthers Zeiten.* Heidelberg: Carl Winters Universitätsbuchhandlung, 1920.

――――. "Bilder aus dem Gebiet der Pueblo-Indianer in Nord-Amerika," in *Werke in einem Band. Auf der Grundlage der Manuskripte und Handexemplare.* Edited by Martin Treml, Sigrid Weigel and Perdita Ladwig. Berlin: Suhrkamp, 2018, 524–566.

――――. "Reise-Erinnerungen aus dem Gebiet der Pueblo Indianer in Nordamerika (1923)," in *Werke in einem Band. Auf der Grundlage der Manuskripte und Handexemplare.* Edited by Martin Treml, Sigrid Weigel and Perdita Ladwig. Berlin: Suhrkamp, 2018, 566–600.

――――. "Symbolismus als Umfangsbestimmung," in *Werke in einem Band. Auf der Grundlage der Manuskripte und Handexemplare.* Edited by Martin Treml, Sigrid Weigel and Perdita Ladwig. Berlin: Suhrkamp, 2018, 615–628.

――――. "Mnemosyne Einleitung," in *Werke in einem Band. Auf der Grundlage der Manuskripte und Handexemplare.* Edited by Martin Treml, Sigrid Weigel and Perdita Ladwig. Berlin: Suhrkamp, 2018, 629–639.

Wariboko, Nimi. and Amos Yong. Editors. *Paul Tillich and Pentecostal Theology. Spiritual Presence and Spiritual Power.* Bloomington; Indianapolis: Indiana University Press, 2015.

Wedepohl, Claudia. "Pathos – Polarität – Distanz – Denkraum. Eine archivarische Spurensuche," in *Warburgs Denkraum. Formen, Motive, Materialien.* Edited by Martin Treml, Sabine Flach and Pablo Schneider. München: Fink, 2014, 17–49.

Weiss, Johannes. *Die Predigt Jesu vom Reiche Gottes.* Göttingen: Vandenhoeck & Ruprecht, 1892.

Wenz, Gunther. "Theologie ohne Jesus? Anmerkungen zu Paul Tillich," in *Kerygma und Dogma* 26 (1980) 128–139.

Windelband, Wilhelm. "Kulturphilosophie und transzendentaler Idealismus," in *Logos* 1 (1910/11) 186–196.

_____. "Das Heilige. Skizze zur Religionsphilosophie," in *Präludien. Aufsätze und Reden zur Philosophie und ihrer Geschichte*. Volume Two. Seventh Edition. Tübingen: Mohr Siebeck, 1921, 295–332.

Wittekind, Folkart. *Geschichtliche Offenbarung und die Wahrheit des Glaubens. Der Zusammenhang von Offenbarungstheologie, Geschichtsphilosophie und Ethik bei Albrecht Ritschl, Julius Kaftan und Karl Barth (1909–1916)*. Tübingen: Mohr Siebeck, 2000.

_____. "Das Erleben der Wirklichkeit Gottes. Die Entstehung der Theologie Hans Joachim Iwands aus der Religionsphilosophie Carl Stanges und Rudolf Hermanns," in *Neue Zeitschrift für Systematische Theologie und Religionsphilosophie* 44 (2002) 20–42.

_____. "'Sinndeutung der Geschichte.' Zur Entwicklung und Bedeutung von Tillichs Geschichtsphilosophie," in *Theologie als Religionsphilosophie. Studien zu den problemgeschichtlichen und systematischen Voraussetzungen der Theologie Paul Tillichs*. Edited by Christian Danz. Wien: LIT, 2004, 135–172.

_____. "Gottesdienst als Handlungsraum. Zur symboltheoretischen Konstruktion des Kultes in Tillichs Religionsphilosophie," in *Das Symbol als Sprache der Religion. International Yearbook for Tillich Research*. Volume Two. Edited by Christian Danz, Werner Schüßler and Erdmann Sturm. Wien: LIT, 2007, 77–100.

_____. "'Allein durch den Glauben.' Tillich's sinntheoretische Umformulierung des Rechtfertigungsverständnisses 1919," in *Religion – Kultur – Gesellschaft. Der frühe Tillich im Spiegel neuer Texte (1919–1920)*. Edited by Christian Danz and Werner Schüßler. Wien: LIT, 2008, 39–65.

_____. "Von der Bewußtseinsphilosophie zur Christologie. Theologie und Moderne bei Karl Heim, Paul Tillich und Hans Joachim Iwand," in *Der "frühe Iwand" (1923–1933)*. Edited by Gerard den Hertog and Eberhard Lempp. Waltrop: Spenner, 2008, 59–114.

_____. "Grund- und Heilsoffenbarung. Zur Ausformung der Christologie Tillichs in der Auseinandersetzung mit Karl Barth," in *Jesus of Nazareth and the New Being. International Yearbook for Tillich Research*. Volume Six. Edited by Christian Danz, Marc Dumas, Werner Schüßler, Mary A. Stenger and Erdmann Sturm. Berlin; Boston: de Gruyter, 2011, 89–119.

_____. "Das Sein und die Frage nach Gott," in *Paul Tillichs 'Systematische Theologie'. Ein werk- und problemgeschichtlicher Kommentar*. Edited by Christian Danz. Berlin; Boston: de Gruyter, 2017, 93–116.

_____. *Theologie religiöser Rede. Ein systematischer Grundriss*. Tübingen: Mohr Siebeck, 2018.

_____. "Herrmann, Treoltsch und Tillich über die Konstruktion der Theologiegeschichte," in *Paul Tillich in der Diskussion. Werkgeschichte – Kontexte –*

Anknüpfungspunkte. Festschrift für Erdmann Sturm zum 85. Geburtstag. Edited by Christian Danz and Werner Schüßler. Berlin; Boston: de Gruyter, 2022, 133–170.

_____. "Tillichs Dresdener Dogmatik im theologiegeschichtlichen Kontext," in *Paul Tillich in Dresden. Intellektuellen-Diskurse in der Weimarer Republik.* Edited by Christian Danz and Werner Schüßler. Berlin; Boston: de Gruyter, 2023, 247–276.

Wrede, William. *Das Messiasgeheimnis in den Evangelien. Zugleich ein Beitrag zum Verständnis des Markusevangeliums.* Göttingen: Vandenhoeck & Ruprecht, 1901.

Zachhuber, Johannes. *Theology as Science in Nineteenth-Century Germany: From F. C. Baur to Ernst Troeltsch.* Oxford: Oxford Academic, 2013.

Index of Names

Index of Subjects